A Reader's Guide to Herman Melville

A Reader's Guide to
Herman Melville

JAMES E. MILLER JR.

THAMES AND HUDSON · LONDON

FIRST PUBLISHED IN GREAT BRITAIN 1962
COPYRIGHT © 1962 BY JAMES E. MILLER JR.
PRINTED IN GREAT BRITAIN BY
LOWE AND BRYDONE (PRINTERS) LTD. LONDON

. . . there is a Catskill eagle in some souls that can alike dive down into the blackest gorges, and soar out of them again and become invisible in the sunny spaces. And even if he forever flies within the gorge, that gorge is in the mountains; so that even in his lowest swoop the mountain eagle is still higher than other birds upon the plain, even though they soar.

Acknowledgments

A number of the chapters of this book appeared, sometimes in different form, in a variety of periodicals. I am grateful to the editors for their kind permission to reprint in whole or in part: "Melville's Quest in Life and Art" from *South Atlantic Quarterly;* "The Complex Figure in Melville's Carpet" from *Arizona Quarterly;* "The Many Masks of *Mardi*" from *Journal of English and Germanic Philology;* "*Redburn* and *White Jacket:* Initiation and Baptism" from *Nineteenth Century Fiction;* "*Moby Dick:* The Grand Hooded Phantom" from *Annali Dell' Istituto Universitario Orientale* (Naples, Italy); "*The Confidence-Man:* His Guises" from *PMLA;* "*Billy Budd:* The Catastrophe of Innocence" from *Modern Language Notes;* "The Achievement of Melville" from *University of Kansas City Review;* "Melville's Search for Form" from *Bucknell Review.*

My debt to Melville scholars and critics cannot be listed on a page. The bibliography at the end of this book suggests the extent but not the depth of that indebtedness.

To my Melville seminar at the University of Nebraska I must express my special thanks. My students listened patiently to my ideas, and generously contributed their own. It was, indeed, frequently difficult to distinguish the teacher from the pupil.

I am grateful to the Research Council of the University of Nebraska for a summer fellowship which gave me time to write and for a grant which helped me prepare the manuscript.

Preface

One of the reasons that Melville continues to fascinate ever-increasing numbers of readers is his ambiguities. Their central position in his work is suggested by his use of the word as a subtitle to one of his important novels, *Pierre; or, The Ambiguities*. The word serves as both a proclamation and a warning—a proclamation that the truth, of life or of fiction, is contradictory and complex; a warning that superficial reading and hasty interpretation will lead the reader astray. Few are Melville's readers who, upon a first reading of a novel, have not made interpretations that they have reluctantly abandoned on subsequent and deeper reading. These experiences have cut deep because frequently the first assumed meaning is precisely the opposite of that which eventually displaces it.

In writing about Melville, the temptations are to withhold any interpretive judgment at all, or to collect all those that have been ventured and attempt some indecisive synthesis, or to restrict the material and narrow the vision to a single, simple element. I have avoided all of these temptations, perhaps in pursuit of others. I have taken my stand on the key interpretive questions, and I have tried to identify the patterns of meaning that recur throughout Melville's work. I have kept these patterns to the fore in my analyses because I feel that intepretation of *Mardi* will illuminate *Moby Dick*, that the meanings of *Pierre* have significance for *Billy Budd*. I would be surprised if anyone agrees with me on every point, or if everyone agrees with me on any single point. But I would hope that even those who disagree might be led by the very defense of their disagreement to deeper insight into Melville's meanings.

Biographical note

When Melville died in 1891, he was remembered not as the author of *Moby Dick*, but, if at all, as the young man who had lived among the cannibals, and who, though he had once shown great gifts as a writer, had not fulfilled his promise. Not until 1921 when Raymond Weaver's biography, *Herman Melville, Mariner and Mystic*, was published, did interest in Melville reawaken. Modern scholars and critics have worked diligently to make up for the long neglect. In the twentieth century, Melville has found a much wider audience than he ever enjoyed in the nineteenth, and one more appreciative of his genius. His example may well serve as a warning to any age, our own included, to avoid haste and dogma in judging the contemporary literary scene, and to view genius, however obscure its manifestation, with a sympathetic eye.

Herman Melville was born in 1819 in New York City. His parents were Allan Melville, a Unitarian, who made a living as a merchant-importer, and Maria Gansevoort Melville of New York Dutch ancestry and a member of the Calvinistic Dutch-Reformed Church. Herman's father was volatile and slightly unstable in character; in 1832, at fifty, he died in debt; his widow, left with eight children to care for, became the pitied poor relation of well-to-do kin. Herman was then thirteen. As a consequence, the Melville children grew up in an atmosphere of rootless, genteel poverty, shuffling from town to town—New York, Albany, Pittsfield. Herman's emotional development may well be imagined: a growing resentment against the father, an intense passion toward the mother, running the gamut from love to hate. His formal education was brief, as school was expensive, and there was the pressing matter of support for such a large family.

It surely is no wonder that in 1837, at the age of eighteen, Herman went to sea. On this first voyage he sailed as a ship's boy on a merchantman bound for Liverpool. The voyage may well have marked Melville's initiation into adulthood, but it may also have temporarily soured his taste for life at sea. He turned to other activities for a time, including school teaching, and he made one significant journey into the West, visiting an uncle in Galena, Illinois, on the banks of the Mississippi.

In 1841, at the age of twenty-two, Melville shipped out of New Bedford as a sailor on the whaler *Acushnet*. He was gone for nearly four years by the calendar, but in the world of literature, his voyage is not likely to see an end: the greatest body of his work was shaped out of the experiences of this voyage. The sailor Melville jumped ship with his friend Toby in the Marquesas Islands and lived for a time as a captive among the "cannibalistic" Typees. After being rescued he took part in a mild mutiny and was imprisoned on Tahiti. When released, he roamed the islands with his vagabond friend, Long Ghost, a deposed ship's doctor, and sailed finally on another whaler which took him to Honolulu. From there he shipped on the man-of-war, the U.S.S. *United States*, thus becoming a sailor in the U.S. Navy, and after a fourteen-month voyage was discharged at Boston in October, 1844.

After so much high adventure in so few years, the remainder of Melville's life seems tame indeed. Beginning in 1846, the books began to pour out seemingly without end: 1846, *Typee* (life as a captive of the savages in the Marquesas); 1847, *Omoo* (life as a vagabond sailor, on shipboard and in Tahiti); 1849, *Mardi* (voyages in the South Sea Islands transmuted into fantasy and allegory); 1849, *Redburn* (life on a merchantman to Liverpool and return); 1850, *White Jacket* (life on a man-of-war homeward bound); 1851, *Moby Dick* (life in a whaler on a sea of metaphysics). This last, great book was the climax to his furious and sustained outburst of creativity—in six years he had published six books; and, indeed, *Moby Dick* seems to have been the climax of Melville's life; the rest was decline.

Melville had, actually, largely used up his early experiences, and he seemed at a loss to discover new and usable material. After his youthful, vagabond voyages and his captivity among the savages, his civilized experiences seemed incapable of a primary appeal to his imagination. He developed a number of literary friendships, particularly with Evert and George Duyckinck. There were, too, relationships with numerous intellectual companions—Shakespeare, Milton, Hobbes, Spinoza, Rousseau, Hume, Hegel, Kant. Certainly, the two most crucial relationships were those with his wife, Elizabeth Shaw, and with his friend, Nathaniel Hawthorne.

Elizabeth Knopp Shaw was one of the four children of Judge Lemuel Shaw, Chief Justice of Massachusetts. When she married Melville in 1847, she was twenty-five, he twenty-eight. Melville's choice is puzzling for one of the salient facts of Elizabeth's emotional constitution was her total lack of imagination. Their families, however, were close. Lemuel Shaw had been in love with Nancy Melville, sister to Herman's father Allan, and after her early death, had continued his close association with the Melville family, advising and aiding the widow after Allan Melville's death. Herman's sense of gratitude was very strong, and in fact he dedicated his first book, *Typee*, to Lemuel Shaw. If it is possible that in marrying Elizabeth Shaw, Melville felt a sense of duty in the fulfillment of an obligation, he may also have felt, below the levels of consciousness, a sense of guilt in the commitment of an incestuous sin. For if Lemuel Shaw acted like a father, Elizabeth must at times have seemed a sister.

Although the relationship between Melville and Hawthorne is one of the most interesting in all American literature, so little is known about it that its significance remains largely a matter of speculation. They met when Melville was thirty-one and Hawthorne forty-six. The master had just finished his great work, *The Scarlet Letter*, and the disciple was struggling to finish *Moby Dick*—the whale among his books. Melville's dedication of his masterpiece to Hawthorne, in "admiration for his genius," stands as testimony to the impact of the friendship on Melville, and suggests an imaginative indebtedness almost impossible to measure. They enjoyed each other's intellectual companionship for some months during 1850-51 in the Massachusetts countryside, where their houses were close enough to make frequent visiting possible; they were then separated, to have only one major, though brief, meeting in 1856 in Liverpool, England, where Hawthorne was then American Consul. In these encounters, the vigorous young Melville seemed the pursuer, and the reserved, retiring Hawthorne the reluctant object of pursuit. At the end, the younger man had to confess to himself that he was unable to break down the older man's reserve.

The works published after *Moby Dick*, though they did not reach its grandeur nor strive for its epic scope, had a classic quality of their own. *Pierre* (1852) made uncharted journeys into the human psyche, and the discoveries still startle readers. *Israel Potter* (1855) illuminated the national character in an adventurous excursion into history. *The Piazza Tales* (1856), delightful and daring, portrayed the price of withdrawal from the human scene. *The Confidence-Man* (1857) dramatized in bitter comedy the fantastic drift of America—and man—down the treacherous Mississippi in the steamer *Fidèle*. By 1857, Melville must have felt that even the leftover scraps of his central experiences had been consumed; he never published fiction during his lifetime again, though in his last years he returned to it for the Christ-like story of *Billy Budd*, first published in 1924, long after Melville's death.

The rest may not have been silence, but it was a retreat

to privacy where the imagination need not strain for a vain popular appeal. There were volumes of verse, and even a long narrative poem, but these were in the main privately printed for limited circulation. The narrative poem, *Clarel* (1876), was based on a long voyage of 1856-57, during which Melville visited England (to see Hawthorne) and then journeyed on to the Holy Land to work out alone an obscure personal anguish which neither his relatives nor his friends could understand or mitigate.

The last, long years were lived out quietly in New York, where the author of *Moby Dick* worked as an anonymous District Inspector of Customs. Though these years gave leisure for the reading of innumerable books and for the writing of a quantity of verses, there must have been a residue of restlessness if not of bitterness deep within. Two of his four children died before Melville: his son Malcolm shot himself at the age of eighteen; Stanwix died of an illness at thirty-five. Melville himself died in 1891 at the age of seventy-two.

Contents

2

a reader's guide to HERMAN MELVILLE

1

The complex figure in Melville's carpet

Hugh Vereker, the elusive novelist in Henry James's "The Figure in the Carpet," tantalized his puzzled critic by telling him: "there's an idea in my work without which I wouldn't have given a straw for the whole job. . . . It stretches, this little trick of mine, from book to book, and everything else, comparatively, plays over the surface of it. The order, the form, the texture of my books will perhaps someday constitute for the initiated a complete representation of it." When James's critic asks the novelist whether this element running through the work isn't like "a complex figure in a Persian carpet," Vereker approves the metaphor with enthusiasm.

Perhaps the failure of the critic, in spite of diligence and persistence, to discover the novelist's "complex figure" should appear as a warning. But Herman Melville's work, like Vereker's, is too tantalizing for critics to resist. And although much of its complexity has been revealed, the figure itself remains dim, and in its alleged recurrence frequently assumes a grotesque shape.

1 *The intricate design*

When the critic in James introduced the carpet figure, the novelist countered with the metaphor of the string of pearls. In seeking the figure in Melville's carpet, in tracing the

thread that runs through his pearls, we shall not reduce the
work to a convenient simplicity, but attempt to discover in
the complexity both the open and the subterranean connec-
tions that make of Melville's work a single vision. Hereto-
fore it has been customary to look at Melville's work as shifting from celebration to pessimism, or from faith to cynicism,
or from defiance to acceptance. This view, which assumes
that Melville's books reflected his inner turmoil and conflicting moods at various stages of his life, emphasizes certain
peaks of elation and valleys of despair.

My use of the figure of the carpet is meant to suggest that
this peak-valley view is, if not incorrect, at least misleading.
Too much emphasis has been placed on so-called abrupt
shifts in Melville's emotional point of view and even on contradictions in his themes. One account has received considerable acceptance: Melville, at the beginning of his career, identified himself with Taji's ultimately suicidal search
in *Mardi,* and hovered between Ishmael's purgation and
Ahab's cosmic defiance in *Moby Dick;* in mid-career Melville's extreme bitterness burst forth in *The Confidence
Man's* vicious misanthropy; and, finally, at the end of his career, Melville achieved a calm Christian acceptance with
Billy Budd.

Although I would not contend that Melville's entire work
is one grand emotional monotone, I do desire to cast doubt
on the extreme fluctuations now identified in the line of his
artistic development. Indeed, I want to abandon the verti-
cal for horizontal metaphor, to flatten the peaks and fill the
valleys and end with some rolling hills. Instead of viewing
Melville's work as a series of heights and depths, I wish to
view it as essentially steady and straight in theme, though
shifting radically in focus and form.

The straight line running from *Typee,* 1846, through *Billy
Budd,* 1891, may be intellectually formulated first as a question and then as an answer. What should be man's response

to his situation in the universe, where evil is omnipresent and where man by the involuntary act of birth becomes inevitably involved? In examining this question, Melville dramatized a series of human beings in the act of responding, some in violence, some in apathy, and some in ambiguity. And throughout his dramatizations, Melville pondered and questioned, evaluated and judged. But his own attitude did not change and shift so much as simply deepen in complexity. In brief, from the beginning to the end, Melville asserted the necessity of man to compromise with his ideals, frankly and without private or public deception, in order to come to terms with the world's evil and his own.

But Melville's assertion was invariably linked to vital qualifications, extensions, reservations, all in the midst of deep probing. In working out his assertion, Melville wrote book after book in an extended drama of masks. The dominant figures in this drama, from Taji to Billy Budd, all hold in common their vast pretense, conscious or unconscious, that things are not as they are. They all protest their innocence and their desire for good; most frequently they are crusaders destroying the world in an attempt to set it right.

In the world of Melville's novels, man's characteristic response to his situation is to don a mask of innocence. Melville conceived it as his artistic task, if not to rip off the mask, to explore the depths of the mind behind it and to reveal what was hidden there. Melville's characters who wear masks are of two kinds: those who don the mask to conceal nefarious purposes and those who put on masks unconsciously and mistake them for their own true face. The degree of self-consciousness of the masquerade does not determine the extent of the evil wrought; for the most apparently innocent may perpetrate the greatest evil. It was Melville's finest achievement to plunge deep into men's souls and to surface with much that was barely visible to their own inner eye.

In addition to the masked figures there are in Melville's books the maskless men, those rare creatures who stand naked and exposed before the world, but balanced and poised within. Their greatest claim to innocence, ironically, is that they do not don its mask. They accept with equanimity their share of the world's guilt, trying neither to hide nor disclaim it. And between the masked and the maskless are the wanderers and seekers, the Omoos and the Ishmaels, who, in the progress of their quest, must decide with what face to confront the world.

An examination of this dramatic masquerade running through the whole body of Melville's work may enable us to trace out the figure in his complexly woven carpet. We shall perhaps discover that the design is intricate, its recurrence sometimes vividly detailed on the surface, sometimes submerged deep within the thickly entangled threads.

2   *The young seekers*

Typee (1846) and *Omoo* (1847) must be considered as two volumes of a single work, an extended quest for innocence by the Young Seeker, Tommo-Omoo. Throughout his search for the "uncontaminated island" in the South Seas, he constantly contrasts three states of society—the primitive level as represented by the pristine savage life, the primitive level as contaminated by merchant and missionary, and (indirectly) the civilized level of which the protagonist is a protesting product. From the very beginning of *Typee*, as he prepares to abandon ship, disillusioned Tommo directs his criticism at civilization, particularly as it is represented in miniature in the world of the ship. But his keenest criticism is saved for merchants and missionaries who bring misery and destruction in the guise of merchandise and the gospel to the innocent islands of the Pacific. These merchants of death and missionaries of sin perpetrate an evil which is increased in enormity by their pretensions to innocence and their protestations of godliness. Tommo-Omoo's highest praise is saved for the purely primitive society in which he seems to believe—at first—that he has discovered natural goodness. But gradually he becomes aware that the primitive goodness exists on an instinctive level where dwells, too, alas, primitive hostility that may flash forth at any moment. The central discovery of the protagonist in *Typee-Omoo* is that the happiness of the primitive life is peculiarly mindless and soulless, and that its attractive instinctive love can be matched by a terrifying instinctive hate. At the end of his search in *Omoo,* the Young Seeker sails out into the wide Pacific, still uncommitted in a world of apparently infinite possibilities.

The Young Seeker of *Mardi* (1849), unlike his counterpart in *Typee* and *Omoo,* is deeply committed, even to his own doom, by the end of his lengthy voyage. But before he reaches that commitment, he travels widely and discovers the many masks which hide the terrible faces of the world. Accompanying Taji, the sailor turned demigod, in his search for the beautiful, ethereal Yillah, are a king, a historian, a poet, and a philosopher. As the search progresses, Babbalanja, the philosopher, gradually penetrates into the truth of things as they are, through his ancient prophet, Bardianna and his contemporary devil, Azzageddi. Babbalanja, the mad mystic, becomes Melville's first maskless man, advocating, finally, a recognition and confrontation of evil in Serenia as against a suicidal pursuit of a purity that exists nowhere. But Taji the Young Seeker will not listen and will not accept. Even as he observes the hardening of his own heart, Taji determines on the endless pursuit of Yillah. In this determination he moves from the position of Young

Seeker to the role of a Melvillean masked man, pretending an innocence he knows he no longer has, hiding an evil he recognizes deep within. In his refusal to compromise and in his perseverance in the path of destruction and death, Taji becomes committed to an evil greater than any he has observed in Mardi, intensified, not mitigated, by his mask of innocence.

Like *Typee* and *Omoo, Redburn* (1849) and *White Jacket* (1850) must be considered as two parts of the same whole. The young Wellingborough Redburn who ventures from home for the first time on his voyage to Liverpool begins an initiation into the world's evil that is not completed until the closing pages of the story of White Jacket. The green hunting jacket which Redburn dons when he starts out on his adventures is not really disposed of until the floundering White Jacket rips himself out of his accursed garment to save himself from sinking in the sea. Also the Young Seeker, Redburn-White Jacket's education in the nature of the world begins the moment he steps out of his mother's house. Every event kills a comfortable myth, every experience destroys an illusion. Whether on board the brutal merchant vessel, amid the swarming streets of Liverpool, in the elegant apartments of London, or on the man-of-war seething with public and private vice, Redburn-White Jacket's recurring discovery is that the world is full of evil concealed beneath a thin veneer of innocence. But out from the midst of iniquity step two characters who become the protagonist's best friends. The first, Harry Bolton, emerges from Liverpool into Redburn's ken and becomes a fast friend: though largely untainted by the evil with which he has had to struggle, Harry has neither the means nor the virility to come to realistic terms with the world. His effeminate innocence spells his ultimate doom. But Jack Chase, captain of White Jacket's maintop, has all of Harry's attractions without his weaknesses, and emerges vividly as the prototype of the Melvillean maskless man, not vulnerably innocent, but frank, courageous, and firmly balanced in heart and mind in confrontation of evil.

While Tommo-Omoo sailed off into the Pacific uncommitted, and Taji donned the mask of innocence and sailed on in suicidal pursuit of Yillah, the Young Seeker Redburn-White Jacket finally discards his mask, the jacket of innocence, and becomes a maskless man. In portraying White Jacket ripping off the garment that has kept him isolated from his fellows, Melville brings to a close his extended treatment of the Young Seeker, whom he has dramatized in all of his possible roles, confronting all the possible choices. White Jacket's act is an affirmation not of innocence but of involvement. In discarding his jacket he joins the human race. In descending into the waters of the sea, he is cleansed not of his guilt but of his pretensions of innocence, and he rises reborn not into the sainthood of purity but into the communion of complicity.

3 Idealists and innocents

Although Ishmael introduces himself at the opening of *Moby Dick* (1851) in the familiar manner of Melville's other Young Seekers, by the time the book is ended he is clearly on the periphery of the story revolving about the *Pequod*. The magnificent Ahab has at some point assumed the central position, center stage, and does not relinquish it until his violent death. Clearly Melville's imagination has spent its force on the Young Seeker in the five books that have gone before. In *Moby Dick* his imagination is fired by the figure of the titanic rebel—the kind of character that Taji was becoming at the very close of *Mardi*.

Ishmael is the sole survivor of the catastrophe that concludes *Moby Dick;* implicit in this is the suggestion that
there were deficiencies, whether subtle or grotesque, in all
the doomed—and not in Ahab alone. Ishmael's immersion
in the sea, like White Jacket's, signifies a baptism into the
human condition, an acceptance of the human burden of
guilt. The only other maskless man of the *Pequod* is Bulkington, and he is buried in an early chapter to prevent his avert-
ing the necessary catastrophe. But the masked figures of
Moby Dick are legion. The society which Ishmael escapes
and which Queequeg observes is, like the society of *Mardi,*
thick with vice thinly veneered with innocence. And even
aboard the *Pequod,* evil masquerades as its opposite. The
savage harpooners, for all their innocence of civilized vices,
live, like the savages of *Typee,* on an instinctive level that
barely distinguishes blow from embrace. The mates Stubb
and Flask hide their mediocrity and their indifference behind a show of bravado. Starbuck and Pip are rendered ineffectual by their imbalance of mind and heart. Though all
of these pretend or protest their innocence, they are all
guilty participants, direct or indirect, in the fatal action.

But of course the deepest guilt of all is Ahab's. And he
would claim the purest innocence. Ahab's evil must be
measured by the extent of his self-awareness, and his self-
awareness may be assessed only in terms of the book's symbolism. Crazy Ahab wants to rid the world of evil by destroying the white whale who once reaped away his leg.
What nobler task could man set himself? But observe the
shadowy character Fedallah, lurking about in lonely, hidden places—like Ahab's deep sense of guilt. Fedallah is
smuggled on board by Ahab before the ship sails; Fedallah
merges with and extends Ahab's shadow in the course of the
voyage; Fedallah's reflection gazes up from the sea into
Ahab's eyes to claim his soul just before the final pursuit of
Moby Dick. This entire drama of silence and secrecy is the

symbolic drama of Ahab's internal struggle with evil and his ultimate dedication to it. Ahab never reveals this private drama to the world. Even to his death, he insists on his innocence as he conceals his guilt. Like Taji before him and Pierre after, he deceives himself as well as the world.

Pierre (1852) is a domesticated *Moby Dick*. But although the setting changes to the domestic romance and the scale of action is appropriately reduced, the terms of the tale remain unchanged. The society of *Pierre*, like that of *Moby Dick*, is evil compounded by hypocrisy. But in *Pierre* the society is brought vividly to life in such characters as the haughty, proud, "Christian" mother of Pierre, Mrs. Glenndinning, and the superficial, snobbish, self-seeking cousin of Pierre, Glen Stanly. The mask of virtue worn by these two relatives conceals deep and grotesque deficiencies in human sympathy. And these two are but society writ small. Hidden beneath a genial exterior, these deficiencies become monstrous in society en masse—as penniless Pierre discovers when he arrives in New York and seeks assistance.

The maskless man of *Pierre* is not a character in the action so much as a chorus silently and knowingly watching the inevitable working out of Pierre's doom. Plotinus Plinlimmon, like Babbalanja in *Mardi*, is a mad mystic with a practical bent. The Plinlimmon pamphlet, which Pierre discovers in his carriage on the way to New York, does not affect so much as illuminate the course of the novel's events. Plinlimmon's doctrine of "virtuous expediency" would have saved Pierre from his "unique follies and sins"—but Pierre did not—because he would not—understand. The pamphlet lost in the lining of his coat is like the self-knowledge submerged in his unconscious: both are "lost" because Pierre prefers not to confront them. Plinlimmon's penetrating gaze into Pierre's fearful soul is a frank revelation of the impure motives that Pierre himself, as he instinctively realizes, refuses to recognize.

Although Pierre has much in common with the Young Seekers, particularly with Taji after he rejects Serenia or White Jacket before he removes his badge of purity, the young idealist shares much more with Ahab. Though drawn to a reduced scale as necessitated by a landlocked domestic situation rather than an open-sea cosmic drama, Pierre is a youthful Ahab spiritually maimed by a seemingly inexplicable and apparently hostile force. We see Ahab long after his injury when his monomania has come to full fruition; we see Pierre in the process of discovery—as his monomania is developing in embryo. Pierre's Fedallah hides not below deck as in *Moby Dick* but in the dim recesses of his mind. The most exciting moments in *Pierre* are those in which he glimpses with horror the obscure sexual nature of his "pure" love for his half-sister, Isabel. But invariably he suppresses his self-awareness and dons the mask of innocence in a vain effort to convince not only the world but also himself. *Pierre's* concluding catastrophe, like *Moby Dick's*, is the inevitable result of the protagonist's uncompromising idealism and persistence in the pretense of purity.

4   A *miscellany of masks*

After *Moby Dick* and *Pierre*, Melville was never again able to muster his power to such terrible and massive focus. But there remained many brilliant moments, patricularly in the short tales and *Israel Potter*, and reaching a climax in *The Confidence-Man*, after which—silence. The works of this period (1853-1857) are miscellaneous in nature but even in his short pieces, Melville sought to present anew his old, unchanging vision.

In *Israel Potter* (1855) Melville probed his country's past to discover something of its character. For the first time he chose as his hero, who was to suffer forty years of exile from his native land, neither a young seeker nor a masked idealist —but a maskless man, a Yankee who had both the wisdom of the serpent and the gentleness of the dove to enable him to survive in an indifferent and hostile world. Potter endures to a ripe old age in spite of the unwillingness of his country to reward his services. He seems to hold all of the fine traits of mind and heart in stable balance. In contrast, some of his fellow countrymen, encountered during his Revolutionary War adventures, exhibit national virtues which, only slightly exaggerated, could become gross national defects. Ethan Allen, the embodied Western spirit, and John Paul Jones, symbol of the very nation itself, display a courage and righteous wrath that could, undisciplined, become a suicidal pursuit of the unattainable. Benjamin Franklin, the national genius, shows a contrasting cunning at compromise that, undisciplined, could become the duplicity of a swindling confidence man.

In two of his short stories, "Benito Cereno" (1855) and "Bartleby" (1853), Melville treats a new aspect of his old theme. Although he presents again the familiar masked innocent (the title character in each case), for the first time he portrays a withdrawing rather than a rebelling protagonist. Benito Cereno and Bartleby refuse to adjust to the evil in the world. And when it becomes overwhelmingly present, instead of coming somehow to terms with it, like White Jacket, or rebelling against it, like Ahab or Pierre, Don Benito and Bartleby withdraw into themselves and finally into death. Their masks prevent them from seeing the world's evil and their own intimate relationship to it. In "Benito Cereno" there are others who wear masks. The entire ship of blacks, and their master Babo, pretend subservience when they are actually conducting a reign of terror. Captain Delano at first cannot comprehend evil of such magnitude, but when he finally understands its imminence, he does not shrink from the involvement of coping with it. The Wall Street lawyer in "Bartleby," though he sardonically confesses many hard-hearted compromises with existence, exhibits a warm humanity in his concern for the fate of poor Bartleby: beneath his crusty exterior beats a human heart.

In *The Confidence-Man* (1857) Melville wrote a fine prelude to his prolonged silence. He had in his previous books dramatized a variety of Young Seekers and their various fates, and he had portrayed man masked and maskless in a variety of poses and postures. But though he had presented man grown Satanic, he had not shown Satan become man. In *The Confidence-Man* Melville chose as his protagonist the devil himself and presented him in a series of human guises. And each guise, though unique, shares with the rest a preposterous pose of innocence. The confidence man repeatedly gulls his fellow men by pretending a total faith and confidence in human nature. The irony is the repeated demonstration, in the victims' wickedness, greed, and selfishness, of the depravity of human nature. But even innocence is no defense against the confidence man. To cope with this masquerading evil requires wisdom as well as sympathy, mind as much as heart. Only the clever mystic, Mark Winsome, and his disciple, Egbert, are able to turn the tables and gull the devil. In thus coping with evil they demonstrate a realistic—and maskless—adjustment to the world as it is. Their practicality, like Babbalanja's of *Mardi* and Plinlimmon's of *Pierre,* provides ballast for their mystic vision.

The Confidence-Man is not, as sometimes claimed, Melville's anguished cry of despair. It is a comic allegory which takes as its central subject the world's evil. Melville's world had always been full of such evil, as witness the "contaminated" islands of *Typee* and *Omoo,* the mythical islands of *Mardi,* the Liverpool and London of *Redburn,* or the New

York of *Pierre*. Melville simply chose in *The Confidence-Man* to bring into clear focus what had always been a part of his vision, sometimes at the periphery, but never really absent.

5   *Backward glances*

Long after *The Confidence-Man* Melville was to make two major efforts to recreate the complex world of his fiction. *Clarel* (1876) and *Billy Budd* (finished in 1891, published 1924) represent Melville's final and somewhat reflective treatment of his old themes. Clarel is a direct descendant of those early Young Seekers—Tommo, Taji, Redburn, White Jacket, and Ishmael. Billy Budd is, in spite of major modifications, directly related to those earlier figures cloaked in innocence—the obsessed Taji, Ahab, and Pierre. But *Clarel* and *Billy Budd* do not merely repeat and restate. They extend and complete Melville's complex figure in the carpet. Without these later works, which are an intricate working out of the implications of the earlier books, we would sense an incompleteness in Melville's vision, particularly as brought to an abrupt halt by *The Confidence-Man.*

The Young Seeker Clarel is an American student touring the Holy Land in search of faith. As the earlier Young Seekers turned West and explored the primitive islands of the Pacific, Clarel travels East to examine at firsthand the ancient sources of modern Christian culture. In a journey more philosophical than physical, narrated in a persistently rhyming iambic tetrameter, Clarel discusses with his companions the nature of the world and the construction of the universe. He witnesses the death of Nehemiah, who is a religious fanatic, and of Mortmain, who is obsessed with re-

vealing the world's evil. He is at first attracted by the Angli-
can clergyman Derwent's optimism, and then repelled by
his shallowness and hypocrisy. He is drawn to the shy and
sensitive Vine, but ultimately rebuffed and wounded by
Vine's self-sustaining isolation and poverty of human feeling. He finally finds in Rolfe, spiritual descendant of Jack
Chase, the courage and balance and frankness of the maskless man he can admire. At the conclusion of his journey,
when he is stricken with grief at the death of his betrothed
(in the somewhat contrived and unconvincing narrative
frame), Clarel chooses his course—as did all those Young
Seekers who went before. Like White Jacket, Clarel chooses
life over death, involvement over withdrawal, complicity
over innocence. Clarel is last seen disappearing in the min-
gling throngs wending their way on the *Via Crucis*—the
lane along which, legend tells, Christ bore his cross. Like
White Jacket, Clarel makes his peace and accepts his burden.

   Billy Budd, like *Clarel*, introduces as its dominant metaphor the Christian myth. This metaphor has led some to con-
clude that the work is simply a retelling of the Christ story
in modern dress. But Billy's radical innocence, like innocence always in Melville, ends in catastrophe. The innocence is not only Christlike, but it is also childish, animal-
istic, primitive and barbaric—like that of the savage Typees.
All of these metaphors appear, as well as the Christian, and
operate in Melville's meaning. Like Taji, Ahab, and Pierre,
Billy Budd can neither comprehend nor cope with the evil
of this world—and yet he partakes of it in his Satanic stutter.
Though infinitely less intellectual than these predecessors
—indeed, he is almost mindless—Billy's encounter with
evil, like theirs, results in destruction, disorder, and death.
Billy's relation to the devilish Claggart, though dramatized
in radically different terms, is not ultimately far different
from Ahab's relation to Fedallah. And his welcoming death

as he does partakes of the suicidal drives of Taji, Ahab and Pierre. Billy Budd in his assumed but far from flawless innocence rightfully belongs in this gallery of Melville's masked men.

Captain Vere, who must impose the death sentence on Billy in order to preserve order in the Navy and the nation, is Melville's final, mature portrait of the maskless man. Throughout his characterization, Vere is given virtues in balance which in isolation or exaggeration could quickly become vices. With the wisdom and insight of Babbalanja and Plinlimmon, with the frankness and courage of Jack Chase and Rolfe, Captain Vere discovers the realities and necessities of the situation not as it ought to be but as it is, and then acts to prevent a personal catastrophe from engulfing an entire ship or an entire state. Captain Vere's act is a renunciation of personal innocence and a clear assertion (like White Jacket's and Clarel's) of involvement and complicity.

Melville's drama of the masks might be likened to one prolonged morality pageant. In work after work he extended and elaborated as he explored the labyrinths of his complex vision. From the beginning to the end, in the total design of his work, we may trace the intricate pattern as it reiterates the basic truths he discovered and dramatized: the impossibility and catastrophe of the assumption of innocence; the necessity of connecting with the chain of human sympathies in an acceptance of the universal burden of guilt. Though Melville shifted his form, changed his settings, varied his characters, we shall find that this basic view persisted. He must have come to realize (as we have come to know) that this singular vision nourished his creative imagination and at the same time gave it form and shape.

2

Typee *and* Omoo: *the quest for the garden*

Typee (1846) and *Omoo* (1847) are not only Melville's first but also his most neglected works. They are the basic books that gained him the small literary fame he enjoyed during his own time and caused him to predict his fate as the writer who would be remembered if at all as the man who lived among the cannibals. Melville's prophecy has proved wrong: he is remembered as the man who went whaling; and his life among the cannibals is generally regarded as an interesting footnote to his career. Both *Typee* and *Omoo* would lie unread today were they not by the author of *Moby Dick*.

It is surely a mistake to judge *Typee* and *Omoo* as conventional novels, for they have no plot, no central action springing from a basic conflict. They are rather books of adventurous travel written in the same tradition, and in much the same spirit, as R. H. Dana's *Two Years Before the Mast*, which had appeared in 1840 and had enjoyed a popular success. Dana's book emphasized the "wonders" of the California coast, then a remote and unexplored land, and devoted much space to the inhabitants, their customs and their means of livelihood. Intermixed with these descriptions and never far in the background was a detailed account of life aboard a merchant vessel, its excitements and its boredoms, its dangers and its calms, together with a running commentary on the customs of government and misgovernment on ships at sea.

Melville's books, too, dwelt on wondrous and distant lands filled with a strange and pagan people. But these lands were the even more distant islands of the South Pacific and the people the still more remote Polynesians. Alongside his observations of life in the South Seas in all its varied facets appears an account of the life of a roving sailor both as a seaman at sea and as a vagabond at his ease in the world at large. Melville's critical sights are set in every direction, but they are especially trained on civilization and its appalling inroads in a primitive culture. As always when Melville adapted a particular tradition to his artistic needs, he transcended the limitations of the borrowed form and wrote as he pleased. He knew better than Dana that, though the travel account demanded truth, fiction is sometimes more faithful than fact to reality.

From the beginning, critical discussion of *Typee* and *Omoo* revolved around the question as to whether the tales contained in them were true. Several studies addressed themselves to this question with the primary aim of discovering how reliably the works might contribute to a reconstruction of Melville's life. When it was discovered that the books contained fiction as well as fact, it was upsetting to those who saw their chief value in biographical revelation.

Commentary has been confined largely to *Typee*, with *Omoo* generally neglected because it is considered inferior. And in *Typee*, according to most critics, Melville identifies with the Rousseau tradition which assumes the fundamental superiority of the primitive over the civilized society. Indeed, the image of *Typee* sustained through a large body of criticism is of an idyl, a relaxed description of an instinctual society to which the narrator is unreservedly committed. Only Tommo's flight at the conclusion of *Typee* causes some critics to speculate on Melville's possible reservations about the life in Typee Valley.

Those critics who have attempted comprehensive interpretations of Melville's work have tended to be embarrassed by these two early books, not because they are inferior but because they do not seem to conform to the concepts of the world and man that inform the main body of Melville's fiction. Melville's primary works clearly place him, alongside Hawthorne, in the Calvinistic tradition of American literature as contrasted with the transcendental line running through Emerson, Thoreau, and Whitman. Melville's classic statement of his own attitude appears in his review, "Hawthorne and His Mosses," written in 1850 or only some three or four years after his South Sea island books. In defining Hawthorne's dark center, Melville speculates that the "great power of blackness in him derives its force from its appeals to that Calvinistic sense of Innate Depravity and Original Sin, from whose visitations, in some shape or other, no deeply thinking mind is always and wholly free. For, in certain moods, no man can weigh this world without throwing in something, somehow like Original Sin, to strike the uneven balance."

The implications for Melville of these remarks are borne out and in a sense confirmed by his major work. Yet *Typee* and *Omoo*, with their vivid contrast of pagan and Christian societies, have seemed to many readers paeans in praise of the noble savage. Thus we arrive at the central dilemma in the criticism of Melville's first books: how may we reconcile these apparently Rousseauistic works with an essentially Calvinistic temperament. We can assume, as a number of critics have, that Melville changed. But such an assumption involves the notion that Melville acquired his "Calvinistic sense" late and in spite of his earlier "noble savage" ideas confirmed by his Polynesian experience. It is difficult to believe that so deep a mind as Melville's could so readily and completely shift its orientation.

1   Some yet undiscovered island

Typee and *Omoo* should be read as one continuous work
just as they recount one continuous adventure. Moreover,
the informing sensibility in each is identical, and the serious
thematic content does not alter. In a prefatory note to the
second volume, Melville said that *Omoo* "necessarily begins
where 'Typee' concludes, but has no further connection with
the latter work." In other words, *Typee* and *Omoo* form one
continuous picaresque tale which is divided merely for the
sake of convenience into two volumes. Melville himself fills
the central role of the wanderer.

Neither strictly a travel account nor by any means a conventional novel, *Typee-Omoo* is a half-humorous, semi-
serious narrative of episodic adventure. Like a medieval
romance portraying the hero's quest for the Holy Grail,
Typee-Omoo dramatizes the protagonist's search for an innocent and untouched Garden of Eden. Early in the first
volume the hero exclaims of the pagans, "Thrice happy are
they who, inhabiting some yet undiscovered island in the
midst of the ocean, have never been brought into contami-
nating contact with the white man." In the recurring pattern of exploration, discovery, and flight throughout *Typee-
Omoo,* the constant thread is the quest for the "undiscovered island." Like the Holy Grail, the uncontaminated isle
surrounded by the sea glitters in bright vision luring the
seeker on. The pace of the narrative is at first slow and rela-
tively serious but gradually livens into a kind of frolicsome
vagabondage as one island after another is examined and
found wanting. Typee Valley is succeeded by Tahiti, followed by Imeeo, and, finally, the isolated inland village of
Tamai. But the Garden remains at the last unfound, the perfect innocence undiscovered. The ultimate meaning of

Typee-Omoo is to be found not primarily in the successive primitive societies scrutinized but in the increasingly complex reaction of the rover-observer to the pagan life he witnesses.

Although *Typee* and *Omoo* are basically episodic in nature, the high narrative interest sustained in them is evidence of an artistic instinct in process of self-discovery. "Six months at sea! yes, reader, as I live, six months out of sight of land; cruising after the sperm whale beneath the scorching sun of the Line, and tossed on the billows of the wide-rolling Pacific—the sky above, the sea around, and nothing else!" So opens *Typee*. And many pages later, *Omoo* closes: "By noon, the island had gone down in the horizon; and all before us was the wide Pacific." Out of the wide Pacific, back into the wide Pacific: Melville in *Typee* and *Omoo* looms up suddenly, is vividly there, and then returns to the vast, rolling waters, a true son of the sea. But while he is *there,* the wanderer Melville leaves his mark.

Grown restless at the confinement of a whaler at sea, Melville decides while his ship, the *Dolly,* is harbored in the Marquesas to desert with his companion Toby to go exploring among the islands. Melville asserts that Toby is of "that class of rovers you sometimes meet at sea, who never reveal their origin, never allude to home, and go rambling over the world as if pursued by some mysterious fate they cannot possibly elude." Melville understands this nature because he partakes of it himself. After struggling across a rugged, mountainous area and becoming lost, the two sailors find themselves, not in the land of the peaceful Happars, which they were seeking, but in the land of the dreaded Typees, warlike and cannibalistic—at least by reputation.

Two narrative threads tighten the loosely connected adventures: Melville—or Tommo, the name he assumes—is beset by recurring fears that he will become the victim of the cannibalistic appetites of the Typees; and the sailor's romance with a beautiful, young island girl. A dash of realism is added by the annoying injury to Tommo's leg which causes it to swell and to immobilize and confine him periodically. By and large, however, *Typee* consists of a systematic account of the social organization of the Typees, their mores and customs, their government and their religion, their marriage practices and their food habits, their rituals and their taboos. Interspersed with this account is an idyllic picture of island life as Tommo lives it with his constantly present and ingratiating servant Kory-Kory, and with his innocent and affectionate female companion, Fayaway. When Toby one day disappears, perhaps into food for the Typees, Tommo's fears for his own fate increase. But finally, through the help of the handsome, taboo islander, Marnoo, he discovers the opportunity to escape and does so over the physical protests of his captors. Years later he discovers that Toby had not been eaten but had also escaped.

Omoo (a Marquesan word meaning rover or wanderer) begins with Melville's escape from the Typees aboard the whaler *Julia*. The first half of the book is devoted largely to the appalling state of the life of a sailor aboard ship and the subsequent attempt by the crew, when the *Julia* reaches Tahiti, to escape. This whole affair, like the escape from the Typees, though matters of the utmost seriousness are implicit, seems somewhat lightly treated.

Indeed, it would be difficult to find elsewhere in Melville a finer series of comic portraits than those of the ineffectual and incompetent Captain Guy; the robust drunkard who is first mate, John Jermin; the black Baltimore, the ship's cook; Chips and Bungs, the carpenter and the cooper; and many more. Liberally sprinkled throughout are brief, brilliant characterizations, such as that of Old Gamboge of the French ship *Reine Blanche:* "His whole physical vigour seemed exhausted in the production of one enormous moustache." On the voyage and in the brief "imprisonment" on

Tahiti that follows the "mutiny," Melville becomes a close friend of the most fascinating character of them all, Doctor Long Ghost, a carefree, intellectual vagabond who has been deposed as the ship's physician.

Melville and his companion "escape" from their imprisonment and begin roaming about the islands, going first to the island of Imeeo to work for two farmers, Zeke and Shorty. After becoming bored with this life, the two sailors start out for a visit to Tamai, an area more remote and not yet so "civilized" as more accessible areas. After a good deal of roving, including an abortive interview with the queen of Tahiti, they make their way to the Bay of Taloo where a whaler lies at anchor in search of a crew. The Captain will sign on Melville but not his companion, the doctor. After considerable self-examination and after turning over part of his advance pay to Long Ghost, Melville parts from his buddy and sails off across the sea.

2   *Examples of civilized barbarity*

In all these adventures, Tommo-Omoo-Melville discovers much about man and his many masks. A symbolic note is struck in the opening chapter of *Typee*. Melville tells the tale of the missionary in the South Sea Islands who, faced with the problem of converting the reluctant savages, set up his wife as a divinity. The natives were impressed until they had penetrated the "sacred veil of Calico" and discovered the sex of the unfamiliar creature. Enraged at the deception, the savages became so unmanageable that the missionary and his wife had to throw up their mission and depart. Humorous as this anecdote is, it contains the major ingredients of Melville's most serious criticism in *Typee*-

Omoo—the evil wrought in the name of virtue by the Christian missionaries.

Unfortunately the opportunity was not given to all the natives to unmask their harmful "benefactors." And perhaps the greatest misfortune, for both native and Christian, was that the missionary could not unmask himself. He wore his mask so oblivious of its existence as to deceive himself utterly. He was so certain of his good intentions that he frequently was blind to his own cruelty.

In *Omoo,* Melville discovers a single scene which is able to convey some sense of the true situation behind the mask of missionary innocence. The Royal Mission Chapel of Papoar was built with the blessing of native royalty and was without equal in its vast dimensions. It was over seven hundred feet in length, and the ridgepole was supported by thirty-six breadfruit trees. The site was magnificent, the lofty structure spanning a murmuring mountain stream that swept down to the valley. All of three weeks had been consumed in erecting the structure. But what did Melville see? Not the chapel in all its glory but the decayed edifice long since reclaimed by woods and stream. "But the chapel of the Polynesian Solomon has long since been deserted. Its thousand rafters of hibiscus have decayed, and fallen to the ground; and now, the stream murmurs over them in its bed." The Royal Mission Chapel of Papoar, in its speedy erection and speedier decay, symbolizes the essential nature of the work of the missionaries—the hasty completion and the swift disappearance of their superficial achievement.

Inasmuch as the missionaries themselves have spread the impression, perhaps with no intention of deception, that the numbers of pagans converted have been enormous, Melville takes pains to point out that the figures are misleading. "The Tahitians can hardly ever be said to reflect: they are all impulse." As a consequence, a genuine and "permanent" conversion is almost impossible. The so-called "Great Revival at the Sandwich Islands" of 1836 was supposed to have converted several thousand. But the results were transient. There was an "almost instantaneous relapse into every kind of licentiousness" among those converted. The initial conversion "was the legitimate effect of a morbid feeling, engendered by the sense of severe physical wants, preying upon minds excessively prone to superstition." Such conversions are in a sense the wearing of masks—masks of sophistication to conceal elemental innocence. But the missionaries are not merely ineffectual: they bring in their wake wholesale death. Melville cites census estimates to demonstrate that the inroads of Christianity have not so much increased morality as decreased the population. The conclusion is clear: "Who can remain blind to the fact that, so far as mere temporal felicity is concerned, the Tahitians are far worse off now, than formerly; and although their circumstances, upon the whole, are bettered by the presence of the missionaries, the benefits conferred by the latter become utterly insignificant when confronted with the vast preponderance of evil brought about by other means."

These "other means" may best be comprehended under the sweeping and ambiguous term, "civilization." The villain behind the villain in *Typee-Omoo* is, in all its complexity—civilization. After excoriating the missionaries unmercifully, Melville adds: "In justice to the missionaries, however, I will willingly admit, that whatever evils may have resulted from their collective mismanagement of the business of the mission, and from the want of vital piety evinced by some of their number, still the present deplorable condition of the Sandwich Islands is by no means wholly chargeable against them. The demoralizing influence of a dissolute foreign population, and the frequent visits of all descriptions of vessels, have tended not a little to increase the evils alluded to. In a word, here, as in every case where civilisation has in any way been introduced among those whom we call

savages, she has scattered her vices, and withheld her bless-
ings."

If Melville singled out the missionaries for special criticism, it was because the gap between their voiced aims and
their real achievement was so great. The missionary at least
"meant well"—or thought he did, or deluded himself into
believing he did; his was a complex mask involving a strange
mixture of public and private, conscious and subconscious,
motives. When "civilization" assumed the mask, the frank
purpose was self-interest, not self-deception, and the mask
was designed to delude the savages—at least temporarily.
The hypocrisy of "civilization" was not compounded by self-
hypnotism involving lofty and spiritual aims. The reader is
dimly aware in *Typee* and *Omoo* that on the distant periphery of the action an imperialistic struggle is in progress.
Brief vignettes of the machinations of the French are
glimpsed. Disease and death, depopulating the Polynesian
Islands, have followed in the wake of political and com-
mercial struggles which are a permanent part of the pattern
of the white man's "progress." Though less obvious because
more conniving than the propagators of the faith, these
propagators of profit have done their full share to demonstrate the transcendent barbarity of "civilization." As Melville watches, at the opening of *Typee,* the gratification of
the "unholy passions" of the crew, he observes of the "Savages": "Unsophisticated and confiding, they are easily led
into every vice, and humanity weeps over the ruin thus re-
morselessly inflicted upon them by their European civilizers."

3 *The decayed fruit of the Polynesian paradise*

Though civilization is evil, can primitive life in its innocence
be preferable? If so, we are then confronted with the para-

dox of Tommo's flight, not only from the valley of Typee, but also from his pleasant incarceration in Tahiti, his idyllic life on the farm in Imeeo, the attractive life discovered in Tamai, and, finally, his desertion of the primitive South Sea islands altogether for a whaling ship that will carry him home eventually to civilized America.

At first glance, indeed, it would seem that Melville had discovered Paradise in the South Seas. From the time that he and Toby stumbled upon the lovers of Typee Valley, the boy and girl, both innocently naked and oblivious of their nakedness, we seem to be entering a society as guileless as the garden of Adam and Eve before the Fall. The Garden of Eden metaphor recurs in *Typee* and *Omoo* to suggest the unsophisticated and primal innocence of the "Savage" society, to imply that the idyllic state enjoyed by the natives was once possessed and lost by "civilized" man. Melville explores the varied facets of a simple yet subtly complex social structure which seems to allow, as "civilization" does not, for the natural expression and fulfillment of man's basic impulses, appetites, and desires. What has become corrupt or grotesque in the civilized world retains in Polynesia some of its primordial innocence. Evil does not masquerade as good; the frank and open social order does not give rise to the self-deluding crusader. Even the material transcendence of civilization appears challenged. Only three times (and those trivial) do the natives of Typee avail themselves of what Melville ironically calls his "superior information." In view of his experiences, Melville feels justified in generalizing: "Civilization does not engross all the virtues of humanity; she has not even her full share of them. They flourish in greater abundance and attain greater strength among many barbarous people."

In the South Pacific the degree of innocence of the society is determined by the amount of traffic with civilization. The seclusion and natural isolation of Typee make it the ideal place for close study; Tahiti demonstrates the inroads into innocence made by civilization; Imeeo may be located at some point in transition between Typee and Tahiti, the bay areas corrupted by intercourse with the white man, but some valleys, such as the secluded Tamai, still largely preserving their aboriginal and pristine way of life. In the long sought Tamai, Melville and Dr. Long Ghost are "struck by the appearance of these people, both men and women; so much more healthful than the inhabitants of the bays. As for the young girls, they were more retiring and modest, more tidy in their dress, and far fresher and more beautiful than the damsels of the coast." This idyllic description, coming near the end of the roving in *Omoo,* is allied with that of the innocent boy and girl which stands at the beginning of the adventure in *Typee.* Both suggest the uncorrupted and maskless innocence of the first Garden.

But if Melville really discovered Paradise in Polynesia, why did he repeatedly flee? A more thorough scrutiny of this South Sea Garden reveals some vital differences from the archetype. Melville suggested these differences symbolically in depicting the arrival of Toby and Tommo in Typee Valley. Like Christian in *Pilgrim's Progress,* they endure all kinds of dangers and hardships, moving over mountains, across streams, down cliffs, emerging finally from a rugged and hostile world into the beautiful green valley which promises food, drink, and rest. Having arrived in a virtual paradise, they seek their immediate reward: "How to obtain the fruit which we felt convinced must grow near at hand was our first thought." The fruit of Paradise is soon caught sight of, and there is a race to the inviting trees and its abundant "delicious fruit." But just as they are about to achieve fulfillment in consuming the fruit, they discover a disheartening truth: "[Toby] quickly cleared one of the trees on which there were two or three of the fruit, but to our chagrin they proved to be much decayed; the rinds

partly opened by the birds, and their hearts half devoured."
The reality turns out to be far short of the expectation. But
even half-devoured fruit has its attraction to hungry men:
Tommo and Toby quickly eat the fruit, "and no ambrosia
could have been more delicious." The symbolism seems clear
and pointed: this Polynesian retreat, though a Paradise in
many respects and particularly to one weary of the outrageous behavior of civilization, still falls far short of the
original Garden. Discovery of decay in the inviting fruit
proves to be a recurring experience.

There are two counts upon which Polynesian life is apparently declared superior to civilized life in *Typee-Omoo:*
primitive man is happier and he is more virtuous than civilized man. Of these, the Polynesian's idyllic happiness seems
to dominate. At the very outset of *Typee,* Melville brings
dramatically together two seemingly supreme specimens of
two vastly different cultures, a French admiral and a Polynesian king: "In the one is shown the result of long centuries
of progressive civilisation and refinement, which have gradually converted the mere creature into the semblance of all
that is elevated and grand; while the other, after the lapse
of the same period, has not advanced one step in the career
of improvement." Melville then poses what appears to be
the working hypothesis of his books: "Insensible as he is to
a thousand wants, and removed from harassing cares, may
not the savage be the happier man of the two?"

Even in this very scene may be detected an element subtly modifying and ultimately destroying the serious point
made: an elusive but frequently decisive humor which sometimes lurks mockingly behind the sober statement. This
humor seems at times so overwhelming that it leaps out of
Melville's control. If the Polynesian king seems superior to
the French admiral, what can one say for the Queen of Naku-
heva on her state visit to the flagship of an American squad-
ron and in the presence of a number of French officers? In

front of the entire group assembled for the ceremony, she
becomes intensely and insistently interested in an old
salt's tattoos and begins to beg him to let her see all. Carried away with the possibilities for farce, Melville concludes
the scene: "But picture their consternation, when all at
once the royal lady, eager to display the hieroglyphics on
her own sweet form, bent forward for a moment, and turning sharply round, threw up the skirts of her mantle, and revealed a sight from which the aghast Frenchmen retreated
precipitately, and tumbling into their boat, fled the scene
of so shocking a catastrophe." This tattooed lady is more
likely to become deeply lodged in our consciousness of
Polynesia than is the dignified king. And the writer who
brings both to life with such gusto is surely not willing to
leap to easy and hasty conclusions about a people so obviously volatile.

At one point in his observation of the Typees, Melville
begins his remarks on their happiness with a small word of
great reservation: "But the continual happiness which, so
far as I was able to judge, appeared to prevail in the valley,
sprung principally from that all-pervading sensation which
Rousseau has told us he at one time experienced, the mere
buoyant sense of a healthful physical existence." How much
emphasis can be placed on "mere" might be questioned, but
its force of reservation is great. In fact, throughout *Typee*,
the primitive society is depicted as far more materialistic
than America's. In Typee Valley there is abundance and
life seems to consist of one sensual satisfaction after another
in almost dreary succession. Such a glutted happiness
might well begin to cloy. Melville pauses in his narrative to
note the ability of the Typees to "endure" sleep: "To many
of them, indeed, life is little else than an often interrupted
and luxurious nap." Such a life might be happy, but for one
of restless intellect it cannot seem very significant. So nearly
devoid of any life of the mind or of the spirit, the Typees

4

seem subhuman, closer to fine, healthy, instinctive animals than to human beings. Even their complicated religion they take very lightly; when Tommo wanders into the Taboo grove he discovers "mouldy fruit . . . hanging in half-decayed baskets": "In fact, religious affairs in Typee were at a very low ebb. All such matters sat very lightly upon the thoughtless inhabitants; and, in the celebration of many of their strange rites, they appeared merely to seek a sort of childish amusement." The religious leaders, the priests, were the "merriest dogs in the valley." The recurring child and animal metaphors tend to deprive the Typees of those distinctively human attributes, a mind and a soul.

The other superior attribute of the Typees, their virtue, also begins to assume a strange configuration when examined closely. In the midst of his description of the virtues of the Typees, Melville pauses for an aside that is a kind of warning as it is also a direct revelation of his disbelief, despite the Polynesians, in any theory of natural goodness: "I will frankly declare, that after passing a few weeks in this valley of the Marquesas, I formed a higher estimate of human nature than I had ever before entertained. But alas! since then I have been one of the crew of a man-of-war, and the pent-up wickedness of five hundred men has nearly overturned all my previous theories." This casual remark clearly defines the two points of view operative in both *Typee* and *Omoo,* the view of the young rover in the midst of his romantic experiences tempered by the view of the maturer writer recalling an earlier day. It is frequently the reservations of the latter imposed on the rashness of the former which reveal Melville's deepest meanings.

As a hearty humor tends to modify the extravagant praise of the Polynesian happiness, so a pervasive fear frequently intrudes in the expansive view of savage virtues. Upon Tommo's discovery that he and his companion have arrived in the valley of the terrible Typees, fear becomes dominant: "But what dependence could be placed upon the fickle passions which sway the bosom of a savage? His inconstancy and treachery are proverbial." Although the fear wells up and erupts only occasionally, it is never far beneath the surface, operating not only as a basic device for suspense but as an important element of theme. Tommo's leg injury, which tends to make him passive and immobile, places him in an even more vulnerable position than usual, especially after Toby's mysterious disappearance. Fear of the cannibalistic tendencies of the Typees reaches a climax in the confirming discovery of the three human heads, mummy-like in appearance, two of them islanders but one of them a white man.

The revulsion and horror Tommo feels at the sight of his fantastic discovery is Melville's overwhelming commentary on the society and nature of the Typees. That they could place so small a value on human life has been half-glimpsed already in the minute examination of their essentially materialistic culture. With life so empty of intellectual or spiritual content, it is no wonder that they place such casual value on it. Their cannibalistic deed is exceeded in horror only by their feelings of innocence about it. Like the cannibalism, Tommo's flight at the end of *Typee* is aesthetically if not biographically justified. Jolted out of his passive state by his discovery, Tommo plots his escape and in the execution becomes aggressively hostile to the savages who would detain him, giving one a deathblow in the fierce struggle. The act of escape symbolizes the ultimate recognition of the deficiencies of the Polynesian culture, a recognition of the horror that exists not far beneath the placid surface.

For as Tommo feared at the beginning of his residence among the cannibals, they are swayed by "fickle passions." Like children or animals, their affection and sweetness can be instantly converted to hate and treachery. That same instinct and spontaneity which make them so charming and

attractive can also render them repulsive and horrible. In
Omoo, Bembo, the New Zealand harpooner, acts as second
mate aboard the *Julia*. Rumored to be from a tribe of cannibals, he is universally distrusted. In a fit of pique after a
minor quarrel, Bembo takes the helm and attempts to wreck
the ship: "Bembo's intention to destroy us was beyond all
question. His only motive could have been a desire to revenge the contumely heaped upon him the night previous,
operating upon a heart irreclaimably savage, and at no time
fraternally disposed toward the crew." This same savage
passion can flare up in friendships as intense as they are
apparently whimsical in origin: "In the annals of the island
Tahiti are examples of extravagant friendships, unsurpassed
by the story of Damon and Pythias: in truth, much more
wonderful; for, notwithstanding the devotion—even of life
in some cases—to which they led, they were frequently entertained at first sight for some stranger from another
island." Tommo's experiences with Kory-Kory and Marnoo
in *Typee* and his association with Poky and Kooloo in
Omoo suggest the intensity of the passionate Polynesian
friendships. Kory-Kory was Tommo's constant servant while
the handsome and taboo Marnoo offered him some help to
escape. Poky proved the devoted and faithful "Tayo" while
Kooloo turned out the sponging and fickle friend.

In his debate with himself as to whether to settle down
in Polynesia, Tommo-Omoo-Melville had before him the
frightening examples of two white men who had actually
gone native. In *Typee* a tattooed "grizzled sailor," an "old
rover" by the name of Jimmy, proved to be a "heartless
villain" in his offer of assistance to Toby to escape: his motive
was purely mercenary, his sentiment manufactured. In
Omoo the *Julia* discovers on one of the small islands of the
Pacific "a renegade from Christendom and humanity," one
Lem Hardy, whose most peculiar feature is the tattooing on
his face: "A broad blue band stretched across his face from

ear to ear, and on his forehead was the taper figure of a blue shark, nothing but fins from head to tail." The sailors look upon Hardy "with a feeling akin to horror, no ways abated when informed that he had voluntarily submitted to this embellishment of his countenance." This tattooing seemed "far worse than Cain's" for the "blue shark was a mark indelible." The emotional tone is unmistakable: there is a revulsion at this white man's reversion to savagery even though there is sympathy for the unmerited misfortune that plagued him in the civilized world.

The life of pure instinct led by the Polynesians is characterized by its intensities, and while their virtues seem extravagant, a horrifying hostility can at any moment flash to the surface and strike out in senseless destruction. What Tommo-Omoo-Melville set out to discover at the opening of *Typee* remains unfound at the end of *Omoo*. But the search has been exhilarating and revealing. In a curious reversal of the Garden of Eden myth, Tommo is bitten by a snake in the rugged, mountainous country before reaching the blissful valley. Perhaps the reversal is symbolic of the ultimate failure of the search for Paradise. It is not found in Typee Valley nor in Tahiti nor in the Valley of Martair on Imeeo nor in Tamai. As the quest begins to lose its momentum at the end of *Omoo*, probably out of a growing awareness that Paradise cannot be regained, Melville confesses: "The impulse urging me to sea once more, and the prospect of eventually reaching home, were too much to be resisted." Though full of his island wisdom—Melvillean rather than Rousseauistic—Melville is uncommitted as only a rover can be when he bids Dr. Long Ghost farewell and ships on the *Leviathan*. As he sails into the wide Pacific, the world seems still full of infinite possibilities: though one route is closed, many more beckon ahead. Perhaps that "undiscovered island in the midst of the ocean" can be found—or created —in the midst of a man's soul.

3

Mardi: *the search for innocence*

Herman Melville claimed that since so many readers of *Typee* and *Omoo* had believed fact to be fiction, he wrote *Mardi* "to see whether the fiction might not, possibly, be received for a verity." *Mardi, and a Voyage Thither* (1849) is generally considered an abortive allegory, most interesting as a kind of exercise in preparation for writing *Moby Dick*. But the work has a good deal of intrinsic interest. It shows a talent for romance and philosophy just as the two preceding books demonstrated a talent for realism and criticism. It is a combination of all these practiced talents that is shortly to achieve perfection in *Moby Dick*.

Just as it is a mistake to consider *Typee* and *Omoo* either as novels or as mutually independent works, inasmuch as they are a cross between travel narrative and fiction and together relate a single, continuous, and ultimately fruitless quest for modern man's lost Paradise, so it would be wrong to assume that some single element of *Mardi* is the whole. For the elements are many and diverse. There is, at the beginning, the tale of adventure which seems a continuation of the author's previous books. There is the comic interlude on the abandoned ship, the *Parki*, with its gentle satire on marriage and women. There is the romantic encounter with Yillah, reminiscent of innumerable German mystical romances. There is Queen Hautia and the flower symbolism straight out of the "flower books" of Melville's day. Following Yillah's disappearance, there begins the endless quest, like the quest for the Holy Grail in many medieval romances. As the Yillah-seekers visit island after island in mythical

Mardi, there seems to emerge some strange hybrid descended from Spenser's *The Faerie Queen*, Swift's *Gulliver's Travels*, and Rabelais' *Gargantua* which is, ultimately, none of these but something new and peculiarly Melvillean. In his experimentation with several disparate forms, Melville was creating, though not perfecting, one uniquely his.

The question as to *Mardi*'s origins out of Melville's experiences, reading, and imagination has been rather extensively explored. The question of *Mardi*'s meaning remains yet to be settled. A work of art is something more than simply the sum of all its origins. An imaginative transfiguration takes place in the author's soul. The secret of the new work lies not in the bits and pieces that were somehow transformed into its being, but in that transfiguration, that breath of life the new work has which gives it an independent—and lonely—existence.

Much has been written about *Mardi*, but not many critics have addressed themselves to the book's central problems of meaning—the symbolism of the elusive maiden, Yillah, the significance of the society of Alma in Serenia, the morality of Taji both in the early capture of Yillah and the final rejection of Serenia. When at the conclusion of the work Taji sails on in mad pursuit of the lost Yillah, his purpose and fate have remained largely a mystery among the critics.

One element running consistently through the interpretations of *Mardi* is the identification of Melville with Taji. In the light of such identification, most critics try to define Yillah as a symbol of something, like the Absolute, for which Melville himself was presumably searching. The problem such an interpretation raises, and one never satisfactorily answered, is the role left for Babbalanja and the significance of his acceptance of Serenia. There seems to be general agreement that Babbalanja is the vehicle for Melville's attitudes throughout *Mardi*—up to the end. If so, why should Melville capriciously drop Babbalanja and turn to Taji as

44444444

4444

---

the vessel of his profound and ultimate meaning? The question suggests that the ambiguities of *Mardi* are yet to be resolved.

1 *Mardi's many islands*

The protagonist in *Mardi*, as in *Typee-Omoo*, is the Seeker, whose name is assumed only after he is deeply involved in the adventures of his journey—Taji, demi-god of one of the Mardi islands. But when we first meet Taji, he is a common seaman aboard the whaler *Arcturion* secretly choosing a comrade and making plans for deserting ship. His motive is not dissatisfaction with his lot so much as a burning restlessness and desire for adventure. He escapes with Jarl the Viking in one of the whaling boats—and so begins one of the strangest and longest adventures in all literature. Their first major encounter is with what appears to be an abandoned ship, but they soon discover the sole occupants to be two South Sea Islanders, Samoa and Annatoo, a kind of comic Adam and Eve. Comedy gradually gives way to romance and finally to tragedy, however, in the next encounter. A group of natives are carrying on a raft a beautiful maiden named Yillah to a religious ceremony in which she is to be sacrificed. In the heat of his indignation, Taji slays the old priest standing guard over her tent and saves Yillah from the tribal slaying. There begin simultaneously Taji's deepest sense of sin ("guilt laid his red hand on my soul") and his highest feeling of bliss (Yillah was the "earthly semblance of that sweet vision, that haunted my earliest thoughts"). The bliss is not to last long, for one day Yillah disappears from the bower in Odo to which Taji has taken her on a kind of Eden honeymoon. But the guilt is to haunt

Taji for the rest of his travels; and they are to be long, for
Taji sets out on an endless search for Yillah.

As Taji's search progresses, the reader becomes aware that
Mardi and its islands represent the world and its various
faces; and Taji's search for Yillah is man's yearning for a lost
innocence, for a transcendent ideal, for the transfigured past,
for absolute perfection, for total happiness, for a good unalloyed with evil—all unattainable in this world. Taji's
search begins in Odo, where he lost Yillah but gained the
king, Media (also a demi-god), as a companion in his
search. Three "ordinary" humans are selected to accompany
the "demi-gods" as attendants: Braid-Beard, the historian
or chronicler; Babbalanja, the philosopher and mystic; and
Yoomy, the minstrel or poet. It becomes clear when these
three talkative if not garrulous individuals join the party
that the search for Yillah is to proceed at a leisurely pace,
as each nook and cranny of Mardi arouses their frequently
prolonged comment.

The three canoes bearing this fantastic group make the
grand tour of Mardi, touching all islands where the elusive
Yillah may be found. But there are long stretches of the book
when Yillah, except as a religious, political, or social ideal, is
totally forgotten. Island follows island in a phantasmagorial,
dreamlike sequence of several hundred pages, in which allegory slides into satire, satire slips into allegory. In Mardi the
entire world wears a mask and things are never what they
seem. It is the constant act of the Yillah-seekers to look behind the mask to discover things as they are. Odo, Media's
kingdom, reveals upon probing in its inmost haunts much
misery in spite of the apparently universal happiness; Vala-
pee, the isle of Yams, is ruled by the precocious, ten-year-
old Peepi, who is beset by "contrary impulses" although his
parliament has proclaimed that he can do no wrong; the isle
of Juam is ruled by the comely but effeminate Donjalolo,
confined by tradition to his "impenetrable retreat" as the

"insphered sphere of spheres," who vacillates between vice
and virtue as, to avoid the sun, he divides his time between
his House of the Morning and House of the Afternoon and
apportions his pale affections among his thirty wives; Oh-
onoo, called the Land of Rogues because at one time all of
the malefactors of nearby islands were exiled to it, is ruled
by King Uhia who frets and stews because his dominion is
so small when, as he thinks, it should be the "entire Archi-
pelago"; Mondoldo, the wondrous island where the four fish
ponds "trained" the fish for savory consumption, is ruled by
fat, bald, jolly old Borabolla—these are but the main stopping places in the first half of *Mardi*.

In the second half the criticism becomes more incisive as
the islands begin to assume recognizable shapes. Is Maramma, the island first visited, the dominion of Roman Catholicism or of any religious belief, such as Calvinism, which
has become rigidly and dogmatically and ritually fixed?
Pani, the "chief Divino" of Maramma, disturbed by the daring boy who is a simple, uncomplicated "undoubting
doubter," is plunged into an introspective soliloquy which
reveals the shallowness of his faith. He concludes—"Peace,
peace, my soul; on, mask, again." Pani's tyrannical faith,
paraded ostentatiously before the pilgrims to Maramma,
turns out to be almost no faith at all. Even His Holiness,
Hivohitee, the Pontiff of Maramma, is discovered to be an
old hermit whose claims to divinity are as fantastic as they
are fraudulent. In moderately rapid succession the seekers
discover the reality behind the distortions made by the old
Antiquarian among his antiquities in Padulla, by the "wealthy
old pauper" in Ji-Ji, by the Tapparians enormously busy ele-
vating the trivial and insignificant in Pimminee, by the lords
Piko and Hello engrossed in their perpetual games of war
in Diranda. Suddenly the geography becomes familiar
and the satire is carefully aimed as Taji and his companions visit Dominora (England), Kalleedoni (Scotland),

Verdanna (Ireland), Porpheero (Europe), and, finally, Vivenza (the United States), everywhere uncovering the motives beneath the pretenses and the truths behind the lies. After Vivenza, the seekers travel around the "cape of capes," up the coast, and then west, returning once more to that unidentifiable—but recognizable—area of Mardi already familiar to the reader. The voyage in search of Yillah turns out to be a voyage unmasking the world. The king, the philosopher, the historian, and the poet—all assist Taji in penetrating behind the many masks of Mardi. Whether the masks are moral, religious, ethical, social, political, they all have in common a single purpose: if not to deceive, at least to confuse, the world—but not the wearer.

2 Vivenza and the mask of freedom

As the travelers draw near the shores of Vivenza, they observe a huge inscription chiseled on an arch: "In this republican land all men are born free and equal." Upon closer scrutiny they discover a minute inscription in the nature of a postscript: "Except the tribe of Hamo." This striking difference between appearance and reality in Vivenza is typical of all Mardi. Upon touring the "great central temple" of Vivenza, the visitors observe the chiefs "making a great show of imperious and indispensable business." At the meeting of the "grand council," a chieftain from "a distant western valley" delivers an agitated, violent oration, sounding the alarm in every sentence. Melville notes that his tribesmen (westerners) are "accounted the most dogmatically democratic and ultra of all the tribes in Vivenza; ever seeking to push on their brethren to the uttermost." And Melville adds: "But they were a fine young tribe, nevertheless.

Like strong new wine they worked violently in becoming clear. Time, perhaps, would make them all right."

As they visit the north of Vivenza, the travelers come upon an angry mob gathered about a scroll nailed to a tree. The lengthy scroll is then read aloud as the crowd mutters its indignation. Clearly the scroll represents Melville's reservations about America's optimistic view of itself. The author ("you may ascribe this voice to the gods: for never will you trace it to man") begins by stressing the New World mistake of ignoring the "lessons of history": even though "Mardi's present has grown out of its past, it is becoming obsolete to refer to what has been. Yet, peradventure, the past is an apostle." The "grand error" of Vivenza is "the conceit that Mardi is now in the last scene of the last act of her drama; and that all preceding events were ordained to bring about the catastrophe you believe to be at hand,—a universal and permanent republic." All who believe such things "are fools, and not wise"; for "every age thinks its erections will forever endure," but Oro (God) decrees "vicissitudes."

The reason that Vivenza remains at peace with her neighbors and the world is not some inherent virtue in her people or her nature, but rather the existence of the unsettled West. "Republics are as vast reservoirs, draining down all streams to one level; and so, breeding a fulness which cannot remain full, without overflowing." But Vivenza, unlike Rome, England, or France, has a "wild western waste, which many shepherds with their flocks could not overrun in a day. Yet overrun at last it will be; and then, the recoil must come." Had there not been the West, then the "great experiment might have proved an explosion; like the chemist's who, stirring his mixture, was blown by it into the air." But in addition to the existence of the West is the fact of the nation's youth. Youth is "full of fiery impulses, and hard to restrain; his strong hand nobly championing his heart." Old age

brings a transformation: "he who hated oppressors" becomes an oppressor himself.

Freedom is not so simply conceived nor so easily obtained
as the Vivenzans think. "Freedom is only good as a means; is
no end in itself. Nor, did man fight it out against his masters
to the haft, not then would he uncollar his neck from the
yoke. A born thrall to the last, yelping out his liberty, he still
remains a slave unto Oro; and well is it for the universe that
Oro's sceptre is absolute." Man is always slave to the human
condition, decreed by God, of birth, life, and death: the
"fate" imposed by this condition he cannot escape. Moreover, the truth of freedom is complex: there is "such a thing
as being free under Caesar" and of being slave in a republic
("some despots rule without swaying sceptres"). "Thus,
freedom is more social than political. And its real felicity is
not to be shared. *That* is of a man's own individual getting
and holding. It is not, who rules the state, but who rules
me. Better be secure under one king, than exposed to violence from twenty millions of monarchs, though oneself be
of the number." A tyrannous society can do more damage
to the individual than a ruthless dictator. And a man may
liberate himself though he serve under an absolute monarch.

As for "bloody revolutions" to right the wrongs of Mardi
—they are nowhere necessary: "Though it be the most certain of remedies, no prudent invalid opens his veins to let
out his disease with his life. And though all evils may be
assuaged; all evils cannot be done away." The reason is
simple, and goes far toward explaining the futility of the
search for Yillah in Mardi: "For evil is the chronic malady
of the universe; and checked in one place, breaks forth in
another." No political system, monarchy or republic, and no
social condition, slavery or freedom, will eradicate the evil
in man. This truth the multitude of "kings" in Vivenza might
well ponder.

Once the anonymous scroll is read, a clamor against tory and monarchist arises, and the Yillah-seekers depart hastily, King Media and philosopher Babbalanja jocularly accusing each other of writing the criticism of Vivenza. The travelers depart Vivenza by way of the South, where they observe the institution of slavery flourishing in the land of the "free." This final irony underscores the gap that exists between pretense and reality in the democratic land of Vivenza.

3   Mardi's maskless man

As with Vivenza, so with isle after isle, country after country—the many masks of Mardi are examined and what they conceal and express exposed. Each pause in the journey precipitates a "philosophical" discussion in which the voyagers develop their views of the world; these views, expressing their varied perspectives, are sometimes subtly, sometimes violently in conflict. When the individuals accompanying Taji on his tour of Mardi are introduced, their distinct personalities suggest a variety of ways of looking at the world. Media is a "gallant gentleman and king," not only regal in bearing but handsome in appearance: "Strong was his arm to wield the club, or hurl the javelin; and potent, I ween, round a maiden's waist." Mohi, or Braid-Beard (so-called because of his long, gray beard), "was a venerable teller of stories and legends, one of the Keepers of the Chronicles of the kings of Mardi." Yoomy, or the Warbler, was a "youthful, long-haired, blue-eyed minstrel; all fits and starts; at times, absent of mind, and wan of cheek; but always very neat and pretty in his apparel." His dominant characteristic is his capriciousness, as he is "so swayed by contrary moods."

Although the king Media, the historian Braid-Beard, and the poet Yoomy become distinct, recognizable individuals, each limning the world with regal, historical, or poetic hues, it is Babbalanja the philosopher who emerges as the deepest diver and the book's one wholly unmasked man. He is described as a "man of mystical aspect, habited in a voluminous robe," and as one "learned in Mardian lore" and "much given to quotations from ancient and obsolete authorities." It is significant that upon his appearance he is introduced after Braid-Beard and before Yoomy: this "middle position" suggests the complexity of the truth he ultimately achieves. Babbalanja is the best example in Melville of the terrible struggle entailed in the determination not to don a mask but to confront reality directly. To achieve this insight requires a great deal more than passive acceptance; it necessitates an aggressive exploitation of all the intellectual resources at one's command.

Besides his own restless perceptiveness, Babbalanja draws upon two extraordinary resources. At first he constantly turns to the wisdom of the past, as represented in the old sage of antiquity, Bardianna, whose cryptic sayings Babbalanja applies to various Mardian dilemmas. About the nature of nature: "As old Bardianna has it, if not against us, nature is not for us." About arguments: "As Bardianna has it, like all who dispute upon pretensions of their own, you are each nearest the right when you speak of the other; and farthest therefrom when you speak of yourselves." Of the nature of truth: "Truth is in things, and not in words: truth is voiceless; so at least saith old Bardianna." Of the frailty of man's knowledge: "We are but a step in a scale that reaches farther above us than below. We breathe but oxygen. Who in Arcturus hath heard of us? They know us not in the Milky Way. We prate of faculties divine: and know not how sprouteth a spear of grass." Concerning devils: "Says old Bardianna, 'All men are possessed by devils; but as these devils are sent into men, and kept in them, for an additional punishment; not garrisoning a fortress, but limboed in a bridewell; so, it may be more just to say, that the devils themselves are possessed by men, not men by them.'"

The wisdom contained in the last of these sayings describes the other resource upon which Babbalanja draws more and more as the voyage continues: the prophetic devil he periodically "possesses." Babbalanja describes his devil, called Azzageddi, to his companions, who are startled by the divine frenzy of the philosopher: "He is locked up in me. In a mask, he dodges me. He prowls about in me, hither and thither; he peers, and I stare. This is he who talks in my sleep, revealing my secrets; and takes me to unheard of realms, beyond the skies of Mardi." Vaguely suggested in this brief speech are both the personal and the collective unconscious of the later "new" psychologies. Azzageddi grants (or is granted) a transcendental perception which penetrates far beyond human reason or imagination. The "transcendental" (or even Emersonian) nature of Azzageddi is strongly implied when Babbalanja, accused of inconsistency in his accounts of his devil, answers: "The sum of my inconsistencies makes up my consistency. And to be consistent to one's self is often to be inconsistent to Mardi. Common consistency implies unchangeableness; but much of the wisdom here below lives in a state of transition."

When possessed by his devil Azzageddi, Babbalanja appears sometimes to affirm much, sometimes to deny the possibility of affirming anything. In one of his moments of lucidity he strips his "knowledge" to its essentials: "Let us be content with the theology in the grass and the flower, in seed-time and harvest. Be it enough for us to know that Oro indubitably is. My lord! my lord! sick with the spectacle of the madness of men, and broken with spontaneous doubts, I sometimes see but two things in all Mardi to believe:— that I myself exist, and that I can most happily, or least miserably exist, by the practice of righteousness." Babbalanja's insight on this occasion is in harmony with the basic truths on which Serenia (where he later remains) is founded. When Babbalanja reaches Serenia, what he observes there in effect confirms what he already knows from Bardianna and Azzageddi.

One aspect of Babbalanja's philosophy has an important bearing on the quest for Yillah. When his companions doubt the character of one of the island kings ("There seemed something sinister, hollow, heartless, about Abrazza"), Babbalanja exclaims against the judgment: "For we are all good and bad. Give me the heart that's huge as all Asia; and unless a man be a villain outright, account him one of the best tempered blades in the world." It is this truth that is at the heart of the criticism of Vivenza ("For evil is the chronic malady of the universe"). This knowledge is the one consistent truth Mardi divulges to the seekers. And gradually the relevance for the quest emerges: Taji's Yillah cannot be found wherever evil exists; and since evil is universal, a condition of existence, Yillah can never be discovered—indeed, does not exist. As Babbalanja finally tells Taji, "She is a phantom that but mocks thee."

4   Serenia: Mardi's maskless society

When, at the end of the quest of Yillah, the seekers have reached Serenia, it is Babbalanja's vision, induced no doubt by his demon Azzageddi, which divulges the meaning of existence on that unique island. Serenia is the true land of Alma (Christ) and contrasts vividly with the island which claims Alma—Maramma, where the voyagers discover the sham behind the false faces of piety.

As Maramma is Mardi's hypocritical "Holy Island," so

Serenia is Mardi's maskless society of Alma. In Serenia, the real ruler is "mystic Love," and the law is "true brotherhood." But the people of Serenia do not cling to any false notion about the nature of man. As their spokesman asserts —"Think not we believe in man's perfection. Yet, against all good, he is not absolutely set. In his heart, there is a germ. *That* we seek to foster. To *that* we cling; else, all were hopeless!"

As Serenia takes a candid view of man, so it makes no claims of perfection for its society. When queried on Serenia's social state, the spokesman replies: "It is imperfect; and long must so remain. But we make not the miserable many support the happy few. Nor by annulling reason's laws, seek to breed equality, by breeding anarchy. . . . The vicious we make dwell apart, until reclaimed. And reclaimed they soon must be, since everything invites. The sin of others rests not upon our heads: none we drive to crime. Our laws are not of vengeance bred, but Love and Alma." Throughout Serenia, emphasis is not on an unattainable ideal but on a practically possible virtue. The Society is characterized by its avoidance of masquerade, by its cultivation of simplicity. "Pomp and power" are not needed to "kindle worship." Faith flourishes without "priests and temples."

The conviction of religious faith in Serenia is exceeded only by its tolerance of the views of others. Life in Serenia is not, like life in Typee Valley, deprived of intellectual content and lived solely on the level of instinct. There is provision for philosophical disagreement. Babbalanja asks the fate of the individual who disagrees: is he cast out? "No, no; we will remember, that if he dissent from us, we then equally dissent from him; and men's faculties are Oro-given. Nor will we say that he is wrong, and we are right; for this we know not, absolutely." When the skeptical Babbalanja asserts, "Methinks, that in your faith must be much that

jars with reason," again the reply is ready: "No, brother!
Right reason, and Alma, are the same; else Alma, not reason,
would we reject. The Master's great command is Love; and
here do all things wise, and all things good, unite. Love is
all in all. . . . we hear loved Alma's pleading, prompting
voice, in every breeze, in every leaf; we see his earnest eye in
every star and flower." Man need not deny his mental faculties nor give up reason to accept Serenia.

The reaction of the voyagers is immediate. "Poetry," cries
Yoomy, "and poetry is truth." "Sure, all this is in the histo-
ries," exclaims Braid-Beard. "Thou movest me beyond my
seeming," asserts King Media. Babbalanja, as he kneels, confesses, "Hope perches in my heart a dove;—a thousand rays
illume;—all heaven's a sun. Gone, gone! are all distracting
doubts. Love and Alma now prevail." Because of his "conversion" and his vow ("In things mysterious, to seek no
more; but rest content, with knowing naught but Love"),
Babbalanja is granted an elaborate mystic vision, the primary discovery of which is that "mysteries ever open into
mysteries beyond." Babbalanja is given the privilege of
viewing Mardi's heaven, where man puts off "lowly temporal
pinings, for angel and eternal aspirations." When he asks
where those go who live "thoughtless lives of sin," he is told,
"Sin is death." And when he asks, "Why create the germs
that sin and suffer, but to perish?" he is answered: "That is
the last mystery which underlieth all the rest." None but
Oro may know this mystery. As the archangel returns Babbalanja to earth, he presents his final advice: "Loved one,
love on! But know, that heaven hath no roof. To know all is
to be all. Beatitude there is none. And your only Mardian
happiness is but exemption from great woes—no more.
Great love is sad; and heaven is love." Babbalanja's vision
convinces him beyond doubt that what he had sought
throughout Mardi he had found in Serenia. The simple
truth overwhelms: "within our hearts is all we seek."

5   *Taji and the last, last crime*

But Taji dwells not in the land of Alma, nor does he search there for Yillah. Is it because he has already glimpsed a truth he is unwilling to accept: that Yillah no longer exists? Such self-deception is nothing new in Taji. From the very beginning of his encounter with Yillah, he has manifested a fear of examining his own motives too closely. In his original resolution to free her, there is an unmistakable note of self-revulsion: "Need I add, how stirred was my soul toward this invisible victim; and how hotly I swore, that precious blood of hers should never smoke upon an altar. If we drowned for it, I was bent upon rescuing the captive. But as yet, no gentle signal of distress had been waved to us from the tent." After Taji kills the old priest bearing Yillah to a religious sacrifice, he glimpses but for a brief moment the possible complexity of his motives: "Remorse smote me hard; and like lightning I asked myself, whether the death-deed I had done was sprung of a virtuous motive, the rescuing a captive from thrall; or whether beneath that pretence, I had engaged in this fatal affray for some other, and selfish purpose; the companionship of a beautiful maid. But throttling the thought, I swore to be gay." And to throttle it Taji tries. But the thought recurs periodically in the horrible shape of Aleema's green corpse: "In fancy, I saw the stark body of the priest drifting by. Again that phantom obtruded; *again guilt laid his red hand on my soul.* But I laughed. Was not Yillah my own? by my arm rescued from ill? To do her a good, I had perilled myself. So down, down, Aleema." Taji repeatedly shakes off the "red hand" of guilt in an attempt to maintain his spotless soul. He deceives himself as to his motives and he deceives Yillah as to his origins:

the bliss he achieves with Yillah is the substance of many deceptions.

In killing the priest Aleema and stealing Yillah, Taji performs the ritualistic act of initiation into evil, the old, old act of Adam's eating the apple. By the very nature of the act, the bliss cannot last, reality must finally impinge on consciousness, Yillah must disappear. To Taji, Yillah seems the "earthly semblance" of the "sweet vision" that haunted his "earliest thoughts." In their blissful haven in Odo, Taji wonders: "Did I commune with a spirit? Often I thought that Paradise had overtaken me on earth, and that Yillah was verily an angel." But there are intrusions in this Paradise. There is the haunting scene of the green corpse of the priest Aleema floating in the sea; there arrives one day the mysterious figure of the "incognito" whose solitary eye fixes upon Yillah with a "sinister glance" and which seems to Taji "a spirit, forever prying" into his soul; and finally, there are the "three black-eyed damsels, deep brunettes" who come with their sensual flower messages from Queen Hautia. These intrusions press upon Taji a sense of guilt, a self-acknowledgment of the lure of the senses in his life with Yillah. Taji will deny all and maintain his innocence; because they are denied, these dark forces of the unconscious deprive Taji of his Yillah. In his refusal to admit complicity, in denying his own human nature, Taji deprives himself of Yillah. He cannot remain innocent and have Yillah. He sacrifices Yillah in pursuit of innocence and loses both.

Taji's flight from the three sons of Aleema, who with their fixed spears pursue him throughout Mardi, symbolizes his refusal to accept his human burden of evil. Taji's insistence on his own innocence results in the death of his two original comrades, Jarl and Samoa, who receive the spears meant for him. Thus the individual who will not accept his human guilt wreaks havoc on others. The visits from Hautia's messengers are symbolic of the deep lure of the life wholly

dedicated to the senses. This lure was hidden in Taji's motives when he captured Yillah at the very beginning. It was
this element which came to dominate their paradisaical life
at Odo. Yillah became Queen Hautia's because Taji's lust
transformed her into one of the dark Queen's captives; Yillah disappeared because Taji refused all but a total innocence. Yillah is thus Taji's sacrifice to his own guilt.

Throughout *Mardi*, Yillah symbolizes to Taji a total innocence, a good unalloyed with evil, an ideal perfection. And
this Yillah cannot be found, not even in Serenìa, because the
human fate is inevitably involved in evil. After Taji rejects
Serenia, he sails for Queen Hautia's isle of Flozella: ". . . in
some mysterious way seemed Hautia and Yillah connected.
But Yillah was all beauty, and innocence; my crown of felicity; my heaven below;—and Hautia, my whole heart abhorred. Yillah I sought; Hautia sought me. One openly beck-
oned me here; the other dimly allured me there." Taji can
never attain the perfection and innocence of Yillah nor can
he abandon himself to the totally physical life of the senses
with Hautia. In insisting on the perfect Yillah, he gains only
the evil Hautia: in the very assertion of his spotless innocence lurks the proof of his imperfection. When King Media
exclaims, "Away! thy Yillah is behind thee, not before. Deep
she dwells in blue Serenia's groves, which thou wouldst not
search," he is pointing out the one place Taji rejected without exploring, the one island in Mardi where "love is all in
all" and man lives reconciled to his own shortcomings and
to the limits of his own knowledge. Such a reconciliation
Taji rejects out of hand, as he also rejects Hautia's tempting lures.

In the final pages of *Mardi*, Taji is transfigured from the
seemingly innocent voyager into a monomaniac in mad pursuit of a futile goal—but he maintains the pose of the sinless
seeker. His mask is double, turned toward the world but
turned inward too. Taji becomes a Titanic fraud, his greatest

victim himself. He knows but refuses to accept the nature of
man and the burden of existence. Man, less than perfect, is
doomed to sin; evil exists; "Oro is past finding out, and
mysteries ever open into mysteries." Instead of discovering
the mystic Love of Serenia in himself, Taji observes his own
heart grow "hard, like flint; and black, like night": "Hyenas
filled me with their laughs; death-damps chilled my brow; I
prayed not, but blasphemed." In continuing his search for
Yillah, Taji maintains the outward appearance to both the
world and himself of innocence yearning after unattainable
good; but down within he understands his deepest motives
for the corrupt and fiendish impulses they are. Taji seeks to
disown the heritage of guilt that is his as a man; but in
yearning to become all good, he becomes all evil, in attempting to be God, he becomes a devil.

In spite of Braid-Beard's warning that perdition lies
ahead, and despite Yoomy's plea that he not commit "the
last, last crime," Taji cries out, "I am my own soul's emperor;
and my first act is abdication! Hail! realm of shades!" He
darts wildly into the rushing tide and is last seen fleeing
from Aleema's three sons: "And thus, pursuers and pursued
flew on, over an endless sea." Taji's act is the supreme gesture of a fatal pride. In asserting rule over his own soul, he
usurps the function of God. In abdication of his rule
he abandons his soul by deliberately continuing a suicidal
quest. In shouting "Hail! realm of shades" he asserts a new
allegiance to God's eternal enemy, Satan. Like Ahab and
Pierre, Taji travels the path that leads from heaven's gate to
hell, deceiving the world by self-righteous assertions of
noble intent and half-deluding the self by an insistence on
innocence. Taji lacks, as do Ahab and Pierre, the courage to
peer closely into the darkness of his own deep soul. In attempting to gain all, Taji loses all. In seeking total innocence, he discovers total corruption. In a ruthless quest for
heaven, he wins his way to hell.

4

Redburn *and* White Jacket: *initiation and baptism*

Like his first novels *Typee* and *Omoo*, Herman
Melville's *Redburn* (1849) and *White Jacket* (1850), though
separate volumes, belong together in conception, spirit, and
theme. The "action" begun in the one is not concluded until
the end of the other. If we accept Wellingborough Redburn
and White Jacket as one and the same protagonist, we realize
that the symbolic act of donning the *hunting* jacket at the
opening of the first work is not fully resolved until the loss of
the *white* jacket in the sea at the close of the second volume.
Apparently these books are fictionalized autobiography, but
much closer to fiction than either *Typee* or *Omoo,* and not so
close as *Mardi.* Ostensibly these volumes describe life on two
kinds of vessels—the merchant marine and the man-of-war.
But in spite of these diverse purposes, *Redburn* and *White
Jacket* form a single whole through the unified development
of the protagonist and the informing sensibility of the author.
The two books tell one story of the world's evil—initiation
into it; observation and sampling of it; meditation on and
revulsion from it; and, finally, baptism in it, as the protagonist discovers and acknowledges to himself and the world
his place in the imperfect brotherhood of mankind.

Much of the commentary on *Redburn* and *White Jacket*
has been devoted to the question of their reliability as autobiography. Melville himself is partly to blame for the critical
neglect because of his own seemingly small regard for his
fourth and fifth works. In his 1849 journal of his European
voyage, he calls *Redburn* "a thing which I, the author, know
to be trash" and states that he "wrote it to buy some tobacco

with." In one of his letters he links *Redburn* and *White Jacket* and comments, "They are two *jobs*, which I have done for money—being forced to it, as other men are to sawing wood . . . my only desire for their 'success' (as it is called) springs from my pocket, & not from my heart." Such remarks could not help but lure the critics, and especially those interested primarily in biography, into a self-assured depreciation of the two works.

By the time the biographers had thoroughly exploited *Redburn* and *White Jacket* for comment on Melville's life, the critics began to point out certain deviations from the truth which suggested an artistic purpose. But it took some time and critical daring to find in the books a higher motive than the one Melville casually asserted. Only gradually has it been recognized that Melville is portraying, in both books, the impact of the world on the innocence of the boy. The abundance of the symbols in *Moby Dick* has led some of the critics back to the early work in search of symbolism, but the identification of it in *Redburn* and *White Jacket* has been only tentative and conjectural. The precise significance of Redburn's shooting jacket and White Jacket's distinctive garment remains unsettled. And that impressive scene near the end of *White Jacket,* in which the protagonist makes a dramatic plunge from the weather-top-gallant-yardarm into the sea, and escapes death only by ripping his way out of his hated white jacket—this scene has not yet taken its rightful place in the very first rank of all Melville's scenes as among the most poetically brilliant and symbolically charged.

1 *Initiation of the young seeker*

Like Melville in *Typee-Omoo* and Taji in *Mardi,* the hero
Redburn-White Jacket is an innocent Young Seeker exploring
the world; but whereas Tommo-Omoo-Melville remained at
the end of his narrative the Young Seeker uncommitted and
Taji at the conclusion of *Mardi* appeared resolved on the
pursuit of absolute innocence to self-destruction, Redburn-
White Jacket ultimately and deliberately discards his mask
of innocence and proclaims his common bond of guilt with
all humanity. When he sets off to make his way alone in the
brutal world of the merchant service, Wellingborough Redburn, as his name suggests, is the epitome of "superior" and
almost flamboyant innocence. But Wellingborough's is a
curious innocence alloyed with bitterness. His impulse to
isolate himself springs not primarily from his abhorrence of
evil, as he asserts, but from his fear and suspicion of mankind, as he reveals. When Wellingborough Redburn introduces himself to the reader, he confesses that his "warm
soul" had been "flogged out by adversity," and upon his
young spirit "the mildew has fallen." Redburn-White Jacket's search is a search for the return of that "warm soul," a
soul healthy and vigorous in its fundamental humanity. But
in their bitterness, Redburn and White Jacket gravitate toward evil as an assertion of their moral superiority. They
want to witness sin in order to feel more intensely their self-
righteous goodness. Though they would like to believe that
the world through its wickedness isolates them, in reality it
is they who through their pride isolate the world, and separate themselves from it. The voyage on the merchant vessel
and man-of-war is a voyage for Redburn-White Jacket of
self-discovery.

Redburn is the son of a gentleman—but the gentleman

went bankrupt and died. From an environment of genteel poverty Redburn sets out on his adventure. His appetite for the sea had been whetted by a number of fascinating objects about the house, not the least of which was an old-fashioned, glass ship in a square, glass case—transparent reminder of the fragility of life's dreams. Redburn sets off with his sole inheritance—the shooting-jacket and fowling piece given him by his brother. His education begins immediately upon arrival in New York, as he tries to outwit the pawn shops and ends up gratefully accepting less than he was at first offered for his gun. With the small sum, he outfits himself as best he can for a sailor and bravely launches himself on his voyage. Aboard the merchant ship *Highlander*, bound for Liverpool, Redburn's education is accelerated: his first duty is to clean the ship's pigpen. Because of his profound ignorance of a sailor's duties, his fellow seamen jeer at him and isolate him, and he is singled out for special abuse by one Jackson, an old, unclean, morally and physically deranged sailor who tyrannizes the entire crew. After sundry adventures in which Redburn is initiated into the mysteries of the life of a sailor at sea, he begins to handle his duties with ease and to "hop about in the rigging like a Saint Jago's monkey." But among all the men aboard ship he seeks in vain for a close companion in whom he can confide.

Redburn's isolation and loneliness continue, even on his arrival in Liverpool. He begins his exploration of the city with the aid of an old guide-book which his father had used some fifty years before. To his bitter disappointment, the book proves hopelessly out of date. Left on his own, Redburn wanders around observing the life about him—the ships of all nations in the docks, the churches frequented by the sailors (one of them afloat), the mass of humanity pressing in on the docks and exhibiting every known variety of pleasure and misery, virtue and vice. In the midst of his wandering, Redburn finally finds himself a companion. Harry Bolton, waif of the streets but gallant and noble pretender, emerges from the mass into Redburn's ken and captivates his imagination. After Bolton involves Redburn in a mysterious but obviously evil venture in London, Redburn involves the destitute Bolton in the return voyage of the *Highlander*, a voyage marked primarily by the suffering and death of many of the emigrants aboard ship. Upon conclusion of the voyage, a wiser, more experienced, and tougher Redburn heads for home with a new self-confidence —the poise not of the self-sustained and isolated man, but that of the man whose isolation has been penetrated, and who has discovered in its stead the sustaining warmth of strong human bonds. He has learned more than he realizes both from the hatred of the old sailor Jackson, who plunges to his death in the sea on the return voyage, and from the love of the young comrade Bolton, who after the voyage disappears from view in the complex life of the metropolis.

As *Redburn* is concerned primarily with a boy's first voyage, *White Jacket* focuses on the last lap of an extended sea journey. As Redburn is the novice at sea, White Jacket is the experienced and skilled sailor. Indeed, White Jacket seems but the assumed name of the now nearly mature Wellingborough Redburn. The sensibility is the same, the initiation into life's complex inner nature develops along the same line, and the ultimate baptism in the sea is as surely Redburn's as White Jacket's destiny.

Most of the pages of *White Jacket* are consumed in explanation of the "routine" life aboard a homeward bound man-of-war, the U.S.S. *Neversink*. White Jacket takes it upon himself to analyze the world of the man-of-war with the same exploratory curiosity as Tommo's in analyzing the world of the Typees—the customs and mores, the habits and attitudes, the beliefs and superstitions—and strangely enough, there results a similar series of antitheses. But

whereas in *Typee* the savage life is compared with the civilized, in *White Jacket* the life of the common sailor is contrasted with the officer's. And as virtue rests most frequently
with the Typees, so it is also found in the man-of-war world
most abundantly among the "people," Navy term for the
crew.

White Jacket takes his post in the crew assigned to the top
mast, whose captain, Jack Chase, he comes to know intimately and to admire without limit. His acquaintance is not
—cannot be—wide, but he counts among his friends one
Lemsford, a poet, whose works are uniquely "published" to
the world via the ship's cannon; one Nord, an "earnest
thinker" and "reader of good books" whose learning and
wisdom are so great as to impress the officers and astound
his comrades; and one Williams, a "laughing philosopher"
who has "all manner of stories to tell about nice little country frolics" and who runs over "an endless list of his sweet-
hearts."

White Jacket is caught up in the routine life on a routine
voyage—eating at his mess, standing his watch, sleeping in
his hammock. Some events amuse and some cut deeply.
White Jacket discovers thievery to be so common that out
of desperation he sews up all the pockets of his coat. He observes a flogging, in all of its revolting injustice and inhumanity. And, subsequently, he misses by a hair being
flogged himself. He observes a shipmate die under the "care"
of the ship's surgeon, and he stands by soberly at the burial
at sea. He is caught up with his rebellious fellow sailors in
mutinous resentment against the captain for his order to the
"people" to shave their luxurious beards, grown for the arrival home. But neither flogging, nor death, nor the massacre of the beards delays the voyage: to White Jacket these
may seem unusual happenings, but they are routine events
to both officers and crew. Near the end of the voyage, White
Jacket's plunge into the sea, with the loss of the accursed

coat in the water, symbolizes the final stage of his initiation,
signaling the end of his self-assumed innocence and self-
imposed isolation.

2 *The masked world of the ships*

That Redburn and White Jacket stare at the evil of the
world in sinful fascination makes what they witness no less
evil. The world wears a veil, thin in some places, thick in
others, but always there between the Seeker and reality.
Whether it be in the merchant ship *Highlander* or the man-
of-war U.S.S. *Neversink*, or in the world itself which these
ships symbolize, evil is omnipresent and masked, frequently
parading as its opposite. This world of evil, visible only in
the background of *Typee* and *Omoo* and camouflaged in allegory in *Mardi*, comes in *Redburn* and *White Jacket* to immediate life, overwhelming and engulfing.

At the outset of his voyage, Wellingborough Redburn encounters the fatherly Captain Riga who turns out on board
ship to be remote and hostile, refusing at the end of the voyage to pay proper wages to either Redburn or his companion,
Harry Bolton. Wellingborough discovers what he considers
to be the horrible iniquities of the crew almost as soon as he
becomes a member. Their talk is vulgar and offensive, filled
with words which Redburn cannot hear "without a dreadful
loathing." The sailors appear to hold nothing sacred, least of
all Redburn's feelings for his mother, the "centre" of all his
"heart's finest feelings." They scoff in ignorance at religion.
And they drink. Wellingborough, describing his member-
ship in his hometown's "Juvenile Total Abstinence Association," expresses, in unmistakable tones of superiority, his
shock at the sinful life the sailors lead. Not long after he is on

board, he witnesses the suicide of a sailor suffering from a case of delirium tremens: the individual, clawing and shrieking, rushes from below deck, darts past the frightened crew, plunges into the sea and disappears. To his horror Redburn discovers that he must sleep in the suicide's bunk, a fate suggesting his own inevitable involvement in the very evil he abhors. This terrifying death on the outbound voyage is balanced by another on the return, the "animal combustion" of a sailor pressed into service while unconscious from intoxication. While lying in his bunk, he bursts into flame: "Two threads of greenish fire, like a forked tongue, darted out between the lips: and in a moment the cadaverous face was crawled over by a swarm of worm-like flames." As Wellingborough Redburn gazes in horror, he thinks that he witnesses "a premonition of the hell of the Calvinists" and that the burning sailor is getting "a foretaste of his eternal condemnation." This sailor's death is but the first of many on the return voyage, as a pestilence aboard ship carries off many of the poor and starving emigrants.

There is one sailor aboard the *Highlander* who serves to symbolize the sum total of the crew's evil—one Jackson, who is as repulsive looking as he is brutal and who holds tyrannous sway over his fellow sailors. Jackson's attitude toward Redburn, the natural antipathy of innate depravity toward naïve innocence, foreshadows the situation in Melville's last work, Claggart's spontaneous hatred of Billy Budd. Redburn writes, "it was the consciousness of his miserable, broken-down condition, and the prospect of soon dying like a dog, in consequence of his sins, that made this poor wretch always eye me with such malevolence as he did. For I was young and handsome . . . whereas *he* was being consumed by an incurable malady, that was eating up his vitals." Redburn's resentment and fear of Jackson are intensified by his belief that it is the old sailor's enmity which in turn alienates the crew: "His being my foe set many of the rest against me; or at least they were afraid to speak out for me before Jackson; so that at last I found myself a sort of Ishmael in the ship, without a single friend or companion; and I began to feel a hatred growing up in me against the whole crew—so much so, that I prayed against it, that it might not master my heart completely, and so make a fiend of me, something like Jackson."

This insight into the danger of an obsession with evil corrupting the heart of the one obsessed is perhaps the cause for Redburn's eventual temperate appraisal of Jackson. In spite of his horror at Jackson's appearance and tyranny, Redburn detects in his own feelings a puzzling complexity: "But there seemed even more woe than wickedness about the man; and his wickedness seemed to spring from his woe; and for all his hideousness there was that in his eye at times that was ineffably pitiable and touching; and though there were moments when I almost hated this Jackson, yet I have pitied no man as I have pitied him." On the return voyage, Jackson grows weaker but his terrible treatment of the crew grows worse: "The prospect of the speedy and unshunnable death now before him seemed to exasperate his misanthropic soul into madness; and as if he had indeed sold it to Satan, he seemed determined to die with a curse between his teeth." In the final event of the voyage before arrival home, Jackson is seized by a violent fit of coughing while in the rigging, spews out a "torrent of blood" onto the sails, and plunges to his watery death in the sea. Some of the blood spatters the crew as they watch in horrified silence. Jackson's death seems the crew's baptism in blood. And though the members of the crew never after speak of Jackson, they seem instinctively to realize that "*his* death" is "*their* deliverance." The example of Jackson's fate seems to bestow a dim awareness of the communal nature of evil, a brief glimpse of the shared burden of man's guilt.

The evil of the individual man as represented by Jackson has its counterpoint in the evil of mankind as discovered in the sinful cities of England. Wellingborough Redburn is shocked by the veritable hive of iniquity off the docks in Liverpool, where every conceivable vice flourishes. He is most moved, however, by the sight he sees in Launcelott's-Hey, in the cellar of an old warehouse: "Some fifteen feet below the walk, crouching in nameless squalor, with her head bowed over, was the figure of what had been a woman. Her blue arms folded to her livid bosom two shrunken things like children, that leaned toward her, one on each side." Redburn's shock at the plight of this pitiful family is exceeded only by his horror at the indifference of the people he tries to bring to the scene. They either disclaim responsibility or self-righteously proclaim that as the woman was unmarried, her fate is richly deserved. Redburn is oppressed by his utter helplessness, and his tender heart is torn as he discovers one day the family gone and in their place a glistening "heap of quick-lime."

If in Liverpool Redburn finds that evil is repulsive and sometimes springs from a questionable "justice," he discovers in London that evil can also be attractive. The mysterious Aladdin's Place, where Harry Bolton takes Redburn in London on some obscurely evil expedition, glitters with sumptuous attractions: "The walls were painted so as to deceive the eye with interminable colonnades; and groups of columns of the finest scagliola work of variegated marbles—emerald-green and gold, St. Pons veined with silver, Sienna with porphyry—supported a resplendent fresco ceiling, arched like a bower, and thickly clustering with mimic grapes." Though full of fascination, the rich furnishings are clearly a deceptive façade. Redburn fancifully imagines that within the costly draperies lurks some "Eastern plague." Though swathed in rich damasks, though surrounded by fine furnishings and works of art, evil cannot be transfigured. Redburn muses: "All the mirrors and marbles around me seemed crawling over with lizards; and I thought to myself, that though gilded and golden, the serpent of vice is a serpent still."

In his man-of-war world, White Jacket continues Redburn's discovery of the many masks of evil. Being a member of the crew, ironically called by their officers "the people," White Jacket sees the officer-sailor relationship from the crew's angle. He amuses himself by pointing out the absurdity of the officers' remoteness, of their secret vices (Captain Claret is a tippler), of their dreams of glory in battle. White Jacket poses the question, "Can the brotherhood of the race of mankind ever hope to prevail in a man-of-war, where one man's bane is almost another's blessing?" And he reluctantly answers that, as long as motives remain so mixed and various, the man-of-war "must ever remain a picture of much that is tyrannical and repelling in human nature."

But because he satirizes the officers, White Jacket does not idealize the crew. He specifically disavows the "romantic belief in that peculiar noble-heartedness and exaggerated generosity of disposition fictitiously imputed" to the sailor in literature. And indeed much of White Jacket's tale is devoted to the vice of the crew. Dolefully surveying the members, White Jacket concludes: "The Navy is the asylum for the perverse, the home of the unfortunate. Here the sons of adversity meet the children of calamity, and here the children of calamity meet the offspring of sin." Nevertheless, White Jacket points out that most of the iniquities practiced by the sailors result from "the unjust, despotic, and degrading laws under which the man-of-war's man lives." In a brilliant image, White Jacket describes the sailor's situation: "Like pears closely packed, the crowded crew mutually decay through close contact, and every plague-spot is contagious." The evils practiced are "so direful that they will hardly bear even so much as an allusion."

But White Jacket alludes sufficiently to make his meaning clear: "The sins for which the cities of the plain were overthrown still linger in some of these wooden-walled Gomorrahs of the deep. More than once complaints were made at the mast in the *Neversink*, from which the deck officer would turn away with loathing, refuse to hear them, and command the complainant out of his sight."

But if we may judge by White Jacket's indignation, the sins of the sailors pale beside the evils they suffer. The greatest indignity visited on the sailors is the punishment of flogging, and the practice is its most reprehensible in the occasional instances of "flogging through the fleet," in which the sailor is carried from ship to ship to be flogged before all the crews. White Jacket notes, "There are certain enormities in this man-of-war world that often secure impunity by their very excessiveness." Although White Jacket does not witness a flogging through the fleet, he does record in detail the flogging of four shipmates caught fighting. White Jacket cannot contain his indignation and compassion: "You see a human being, stripped like a slave; scourged worse than a hound. And for what? For things not essentially criminal, but only made so by arbitrary laws." White Jacket is himself "arraigned at the mast" at one point on the voyage and becomes a firsthand witness to the desperate feeling of one about to be flogged: "My blood seemed clotting in my veins; I felt icy cold at the tips of my fingers, and a dimness was before my eyes." Only the unusual and timely intervention of two highly respected shipmates, one of them Jack Chase, to plead White Jacket's innocence, saves him from the cruel "cat."

Among the multitude of sinners aboard the man-of-war, two must be singled out for special mention. Cadwallader Cuticle, M.D., is a renowned surgeon of the fleet: "He walked abroad, a curious patch-work of life and death, with a wig, one glass eye, and a set of false teeth, while his voice was husky and thick; but his mind seemed undebilitated as in youth; it shone out of his remaining eye with basilisk brilliancy." The characterization of Cuticle hovers between the comical and the diabolical, but above all the eminent surgeon appears to be grimly dehumanized. Like Hawthorne's satanic scientists, Cuticle is inflated with a perverted pride in his immense skill and knowledge. In a brilliantly executed scene, Cuticle performs before his assembled officers a "perfect" operation on a sailor with a "blasted thigh" (a gunshot wound). The amputation is a great success. And Cuticle irritatedly brushes aside the death of the sailor as irrelevant to an evaluation of his surgical skill.

Another dehumanized individual aboard ship is the master-at-arms, one Bland, who is charged by the captain with increasing his efforts against the liquor smugglers while at Rio de Janeiro—only to turn out, himself, to be the ringleader of the smugglers. Unlike Redburn's repulsive Jackson, in Bland, "vice *seemed,* but only seemed, to lose half its seeming evil by losing all its apparent grossness. . . . There was a fine polish about his whole person, and a pliant, insinuating style in his conversation, that was, socially, quite irresistible." Only his "wickedly delicate" mouth and his "snaky black eye" hint at the evil concealed within. Bland, it turns out (like Claggart in *Billy Budd*), is innately evil—"wicked deeds seemed the legitimate operation of his whole infernal organization. Phrenologically, he was without a soul. Is it to be wondered at, that the devils are irreligious?"

3 *Some immaculate friend*

But in Redburn-White Jacket's introduction to the world, all is not totally bleak. Their tale is in one sense the tale of

the gradual dissolution of the barriers separating an isolated individual from the world. When Melville's Innocent
ventures out into the world, he holds it at a safe distance,
while he remains critical and aloof. His total independence
is a pose, however, as he secretly confesses to himself his
agonizing need for communion, his soul's lonely yearning
for the "unbounded bosom of some immaculate friend."
Always before, Melville's heroes had vagabond companions
—Tommo had Toby (and later Kory-Kory), Omoo had
Long Ghost, Taji had Jarl. But Redburn and White Jacket
must search for a way out of their lonely isolation. And in
finding a friend, Redburn-White Jacket discovers much
about the involvement of self in the complicated plight of
mankind: he discovers, up close to humanity, that the separation of good from evil is not so simple as he had once, from
a distance, supposed.

Redburn discovers the attractive Harry Bolton in the
midst of iniquitous Liverpool. Like the companions of so
many of Melville's protagonists, Harry is intelligent, gifted,
and extremely handsome, with physical features of almost
feminine beauty: "He was one of those small, but perfectly
formed beings, with curling hair, and silken muscles, who
seem to have been born in cocoons. His complexion was a
mantling brunette, feminine as a girl's; his feet were small;
his hands were white; and his eyes were large, black, and
womanly; and, poetry aside, his voice was as the sound of a
harp." Redburn and Harry in their loneliness discover in
each other the companionship they crave. Harry is by no
means the personification of innocence: he has a proclivity
for fabricating a background for himself but his tales become so fabulous as to arouse the suspicions of even the
naïve Redburn. No doubt Harry Bolton has discovered in
his struggle to survive in the gutters of the world and particularly in the slums of Liverpool that a mask, however fan-

tastic, is a requisite; so he goes about harmlessly romanti-
cizing his past.

Destitute from his gambling losses, Harry ships with Redburn on the *Highlander*'s return voyage, and, because,
through fear, he cannot fill the sailor's role and scramble
aloft, he is ostracized by the crew, enduring passively their
"contumely and contempt," regaining some of their respect
and affection only by singing for them with his melodious
and magic voice—appearing "like Orpheus among the
charmed leopards and tigers." Unable to establish himself
in New York, he disappears from Redburn's ken; but much
later Redburn is to learn that on a whaling voyage Harry
fell between a whale and the ship and was crushed to
death—a creature too finely and delicately wrought for this
world.

Jack Chase in *White Jacket* is a transfigured Harry Bolton, possessing all of his admirable qualities and none of
his weaknesses. If Redburn had reservations about Harry,
White Jacket has none about Jack. In him White Jacket discovers the "unbounded bosom" of an "immaculate friend"
which the lonely Redburn had longed for. In all Melville
there is scarcely another character who arouses such enthusiasm as this "noble first captain of the top": "He was a
Briton, and a true-blue; tall and well-knit, with a clear open
eye, a fine broad brow, and an abounding nut-brown beard.
No man ever had a better heart or a bolder. He was loved by
the seamen, and admired by the officers; and even when the
captain spoke to him, it was with a slight air of respect. Jack
was a frank and charming man." Whereas Harry was a
boy, with many of the girlish traits of youth, Jack is a man,
with the manliness of a man's man. But Jack has many of
Harry's characteristics, such as a keen and cultivated mind
and a fine singing voice. "Jack was a whole phalanx, an entire army; Jack was a thousand strong; Jack would have
done honour to the Queen of England's drawing-room; Jack

must have been a by-blow of some British Admiral of the Blue."

Jack's one past indescretion, the desertion of his ship to join the "cause of Right" in civil disturbances in Peru, redounded to his credit and on his return he was reinstated on his ship with even greater popular acclaim than before. Jack is the paragon of wisdom and courage on the man-of-war, his advice sought in times of confusion, his aid asked in times of stress. It is Jack who has the courage to plead eloquently and learnedly to Captain Claret the case for the crew's liberty in Rio; and Jack is among those who voluntarily and courageously testify to White Jacket's devotion to duty when he is, mistakenly, about to receive a flogging. As Jack Chase is the first shipmate introduced in *White Jacket*, so he is the final figure delineated in that fanciful concluding vision of all the main-top men circling the mast "spliced together" in a "brother-band." Jack is last seen quoting his favorite poet—"straight out into that fragrant night, ever-noble Jack Chase, matchless and unmatchable Jack Chase stretches forth his bannered hand, and, pointing shoreward, cries: 'For the last time, hear Camoens, boys!' "

The progression of Melville's protagonist from the restrained but intense attraction toward Harry Bolton to an unreserved and easygoing comradeship with Jack Chase suggests the final crumbling of the thick-walled isolation of an assumed innocence. Neither Bolton nor Chase is perfect, but the latter is about as near perfection as Melville will ever portray. Frankness, intellectual and literary attainments, and a great heart are virtues for a man to cultivate in himself and to admire in another. And these are the virtues of Chase. That Chase's livelihood is ironically derived from a death-dealing business, that his sustenance is war—these are the paradoxes of life with which the genuine Innocent must ultimately come to terms. The final reconciliation of Redburn and White Jacket to a world of evil is brought about in part by their perception, in the close attachment of comradeship, of the complex entanglement of right and wrong, good and evil.

4 *Baptism of the young Seeker*

The Seeker in *Redburn-White Jacket,* like Taji in *Mardi,* is confronted with the choice of retaining the mask of innocence and intensifying his isolation from mankind, or of discarding the mask and confessing his heritage of guilt and accepting the bonds of human brotherhood. For the first time Melville has designed a concrete symbol for the mask —the jacket. Wellingborough Redburn's hunting jacket, given to him by his brother, is eminently unsuitable for life at sea. It is the jacket which brings him the name "Buttons," and which causes him to stand out from the crew. This landlubber's jacket of many pockets provides a self-sufficiency designed to isolate the wearer. After he is at sea, Redburn begins to realize the inadequacy of his moleskin jacket: it grows smaller and smaller, shrinking with each rain, leaving him more and more exposed and uncomfortable. But only after meeting Harry Bolton and planning the excursion to London does Redburn take off the jacket—and it is, significantly, Harry who provides a new garment. As Redburn's association with Harry develops, his hunting jacket is forgotten. Redburn's relationship with his new-found friend marks the end of his self-imposed isolation and the beginning of his awareness of the possibilities of human comradeship.

The coat which White Jacket provides for himself is the precise counterpart of that given Redburn, but is even more clearly associated with innocence by its color. Like Redburn's hunting jacket, the coat through its conspicuous whiteness makes the wearer a marked man, isolated from the crew. Like the hunting jacket, the white jacket becomes extremely uncomfortable because of its soaking up rather than casting off the rain. And also like the hunting jacket, the white jacket has numerous pockets which the wearer uses for "furniture and household stores" to render himself self-sufficient and independent. To his dismay, White Jacket discovers that the rain ruins many of the provisions he carts around in his pockets; and upon discovery of his multitudinous storage containers some of his fellow sailors skulk about like potential pickpockets. White Jacket abandons his "lockers and pantries" by sewing up his pockets. But his efforts to obtain paint to make the jacket black and waterproof repeatedly fail. And the attempt to auction the jacket off, placing it in the hands of a new owner, also fails. Fellow crew members, and White Jacket too, come finally to curse the jacket and to accuse it of responsibility for much of the evil aboard ship and particularly for the misfortunes which occur in White Jacket's mess. Just before arrival home, White Jacket in his cursed garment falls from the weather-top-gallant-yardarm over a hundred feet into the sea in one of the most dramatic baptisms in all literature.

When White Jacket plunges into the ocean, his soul seems to fly from his mouth and a feeling of death presses in on him. He sinks through the "soft, seething, foamy lull" to the depths of the sea, where he seems dramatically suspended between life and death:

Some current seemed hurrying me away; in a trance I yielded, and sank deeper down with a glide. Purple and pathless was the deep calm now around me, flecked by summer lightnings in an azure afar. The horrible nausea was gone; the bloody, blind film turned a pale green; I wondered whether I was yet dead, or still dying. But of a sudden some fashionless form brushed my side— some inert, soiled fish of the sea; the thrill of being alive again tingled in my nerves, and the strong shunning of death shocked me through.

For one instant an agonizing revulsion came over me as I found myself utterly sinking. Next moment the force of my fall was expended; and there I hung, vibrating in the mid-deep. What wild sounds then rang in my ear! One was a soft moaning, as of low waves on the beach; the other wild and heartlessly jubilant, as of the sea in the height of a tempest. Oh Soul! thou then heardest life and death. . . .

At this moment of high suspense, White Jacket makes his choice. Death in all of its quiet, peace, and order has a strong appeal: the "horrible nausea" of life may be renounced forever for the "deep calm" of death. But the impulse toward death is abruptly reversed by the brush of the "inert, soiled fish of the sea." Life, with all of its corruption, in spite of its falling far short of all conceivable ideals, regardless of its injustice, its evil, its inconsistency—life has a stronger appeal than death. The fish, whether *coiled* or *soiled*, is inert and lives on, and in living reminds White Jacket that they share in common the tingling "thrill" of life. Both fish and human, the two extremes in the ladder of living creatures, assert their union in their choice for life, even though tempestuous, for the "jubilance" of existence, even though "wild and heartless."

White Jacket's descent to and return from the bottom of the ocean symbolizes the recovery of that spirit which had been flogged out of him (as Redburn) by adversity. As he attempts to swim toward the ship, he feels as though he is "pinioned in a feather bed" until he slashes with his knife the strings binding to him the accursed white garment ("I . . . ripped my jacket straight up and down, as if I were ripping open myself"). Deprived of his jacket, he gains his humanity; jolted from his isolation he discovers comradeship; stripped of his innocence, he finds his soul. The protagonist Redburn-White Jacket has learned that man cannot live on earth in perfect innocence: he must throw in his lot with the guilt of mankind or perish—or, perhaps, commit the grossest of sins in the delusion of achieving an impossible moral perfection.

Near the end of his tale, White Jacket accidentally observes a fellow seaman, responsible for the operation of two of the man-of-war's cannon, in silent and fervent prayer. This brilliant vignette of an efficient "killer" in a genuinely religious attitude impresses on White Jacket the great gap between the ideal and the reality in this man-of-war world and he dives deep for a profound insight: "In view of the whole present social framework of our world, so ill-adapted to the practical adoption of the meekness of Christianity, there seems almost some ground for the thought, that although our blessed Saviour was full of the wisdom of heaven, yet His gospel seems lacking in the practical wisdom of earth—in a due appreciation of the necessities of nations at times demanding bloody massacres and wars; in a proper estimation of the value of rank, title, and money. But all this only the more crowns the divine consistency of Jesus. . . ." That the wisdom of earth fails sometimes to coincide with the wisdom of heaven does not mean that one must be discredited but rather that heaven and earth are incompatible. The "Soul and substance" of Christianity, embodied in that passage which enjoins us to turn the other cheek, though magnificent is impractical in the real world of crime and war. Even that noblest of men, Jack Chase, proves a terrible fighter as a soldier in a "righteous" battle. But though the wisdom of Christ must at times be disregarded on earth, the central act of his life may always serve as an example for man: "To be efficacious, Virtue must come down from aloft, even as our blessed Redeemer came down to redeem our whole man-of-war world; to that end, mixing with its sailors and sinners as equals."

Like Taji, Redburn-White Jacket weighs the world and

finds it wanting and yearns for the impossible ideal; unlike Taji, Redburn-White Jacket settles for a Serenia of "sailors and sinners" where man though idealizing Christ makes allowances for humanity's imperfections, where individuals though abhorring sin accept their share of the world's burden of guilt. By his choice, Redburn-White Jacket saves himself from the terrible fate of those tyrants of virtue yet to be created by Melville, Ahab and Pierre, who cannot in their pride come down from aloft.

5
Moby Dick: *the grand hooded phantom*

Resembling none of its predecessors, *Moby Dick* (1851) borrowed from all of them. The most obvious ingredients are the realism of the early tales of adventure fused with some of the allegory of *Mardi* and more of the symbolism of *Redburn* and *White Jacket*. *Moby Dick* has frequently been called an epic, and it is surely one metaphorically if not in fact. It memorializes the fabulous industry of whaling as well as embodies a good share of the complex metaphysical myth of nineteenth-century America, the "myth" born of the collision of the retreating world of puritan Calvinism and the emerging world of industrial materialism.

Moby Dick has also been called a tragedy—a classification which has its justification. Ahab is a heroic figure of impressive stature who seizes and by sheer force paralyzes the imagination. His awesome sway over the souls of his crew extends to the reader too who must bear witness in fascination mixed with dread and even horror. Finally, however, the question remains how to judge the cause of Ahab's downfall. Can it be tragic in any valid sense when it is precipitated ultimately by such a determined devotion to an evil purpose? Ahab's "flaw" is, finally, a chasm in his Soul that all the waters of the ocean cannot fill. But whether a tragic epic or an epic tragedy, or a sea yarn with fragments of both, *Moby Dick* is universally recognized as Melville's leviathan and masterpiece.

Melville's technique is ideally suited to encourage controversy in the interpretation of *Moby Dick*. Melville chose for his narrator one Ishmael, a young vagabond out to see the world and revitalize his soul. But before the book is far along, Captain Ahab takes center stage, and it seems at times that Melville has forgotten his narrator, especially when characters are presented alone, in meditation or reciting soliloquies. At the end of the book, when only Ishmael survives the catastrophe that concludes the three-day chase of the great white whale, the reader is reminded that his endurance had to be assured in order to save someone to tell the tale. Only then, and in retrospect, is the average reader likely to raise a question about the consistency of Melville's technical point of view. It is to the credit of his narrative genius that in the vast solid center of the book, he simply takes the freedom he needs to advance his plot both metaphysically and realistically without resorting to ingenious or awkward devices to maintain Ishmael as narrator—and without violating outrageously the reader's sense of verisimilitude.

However well adapted the point may be to the philosophical substance and technical bulk of the novel, Melville's technique is perfectly suited to underscore many of the book's ambiguities. Is Melville to be identified with Ishmael, or are his feelings to be found in Ahab? Or does Melville divide himself between his narrator and hero, putting a bit of himself in each? Is it possible that Melville effaces himself, remaining aloof from his work, his own voice hidden and his vision sealed? All of these approaches have been elaborately defended, and it sometimes seems that *Moby Dick* has as many and various interpretations as it has readers.

The interpretation that has had the most thorough and prolonged defense identifies Ahab with Melville, making the captain's quarrel with God and his rage against the universe the author's as well. But many critics have split Melville between Ishmael and Ahab and have seen in the split a manifestation of a tension in the author that drove him to conceive *Moby Dick,* and filled him with the fury to finish it, but which remained unresolved when the Herculean task was completed, with Ahab swallowed by the sea and Ishmael plucked from it, drenched but alive. Some critics have seen in Ishmael's survival a kind of death and resurrection that provides the key to the novel, with Melville's affirmative theme complexly interwoven with Ishmael's developing insight and mellowing spirit, both of which run like strong but rarely glimpsed undercurrents throughout the work.

As enigmatic as the chief characters has been the book's chief symbol, Moby Dick. Critics have stared at that huge expanse of whiteness and have, as though hypnotized by the brightness of the glare, found in it everything under the sun, and more. The glistening of the whale's shiny surface has provided a mirror in which readers have found reflected their own deepest fears and desires, their heart's delight and their private horror. Some critics have asserted that the whale was created to serve just such a purpose, an open-ended symbol with its meaning to be supplied by each reader in turn, no one meaning to supplant another. Of course, some readers have said that Moby Dick is a whale— and a whale is nothing more than a whale, mainly blubber and oil. Others have been quick to see Moby Dick as Ahab sees him—as all evil from the beginning of time made living and visible in a single monstrous creature. And if some have seen Moby Dick as the devil incarnate, others have seen him as God Himself, all-powerful and indestructible. Some readers have thought the whiteness to be innocence, while others have identified it with terror. Still others have read the blankness as the essential indifference of the universe. And at least one critic has said that Moby Dick is civilized man's deepest phallic consciousness which he is trying utterly to destroy.

Whatever the validity of these various views, *Moby Dick* is most likely to divulge its deepest meanings in a close reading that holds constantly in mind the thematic drama that recurs throughout Melville's work. In the staggering artistic task of creating his whale, it would be surprising to find Melville radically altering his vision.

1   A *damp drizzly November*

The wanderer Ishmael tells the tale. And in that brilliant opening confession, "Loomings," Ishmael makes two personal revelations vital to his story: his view of the world and the state of his soul. "Whenever I find myself growing grim about the mouth; whenever it is a damp, drizzly November in my soul; whenever I find myself involuntarily pausing before coffin warehouses, and bringing up the rear of every funeral I meet; and especially whenever my hypos get such an upper hand of me, that it requires a strong moral principle to prevent me from deliberately stepping into the street, and methodically knocking people's hats off—then, I account it high time to get to sea as soon as I can." Ishmael reveals, in the very midst of humanity, an emotional and moral isolation, from which in the progress of his sea voyage he is to emerge; the story's movement for Ishmael is away from independence and solitude toward interdependence and involvement.

Balancing Ishmael's view of the world at the opening of this first chapter is his glimpse of his soul at the close, a glimpse dramatized by an image of the book's dominant symbol—the white whale: "The great flood-gates of the wonder-world swung open, and in the wild conceits that swayed me to my purpose, two and two there floated into my inmost soul, endless processions of the whale, and, mid-most of them all, one grand hooded phantom, like a snow hill in the air." This "hooded phantom" is Moby Dick, and here Ishmael identifies him with the spotlessness of his own immaculate soul. Ishmael's illusion of innocence is the root cause of his isolation. Already at the opening of the tale we are confronted with the complexity of Moby Dick's white-ness. Ishmael here envisions him innocent, as Ahab later is to know him evil. When Moby Dick is finally unmasked, un-hooded, he will (like Ishmael's soul), be discovered neither innocent nor evil, but an inextricable entanglement—like life itself.

With his grim and bitter eye and his spotless soul, Ish-mael sets out for the sea where he can contemplate the state of man; for, "as every one knows, meditation and water are wedded for ever." He heads first for the whaling world of Nantucket, where two casual encounters affect him deeply. The Spouter-Inn offers him, through its many tokens of the trade, initiation into the "industry" of whal-ing. But Queequeg the "savage," who turns out to be his bedmate at the inn, offers him a more moving experience —an initiation into the affirmative possibilities of human relationships.

Ishmael and Queequeg, turned "bosom friends" in a cere-mony designed by the simple savage and sealed by a smoke and an embrace, select for their ship the *Pequod* in spite of the warnings about its Captain Ahab ("Old Thunder") from a mad prophet who calls himself Elijah. The whaler embarks on its fated voyage on Christmas, but Captain Ahab does not appear on deck for several days. In his first major encounter with the crew, he enacts a plan carefully designed to instill in the men his own hatred of Moby Dick (who once reaped away his leg) and to fill them with a boundless enthusiasm for the profitless pursuit. These pro-ceedings, in which Ahab gains sway over the very souls of his crew, are climaxed by the diabolical ceremony in which the three Christian mates (Starbuck, Stubb, and Flask) and their three pagan harpooners (Queequeg, Tashtego, Daggoo) drink to the death of Moby Dick. The mad pursuit is assured.

Throughout the long voyage, Ahab restlessly holds his course and drives single-mindedly on in ceaseless search of Moby Dick. When he meets other ships he pauses only long enough to find out whether they have sighted the white whale. He nails a gold doubloon to the mast as a prize for the first man to sight Moby Dick. He smashes the ship's quadrant to the deck in defiance of the sun and devises his own method for plotting his position and determining his course. Finally, having reluctantly rejected his first mate Starbuck's plea to turn back and his cabin boy Pip's appeal to give up the pursuit, Ahab is ready for the terrible and foredoomed struggle with Moby Dick. When the white whale is at last sighted, Ahab sets off in pursuit with the diabolical Fedallah and his dark crew as his harpooner and oarsmen. The three-day chase ends in disaster not only for Ahab but for the *Pequod* and its entire crew. Only Ishmael rises from the sea to tell the fantastic tale.

This skeleton of narrative scarcely accounts for the leviathan bulk of *Moby Dick*. There is more hearty substance there to swell the tale to the size of its namesake. Like a five-act Elizabethan tragedy, *Moby Dick* is not without its multiple plots and multitude of scenes. The novel has been called a whaling handbook, and with good reason. The material on the whale and whaling bulks large and assumes the role of subplot in the drama. The sheer size of *Moby Dick* makes it useful to divide it into parts that can be comprehended one at a time.

The 135 chapters of the novel may be divided into five major parts, each like an act in a play:

    I. Chapters 1-22: Ishmael and Queequeg

II. Chapters 22-45: Ahab and Moby Dick
III. Chapters 46-72: The Business of the *Pequod*
IV. Chapters 73-105: Whales and Whaling
V. Chapters 106-135: The Search and the Chase

It is doubtful that Melville consciously planned his book in these five major blocks, but there can be little doubt that the central focus of the book shifts in the way suggested by the five-part titles. Each of these parts, like the movements of a symphony, is dominated by a single insistent theme, which, however, by no means excludes the major themes of the other parts. In every instance, behind the dominant theme can be heard in complex interplay the various related themes as they continue to run their several courses.

Chapters 1-22: Ishmael and Queequeg. The entire first movement of *Moby Dick* is devoted not to the protagonist Ahab but to the narrator Ishmael, and most of the episodes are constructed around the developing friendship of Ishmael and Queequeg. It is possible to trace through in detail this comradeship as it is set forth by Melville in terms of a metaphorical romance, and with surprising consistency— from the initial bridegroom hug of Queequeg through the "marriage" sealed by the smoking of the pipe, to the "cosy, loving pair" on their "hearts' honeymoon." This climax comes after Ishmael and Queequeg have shared each other's religion, the pagan attending Father Mapple's sermon in the Whaleman's Chapel, the Christian participating in Queequeg's ceremonies with his small idol Yojo. Their bonds of friendship sworn and sealed, the novice Ishmael and the harpooner Queequeg set out to offer their services on a whaler. In Nantucket they encounter the "fighting Quakers," Captains Peleg and Bildad, major owners of the whaler *Pequod*. In spite of the fact that they never see the master of the ship, Captain Ahab, and in spite of the warnings given them by a shabby, shadowy Elijah, they sign up for a share and sail forth on the voyage on a bleak Christmas day. By the time these episodes draw to a close, the stage seems set for heroic, or catastrophic, action: "We gave three heavy-hearted cheers, and blindly plunged like fate into the lone Atlantic."

Chapters 22-45: Ahab and Moby Dick. Although Ishmael and Queequeg dominate the opening part of the book, Moby Dick's ghostly image appeared in the very first chapter (like "a snow hill in the air"), and Ahab's name later recurred so frequently (at the interview on the *Pequod*) that it seemed to brood over the action in a physical and oppressive presence. In this second part, Ahab steps to the fore, and Moby Dick, though he remains invisible, asserts his existence with all the force of his huge and menacing bulk. All of the participants in the drama are introduced, the "knights and squires," the mates Starbuck, Stubb, and Flask, the harpooners Queequeg, Tashtego, and Daggoo. And then—enter Ahab. All this part of the book seems to build to the high passion of the quarter-deck scene, in which the maimed and monomaniac Captain mesmerizes his assembled crew into partaking of the diabolical sacrament that pledges their very souls to the death of Moby Dick. And then a series of scenes, like the smaller waves following a breaker, permits a gradual return to a calmer pulse. Included are the two non-dramatic, speculative and crucial chapters, "Moby Dick" and "The Whiteness of the Whale," which define the central symbolism of the book's metaphysics. Stripping his plot and its tensions to the barest essentials, Melville pauses to sketch a vivid vignette of his action (at the end of Chapter 41): "Here, then, was this grey-headed, ungodly old man, chasing with curses a Job's whale round the world, at the head of a crew, too, chiefly made up of mongrel renegades, and castaways, and cannibals—morally enfeebled also, by the incompetence of mere unaided virtue or right-mindedness in Starbuck, and

invulnerable jollity of indifference and recklessness in
Stubb, and the pervading mediocrity in Flask."

Chapters 46-72: The Business of the Pequod. At the
same time that Ishmael and Queequeg drop to the background in the second part, a new note is introduced, though
it remains muted beneath the high drama enacted in the
foreground. In such chapters as "The Advocate" (24) and
"Cetology" (32), Melville acknowledges his author's responsibility of introducing in some orderly fashion the unfamiliar subject of whales and whaling to his reader. At the
opening of Chapter 46, Melville assures us that Ahab's
monomania is not such as to deflect him entirely from the
main business of the *Pequod*—to harpoon whales and collect oil. And so begins a large section of the book, moving
along at an even pace, devoted largely to the ordinary (but
in many ways extraordinary) pursuit of whales. The sense
of leisurely movement is achieved by the inclusion of inform-
ative and entertaining background chapters on various
aspects of whales—the whale in art, the whale in legend,
the whale in constellations—but the major method of describing the whaling industry is the use of a central narrative stream in which Stubb kills a sperm whale and the
whole elaborate and ritualistic process of converting whale
to oil is set in motion. But although this "collateral prosecu-
tion of the voyage" assumes center state, there remains in
the background the deeper threads of the action. The first
abortive "lowering" brings into action Ahab together with
his shadowy harpooner Fedallah and his mysterious crew;
and it gives Ishmael a memorable ducking and a cold night
in the sea. Ahab's passion to find Moby Dick, though
muted, flares out repeatedly as various ships—the *Alba-
tross*, the *Town-Ho*, the *Jeroboam*—encounter the *Pequod*
and exchange news in gams (visits). And Ishmael continues
his progressive journey of the spirit as his insight into the

nature of man's fate deepens in the ordinary duties of a common sailor, whether weaving mats (Chapter 47) and contemplating the interrelation of free will, necessity, and chance, or (as in the last chapter [72] of this section) hanging onto Queequeg by the monkey-rope and contemplating the inescapable interconnection of all men.

Chapters 73-105: Whales and Whaling. Beginning with Stubb's killing of a Right Whale in Chapter 73, Melville seems to abandon a sustained narrative stream as the basis for conveying information about whales and whaling and resorts more and more to brief and selected episodes and chapters of sheer exposition. In this portion of the book he is remotest from the central action, yet so skillfully has he built up the suspense that even in the most leisurely descriptions the dramatic tension continues to operate through the memory of the reader. An extended discourse on the heads of whales, both inside and outside, leads to contemplation of various other parts of the whale's anatomy, including his jet, his tail, his skeleton, and even his phallus ("The Cassock," chapter 95). Having reached the outermost limits of his subject, having fully described the whale in his "present habitatory and anatomical peculiarities," Melville finishes him off in Chapters 104 and 105 by "magnifying" him in "an archeological, fossiliferous, and antediluvian point of view." This detailed description is interspersed with speculation about whale mythology and detailed accounts of turning blubber into oil. Two ship-encounters, with the German *Virgin* and the French *Rose-Bud,* bring no news of Moby Dick but serve primarily as vehicles for further exposition about whaling, the possible blunders in identifying the whale or the possible ignorance in not realizing the value of the ambergris (used in the manufacture of perfume) of a sick whale. In the episodic progression of this prolonged description, a pair of "visionary" chapters (93 and 94) brings into sharp focus much of the scattered metaphysical speculation. In "The Castaway," the little black cabin boy Pip is abandoned in the ocean in the midst of a chase—and the vision he gains beneath the sea of the "unwarped primal world" drives him "divinely" mad. Immediately following, in "A Squeeze of the Hand," in one of the ordinary duties of a whaler of squeezing sperm oil out of globules of blubber, Ishmael has a vision of human brotherhood that seems a "strange sort of insanity." This quiet, contemplative scene shows how the sour-souled Ishmael of the opening chapter has been transformed, and represents the ultimate depth of his vision—and *Moby Dick*'s thematic climax of affirmative statement. Another pair of chapters (99 and 100) momentarily thrusts to the fore the central action. In "The Doubloon," Ahab's gold Ecuadorian coin, nailed to the mainmast as a prize to go to the sailor first to sight Moby Dick, inspires a variety of interpretations by its cabalistic symbols. In "Leg and Arm," Ahab eagerly exchanges information with the Captain of the British ship the *Samuel Enderby,* the loss of whose arm to Moby Dick excites Ahab to greater determination in pursuit of the white whale.

Chapters 106-135: The Search and the Chase. A new tempo is introduced beginning in Chapter 106 ("Ahab's Leg"), and whale-lore is not permitted to relax the tension of the narrative again. Ishmael, having reached the limits of his insight in the previous part, makes his only significant appearance in this final section at the very end, when he emerges as the sole survivor of the catastrophe. This part of the book is Ahab's, and he dominates it to the bitter conclusion. "Ahab's Leg" appropriately reintroduces the source of Ahab's obsession: as he accidentally twists and splinters his ivory stump, he is recalled with all the fire of his outraged spirit to his monomaniacal purpose on the voyage. In Chapter 119, "The Candles," there is a dia-

bolical ceremony of rededication of the entire crew to the
death of Moby Dick—a final reaffirmation of the pledges
made in the earlier quarter-deck scene of part two. Suspense builds throughout this section as conflicting forces
work on Ahab. Starbuck can neither kill him nor dissuade
him, and even heart-tugging Pip is unable finally to swerve
him from his doom. More and more Fedallah dominates
his will. The ships encountered, the *Bachelor, The Rachel,*
the *Delight,*—the first having prospered by ignoring Moby
Dick, the last two having suffered tragedy by pursuing him
—seem only to steady the mad Captain in his purpose. As
Ahab's self-obsessed defiance builds, through his smashing of the quadrant, his constructing a magnet for his own
compass, his repairing the log and line—as he thrusts himself back more and more on his own powers, his ego swells
to fill the ship, the ocean, the sky. Turning aside from Starbuck, he identifies with Fedallah—and the final three-day
chase begins. One by one Fedallah's once reassuring prophecies turn horribly true: the Parsee goes before, his hearse,
"not made with human hands," is Moby Dick himself; the
Pequod, smashed by the enraged whale, turns into a
hearse "made of American wood," for all its astonished
sailors; and Ahab finally finds his hempen death entangled
in the lines of the harpoon last thrust at the triumphant
whale. Ishmael alone is left floating on the desolate sea, to be
rescued by the sorrowing *Rachel* searching for her lost
children.

2 *Civilized hypocrisies and bland deceits*

Like Tommo-Melville in *Typee-Omoo,* like Taji in *Mardi,*
like Redburn and White Jacket in their tales, Ishmael in
Moby Dick is the Young Seeker. In his original state, with

his grimness of view and wintriness of spirit, Ishmael
most nearly resembles Redburn and his "flogged soul."
What has brought about this hypnotic fascination for death,
this uncontrollable antipathy toward all human beings,
this dark, damp November that Ishmael is attempting to
weather? It is the vast pretense of the world—the world's
mask of innocence—which Ishmael characterizes at one
point as "civilized hypocrisies and bland deceits." Ishmael's mood and its solvent are not unique. As he tells us
in the opening pages, when he confesses his own dark
soul, most landsmen feel, at one time or another, as does he,
and they all head for the sea: "Posted like silent sentinels
all around the town, stand thousands upon thousands of
mortal men fixed in ocean reveries. Some leaning against
the spiles; some seated upon the pier-heads; some looking
over the bulwarks of ships from China; some high aloft in
the rigging, as if striving to get a still better seaward
peep." This silent scene vividly dramatizes mankind's acute
consciousness of its gross inadequacies and the terrible
yearning for the soul-cleansing experience of the sea. There
is, Ishmael reveals, a terrible sickness in the society of men.

As Ishmael is about to enter the Spouter-Inn in New
Bedford, he comes upon a simple scene that embodies in
miniature all the evil which the world's mask of innocence
blandly hides. A beggar lies shivering in the streets. "Poor
Lazarus there, chattering his teeth against the curbstone
for his pillow, and shaking off his tatters with his shiverings,
he might plug up both ears with rags, and put a corn-cob into
his mouth, and yet that would not keep out the tempestuous
Euroclydon." With a real Lazarus before him, Ishmael
creates a Dives out of his imagination—a Dives whose
attitude toward the winter contrasts sharply with the beggar's: "Euroclydon! says old Dives, in his red silken wrap-
per—(he had a redder one afterwards) pooh, pooh! What
a fine frosty night; how Orion glitters; what northern lights!

Let them talk of their oriental summer climes of everlasting
conservatories; give me the privilege of making my own
summer with my own coals." The beggar's misery is the inn-
keeper's comfort. That Ishmael casts his little drama in
biblical terms suggests the ancient nature of the contemporary condition. But though the situation symbolized (human
indifference to human misery) is ancient, it is to Ishmael
still startling.

Ishmael's experiences after his encounter with the savage
Queequeg soon lead him to make some ironic contrasts not
only between civilization and savagery but between the
Christian and pagan religions. In New Bedford, both
Queequeg and Ishmael attend the services in the Whaleman's Chapel, observe the strange behavior of Father Mapple and listen in awe to his vigorous message on Jonah. The
way in which Father Mapple mounts his pulpit provides
the clue to the meaning of his long sermon. The pulpit is
shaped like a prow on a ship, without visible means of
entry. Father Mapple makes a ritual out of climbing a rope
ladder into the pulpit and then pulling the ladder up after
him—leaving him in an impregnable and exalted position
from which to deliver his sermon. As Ishmael contemplates
this elaborate maneuver, he reasons: "Father Mapple enjoyed such a wide reputation for sincerity and sanctity,
that I could not suspect him of courting notoriety by any
mere tricks of the stage." The ironic tone is inescapable: in
spite of the fact that Ishmael decides Father Mapple's action
symbolizes his withdrawal from all "outward worldly ties
and connexions," still there is an ostentatiousness in his
dramatic entry into his pulpit that begins to undercut the
serious posture he assumes before his congregation. The
Christian Father Mapple's isolation and superior, aloof position contrast sharply with the pagan Queequeg's affectionate invitation to Ishmael to join in the worship of his idol.

The sermon on Jonah which Father Mapple delivers ex-

hibits the same stiff, uncompromising attitude that his position in the pulpit suggests. For Father Mapple, the Jonah
story offers a "two-stranded lesson; a lesson to us all as
sinful men, and a lesson to me as a pilot of the living God."
Jonah's sin was the sin of disobedience: he refused to
obey the command of God to go to Nineveh to preach to its
sinful people, and he compounded his sin by trying to flee
God. After prolonged dwelling on the details of Jonah's
actions Father Mapple cites two specific lessons. The first:
"Sin not; but if you do, take heed to repent of it like Jonah."
And second: "To preach the Truth to the face of False-
hood." These seem innocent enough morals to draw from
the biblical tale—but Father Mapple's extension of them suggests the rigidity of the chronometrical (the heavenly) morality, inapplicable to this earth, of *Pierre's* Plinlimmon
pamphlet. "Woe to him whom this world charms from
Gospel duty! Woe to him who seeks to pour oil upon the
waters when God has brewed them into a gale! Woe to
him who seeks to please rather than to appal! Woe to him
whose good name is more to him than goodness! Woe to him
who, in this world, courts not dishonor! Woe to him who
would not be true, even though to be false were salvation!"
This lesson is precisely that which Ishmael, in his association with Queequeg, is in process of unlearning; and it is
the very unalterable view that drives Ahab on to seek out
his wicked Ninevah, Moby Dick. Father Mapple continues:
"Delight is to him, who gives no quarter in the truth, and
kills, burns, and destroys all sin though he pluck it out
from under the robes of Senators and Judges. Delight,—
top-gallant delight to him, who acknowledges no law or
lord, but the Lord his God, and is only a patriot to heaven."
These are the delights of all Melville's uncompromising Titanic rebels—Taji, Ahab, Pierre—who kill, burn, destroy
as they rigidly give no quarter in what they conceive as
the truth.

As Father Mapple sinks in exhaustion to the floor of his pulpit, he breathes—"O Father!—chiefly known to me by Thy rod." In this acknowledgment lies the essence of the inhumanity of his sermon. When Ishmael returns to his room, he discovers that Queequeg has slipped out of the Whaleman's Chapel and preceded him, and sits alone contemplatively fingering his little black idol, Yojo. The pagan scene which follows has all of the warmth and fellow-feeling and humanity that were coldly missing in the bleak Christian world sketched by Father Mapple. For the first time Ishmael learns something of Queequeg's history. Son of the pagan king Kokovoko, Queequeg had in his youth a burning desire to learn something of Christianity, as he wished to enlighten his ignorant countrymen and to increase their happiness. His experience began on a whaler: "Alas! the practices of whalemen soon convinced him that even Christians could be both miserable and wicked; infinitely more so, than all his father's heathens. Arrived at last in old Sag Harbor; and seeing what the sailors did there; and then going on to Nantucket, and seeing how they spent their wages in *that* place also, poor Queequeg gave it up for lost. Thought he, it's a wicked world in all meridians; I'll die a pagan." Queequeg's confessions lead to the bosom friendship, and the bonds of friendship to joint pagan worship. As Queequeg prepares his idol for his evening prayers, he invites Ishmael to share in the ceremony. Ishmael hesitates, but reasons: "But what is worship?—to do the will of God—*that* is worship. And what is the will of God?—to do to my fellow man what I would have my fellow man to do to me—*that* is the will of God. Now, Queequeg is my fellow man." Ishmael thus talks himself into being a pagan—but on Christian grounds foreign to Father Mapple's cold and desolate domain.

Both Ishmael and Queequeg have sampled the world and found it bitter. Out of this profound experience and common knowledge develops their deep tie of comradeship. Their pledge of friendship is a pledge to confront together the world in all its masks. It is Queequeg's idol, Yojo, that makes the decision to allow Ishmael to choose the whaler on which they will sail. And on the *Pequod*, Ishmael once again encounters the inconsistency of the Christian world. The owners, Captains Peleg and Bildad, are Quakers, but they are *fighting* Quakers, and it is clear that they are *materialistic* Quakers from the hard bargains they strike with the sailors. Pious Captain Bildad spends much of his time engrossed in reading the Bible, but his piety does not prevent him from keeping a sharp eye out for a profit or from waiving his rules about hiring only *converted* savages when he discovers Queequeg's skill with a harpoon. Although these scenes have a comic quality that diminishes the seriousness of the Quakers' flaws—makes them human—the religious satire is, nevertheless, telling. For both Ishmael and Queequeg, the episodes merely confirm what they have already learned well about the Christian world—that on every hand, at every turn, one will encounter "civilised hypocrisies and bland deceits," and must develop the craft to cope with them. They little realize, as they board the *Pequod* in spite of the hissed warning of the prophet Elijah, that they are coming under the sway of a masked wickedness that will challenge not merely their considerable ingenuity but the very foundations of their moral being.

3 *Monomaniac revenge and the palsied universe*

Soon after that fateful Christmas day when the *Pequod* embarks on its remarkable voyage, Melville assembles about the brooding Captain Ahab the entire cast of his characters

and launches the central action of his fiction. Ahab has been
amply foreshadowed before his appearance—he is to be "a
mighty pageant creature, formed for noble tragedies." But
the chord is not all harmony: "For all men tragically great
are made so through a certain morbidness. Be sure of this, O
young ambition, all mortal greatness is but disease." When
Ahab finally steps forth on the quarter-deck, he lives up in
appearance to the image created in fancy. "He looked
like a man cut away from the stake, when the fire has over-
runningly wasted all the limbs without consuming them,
or taking away one particle from their compacted aged ro-
bustness." Two physical features command the attention
of the gaping sailors. There is a thin, rod-like scar running
from his hair down the side of his face and into his clothing,
which resembles the "perpendicular seam" made in the
solid trunk of a rugged tree by a bolt of lightning—the visible symbol of his soul sundered in his encounter with the
universe. And there is his "barbaric white leg" made from
the "polished bone of the Sperm Whale's jaw." But these
physical marks do not detract from the majesty of Ahab's
presence—"moody stricken Ahab stood before them with a
crucifixion in his face; in all the nameless regal overbearing
dignity of some mighty woe."

It is this commanding figure who calls together the entire ship's company on the quarter-deck to exact their total
allegiance. As he nails a gold doubloon to the mainmast, a
reward for the first man to sing out for the "white-headed
whale with a wrinkled brow and crooked jaw," the pagan
harpooners Tashtego, Daggoo, and Queequeg start in recognition at the description—they all know Moby Dick. The
mates, Starbuck, Stubb, and Flash, respond immediately
too, and Starbuck boldly asks if it is true that it was Moby
Dick who took off Ahab's leg. Ahab cries out that it was
indeed Moby Dick who "dismasted" him. Of all the assembled crew, it is only Starbuck who raises a question as to

Ahab's motive: "To be enraged with a dumb thing, Captain Ahab, seems blasphemous." Angered by an opposition he cannot tolerate, Ahab cries out a curse on Moby Dick: "He tasks me; he heaps me; I see in him outrageous strength, with an inscrutable malice sinewing it. That inscrutable thing is chiefly what I hate; and be the white whale agent, or be the white whale principal, I will wreak that hate upon him. Talk not to me of blasphemy, man; I'd strike the sun if it insulted me." Though not convinced, Starbuck is silenced by the sheer force of Ahab's will. Ahab is now ready to demand the allegiance of his assembled crew, an allegiance to the death in the pursuit of Moby Dick. The ceremony of the crossed lances, climaxed by the communion of "fiery waters" drunk from the harpoon sockets, delivers the assembled souls to Ahab, and makes them one in purpose with him.

This crew, so eager to shout with Ahab "Death to Moby Dick," is made up of "mongrel renegades, and castaways, and cannibals." The harpooners are all primitives, all sons of darkness assembled from the four corners of the earth. Queequeg is from Kokovoko, an island to the west and south that appears on no map. Tashtego is an American Indian, from Gay Head on Martha's Vineyard—a son, it is rumored, of the "Prince of the Powers of the Air." Daggoo is a Negro savage from Africa, a giant of six feet five. All the harpooners are magnificent physical specimens of humanity, and they exhibit (as in the case of Queequeg) all the barbaric virtues besides. Their simple integrity and fierce strength and dedication contrast with the quality of the *Pequod*'s mates, all civilized but somehow rendered weak or deficient by their civilization in the major, soul-searching tests of life. When, in a later episode, the mates in turn interpret the meaning of the cabalistic doubloon nailed to the mainmast, they reveal their inmost natures. The "mere unaided virtue" of Starbuck causes him, after a tortured moral reading of the symbols, to turn away in fear, "I will quit it, lest Truth shake me falsely." Stubb's "invulnerable jollity of indifference and recklessness" causes him to clown in front of the coin at some length as he reads the merry life of man written out in the symbols of the Zodiac, and he concludes—"Oh, jolly's the word for aye!" The "pervading mediocrity" of Flask causes him to decide at once: "I see nothing here, but a round thing made of gold." These are the men of the *Pequod:* "Such a crew, so officered, seemed specially picked and packed by some infernal fatality to help [Ahab] to his monomaniac revenge. How it was that they so aboundingly responded to the old man's ire—by what evil magic their souls were possessed, that at times his hate seemed almost theirs; the White Whale as much their insufferable foe as his; how all this came to be—what the White Whale was to them, or how to their unconscious understandings, also, in some dim, unsuspected way, he might have seemed the gliding great demon of the seas of life,—all this to explain, would be to dive deeper than Ishmael can go."

If Ahab is the demon that drives his crew on, Moby Dick is the immense magnet that draws the *Pequod* to its destiny. Wild rumors have circulated for some time among sailors about the great white whale—that he is ubiquitous, that he is immortal, that he is, in short, some malevolent deity. But it is no rumor that inspires the hate of Ahab. Moby Dick has reaped away his leg and his "torn body and gashed soul" have "bled into one another." His desire for revenge grown beyond the bounds of human containment, Ahab has become mad, but it is a madness that conserves all its cunning and craft to achieve its end. To Ahab, pursuit of Moby Dick has become the sole reason for existence: "That intangible malignity which has been from the beginning; to whose dominion even the modern Christians ascribe one-half of the worlds; which the ancient Ophites of the east reverenced in their statue devil;—Ahab did not fall

down and worship it like them; but deliriously transferring
its idea to the abhorred White Whale, he pitted himself, all
mutilated, against it. All that most maddens and torments;
all that stirs up the lees of things; all truth with malice in
it; all that cracks the sinews and cakes the brain; all the
subtle demonisms of life and thought; all evil, to crazy
Ahab, were visibly personified, and made practically as-
sailable in Moby Dick. He piled upon the whale's white
hump the sum of all the general rage and hate felt by his
whole race from Adam down; and then, as if his chest had
been a mortar, he burst his hot heart's shell upon it."

After exploring the full and complex meaning of Moby
Dick for Ahab, Ishmael confesses: "What the White Whale
was to Ahab, has been hinted; what, at times, he was to me,
as yet remains unsaid." In thus dissociating himself from
Ahab's view of the whale, Ishmael provides important clues
as to the genuine meaning of Moby Dick. "The Whiteness of
the Whale" (Chapter 42) provides the key to Moby Dick's
complex symbolism. Though whiteness is associated with
many agreeable things—"the innocence of brides, the benignity of age"—still, there "yet lurks an elusive something
in the innermost idea of this hue, which strikes more of
panic to the soul than that redness which affrights in
blood." In short, whiteness both attracts and repels, contains both innocence and terror: "It is at once the most
meaning symbol of spiritual things, nay, the very veil of
the Christian's Deity; and yet is the intensifying agent in
things the most appalling to mankind." In working his
way into the complexity of the meaning of whiteness, Ishmael ultimately ascribes the color (or its absence) to the
entire universe: "And when we proceed further, and consider that the mystical cosmetic which produces every one
of her hues, the great principle of light, for ever remains
white or colorless in itself, and if operating without medium
upon matter, would touch all objects, even tulips and

8

roses, with its own blank tinge—pondering all this, the palsied universe lies before us a leper. And like willful travellers in Lapland, who refuse to wear colored and coloring glasses upon their eyes, so the wretched infidel gazes himself blind at the monumental white shroud that wraps all the prospect around him. And of all these things the Albino Whale was the symbol." The whiteness of Moby Dick is, then, but a reflection of the inscrutable whiteness of the entire universe. In him, as in it, are inextricably bound together both innocence and horror, good and evil. They are the unquestionable conditions of man's existence. In rebelling against man's destiny, man's fate, in pursuing Moby Dick to the death, Ahab would destroy the very foundations of the universe and annihilate life itself.

4 *Whales: manufacture, metaphysics, mythology*

If we may designate Ishmael, as narrator, the spout of our leviathan, and Ahab's pursuit of Moby Dick as the central core and skeleton, then we must label the huge quantity of material on the manufacture, metaphysics, and mythology of whales as that abundant blubber that swells the book to its enormity and keeps it afloat. It is wrong to conceive of all this material as an afterthought, unintegrated, somehow added to the story. On the contrary, the story could not exist without it, any more than a whale could exist without his blanket of blubber. If we are to understand the cause of Ahab's rage and his monomaniac plans for revenge, then we must understand something of whales and whaling. If we are to follow Ishmael's tortured progression, from isolation to comradeship, through the labyrinthine insights that come, never at the high moments of the action but in the routine moments of the daily labor, then we must understand a good many of the details of the business of turning blubber into oil. If we are to sense the epic quality of the tragic action played out before us, if we are to feel that Ahab's pursuit of Moby Dick is something more than simply a sick old man struggling with a malevolent whale, then we must develop some consciousness of the whale in history, in folklore, in mythology—we must acquire some sense of awe and mystery as we contemplate the whale's complexity, antiquity, and immensity.

To the second mate Stubb is given the honor of killing the *Pequod*'s first whale. And as its mountainous bulk is hoisted up at the side of the ship, there begins the long, complicated ritual of manufacturing sperm oil out of the monstrous and uncooperative fish. Stubb's first act is to have himself a steak from his catch, but Stubb's taste is not the crew's. Their task is to massacre the whale before the sharks steal it all. The "cutting in" requires all hands— "The ivory *Pequod* was turned into what seemed a shamble; every sailor a butcher. You would have thought we were offering up ten thousand red oxen to the sea gods." The purpose of the frantic butchery is to remove the whale's blanket of blubber, rich in sperm oil and varying in thickness from ten to fifteen inches. After this removal, the whale is beheaded and the carcass released to drift away, free food for the sharks. The next step is to exploit the riches of the whale's head. In order to make some important distinctions in whales, Melville sends Stubb out to kill a right whale, whose head is hoisted also alongside the *Pequod*. Immediately the poor right whale is beat on the head, for it seems that there is an "immense superiority" in the "pervading dignity" of the sperm whale's countenance. In spite of significant differences (the right whale has two spoutholes, the sperm whale only one), the two heads share certain anatomical peculiarities: "Is it not curious, that so vast a being as the whale should see the world through so small an eye, and hear the thunder through an ear which is smaller than a hare's?" But the heads of the whales are not hoisted for anatomical examination. They contain riches, the purest and most precious kind of sperm oil, which can be lifted out by buckets. It is in the process of scooping up this oil that Tashtego loses his balance and falls into the whale's head as the head itself falls into the sea. He is saved only by the quick manuever of Queequeg, who dives into the ocean and "delivers" Tashtego in obstetrical fashion.

There is a veritable factory set in operation once the blubber and other treasures of the whale are brought on board. Ishmael participates in all these operations, and in the midst of his activity does some of his deepest diving. He sits at one of the tubs of sperm for a time, squeezing congealed lumps back into fluid, and describes how his fingers begin to feel like eels as they "serpentine and spiralize," and how he himself begins to melt at the aroma—"like the smell of spring violets." He describes the strange ritual whereby the whale's huge, jet-black phallus, its "grandissimus, as the mariners call it," is pealed of its dark pelt, which, after drying, forms a "cassock" or "investiture" for the mincer, the man who slices the blubber into thin slices ("bible leaves") for the pots of the try-works. The brick and mortar try-works are built into the ship, between foremast and mainmast, and support two huge try-pots, of several barrels capacity, in which the oil is boiled out of the blubber. Once the shriveled blubber has yielded its oil to the pot, it is extracted and fed into the flames underneath: "Like a plethoric burning martyr, or a self-consuming misanthrope, once ignited, the whale supplies his own fuel and burns by his own body." And then the final step in the production of oil is taken—the oil is decanted into casks and the casks stowed in the hold. After this "stowing down," the enormous and seemingly impossible task of "clearing up" begins. But all of the blood, and soot, and litter are removed, and the sailors themselves perform their ablutions "from top to toe," and soon there remain no signs of the fabulous labor that has been enacted on deck. And all lounge in their spotless ship—until the next cry of "There she blows!" And the entire ritual begins again.

If all the material on whaling were presented simply as information and nothing more, the often-voiced objections to it might well have substance. But rare is the episode which does not set Melville off on a flight of fancy that leads him far from the decks of the *Pequod*. There is so much sense and consistency in Melville's recurring movement from scene to philosophy that it seems appropriate to designate his method as "metaphysical." It is the basic method he uses in plotting Ishmael's progressively deeper insights in the novel. And it provides a kind of musical foundation which weaves together and unites in intricate pattern all of the book's major themes. His chapter on the whale's thick blanket of blubber concludes with the observation that it is this "wall" that enables the whale, a warm-blooded creature, to survive in Arctic waters: "It does seem to me, that herein we see the rare virtue of a strong individual vitality, and the rare virtue of thick walls, and the rare virtue of interior spaciousness. Oh, man! admire and model thyself after the whale! Do thou, too, remain warm among ice. Do thou, too, live in this world without being of it. Be cool at the equator; keep thy blood fluid at the Pole." When the *Pequod* is put on even keel by hoisting the right whale's head to balance the sperm whale's, the ship is "sorely strained": "So, when on one side you hoist in Locke's head, you go over that way; but now, on the other side, hoist in Kant's and you come back again; but in very poor plight. Thus, some minds for ever keep trimming boat. Oh, ye

foolish! throw all these thunderheads overboard, and then
you will float light and right." When the "stowing down
and clearing" are completed, the sailors on the *Pequod* are
ready at any moment to begin again at the beginning the
long, laborious ritual of pursuing and processing the whale:
"Yet this is life. For hardly have we mortals by long toilings
extracted from this world's vast bulk its small but valuable
sperm; and then, with weary patience, cleansed ourselves
from its defilements, and learned to live here in clean taber-
nacles of the soul; hardly is this done, when—*There she
blows!*—the ghost is spouted up, and away we sail to fight
some other world, and go through young life's old routine
again." The whaling scenes of *Moby Dick* may seem at
first glance both extraneous and exterior to the "real" story,
but a little deeper diving (like Pip's involuntary plunge
into the sea) reveals subterranean relationships with both
plot and theme in the "unwarped primal world" of the novel,
and reveals, too, Melville's "foot upon the treadle of the
loom."

But there is still more bulk to this leviathan than we have
yet accounted for. The whaling scenes provide a persuasive
setting of realistic daily life for the precious stone of the
central action, and they weave an intricate background
pattern, with variations, for the book's major thematic state-
ments. But there is more whale still: there is, indeed, a
goodly surplusage of whale. This "excess" exposition spills
over and through and beyond the book with the ubiquity
and immortality of Moby Dick. It becames a veritable sea—
and it provides the mass and the buoyancy with which to
float the fabulous White Whale. This material provides
the means for Melville's myth-making strategy. Through
the manipulation and maneuvering of this material, Melville provides—indeed creates—a leviathan world of the
imagination that has its own vast magnitudes and its own
immeasurable terms of consistency. The materials of this

world had since time began accumulated in the epics and
bibles and wondrous handbooks of the world's cultures, but
Melville was the first to assemble them all in one place to
see what he could make of them. And he massed these materials at the front of his book as a signal that the world it
described offered new deities and new dimensions. That
sub-sub-librarian credited with the scholarship is librarian of
our subconscious bringing together under our conscious eyes
the leviathans that have always floated silently in the
depths within us.

In the first chapter unashamedly devoted to whaling,
"The Advocate" (24), Melville opens an elaborate defense
of the profession: ". . . as this business of whaling has
somehow come to be regarded among landsmen as a rather
unpoetical and disreputable pursuit . . . I am all anxiety
to convince ye, ye landsmen, of the injustice hereby done to
us hunters of whales." In a sense all of *Moby Dick* is an
elaboration of this defense, a massive epic assertion of the
poetic-mythic substance of leviathan and his pursuit. The
threads of this defense are woven so finely into the entire
fabric of the novel that it is impossible to trace them all out,
but there are moments of open and concentrated advocacy.
In "Cetology" (32) Melville presents a "systematized ex-
hibition of the whale in his broad genera," in an attempt to
bring some order out of the chaos of whale science and
whale lore. In the midst of this elaborate classification, he
pauses to exclaim that "the Sperm Whale, scientific or poetic,
lives not complete in any literature. Far above all other
hunted whales, his is an unwritten life"; clearly he sees a
niche—both scientific *and* poetic—for his own book to fill.
In "The Honor and Glory of Whaling" (82), Melville
pushes his "researches up to the very spring-head" of whaling and becomes even more impressed with its "great
honorableness and antiquity." After claiming for his fraternity Perseus, St. George (the dragon was a whale),

Hercules, and Jonah, he adds: "Our grand master is still to be named; for like royal kings of old times, we find the head-waters of our fraternity in nothing short of the great gods themselves." And thus Vishnoo, "one of the three persons in the godhead of the Hindoos, who "became incarnate in a whale," is claimed for the brotherhood. In "The Fossil Whale" (104), Melville glorifies and magnifies leviathan from "an archaeological, fossiliferous, and antediluvian point of view"—in one of the most lyrical passages of his book: "I am, by a flood, borne back to that wondrous period, ere time itself can be said to have begun; for time began with man. Here Saturn's grey chaos rolls over me, and I obtain dim, shuddering glimpses into those Polar eternities; when wedged bastions of ice pressed hard upon what are now the Tropics; and in all the 25,000 miles of this world's circum-ference, not an inhabitable hand's breath of land was visi-ble. Then the whole world was the whale's; and, king of creation, he left his wake along the present lines of the Andes and the Himmalehs. Who can show a pedigree like Leviathan?"

The cumulative effect of this bulk of material on the whale—its anatomy, its antiquity, its divinity and more— is to storm the imagination by sheer mass and magnitude. Out of his unlikely and disparate materials, by the ingenious strategy of alternately infiltrating, concentrating, and dis-persing, Melville creates a mythic setting for his tale. When we reach the final pages of the novel, and see Moby Dick triumphant in the midst of the general catastrophe, we sense in him a lineage and a nature more than flesh, higher than fish; as we watch all the actors but one disappear beneath the waves, and are told that "the great shroud of the sea rolled on as it rolled five thousand years ago," we sense a continuity and cosmic significance in the action that only Melville's massive mythology of the whale could have in-spired.

5   *Ahab's madness maddened*

If the poetic and metaphysical treatment of whales and whaling raises the action of *Moby Dick* to the level of myth, Ahab seems created on the epic scale to act out his role on that high level. Immediately after the soul-exhausting quarter-deck scene, Ahab retires to his cabin and meditates alone. In personal anguish he acknowledges his human deficiency: "Gifted with the high perception, I lack the low, enjoying power; damned, most subtly and most malignantly!" Starbuck thinks him mad—but Ahab realizes that his madness is the result not of a disintegrated mind but of a supreme intelligence: "I'm demoniac, I am madness maddened! That wild madness that's only calm to comprehend itself! . . . The path to my fixed purpose is laid with iron rails, whereon my soul is grooved to run." The self-knowledge evident throughout this soliloquy ultimately gives way to self-delusion in the long pursuit of Moby Dick.

Though outwardly and superficially convinced of his own innocence in his monumental effort to rid the world of evil, Ahab realizes deep within his "unconscious understandings" the magnitude of his gradual and awful commitment to the devil. Until near the time of the sighting of Moby Dick, Ahab's "humanities" make him vulnerable to appeals to give up the chase and turn back toward home. But what began as personal revenge and became an obsessive hatred of evil turns out finally to be a consuming cosmic defiance. Ahab's smashing of the quadrant initiates a series of acts which divest his fixed intent of the least ambiguity and which lead inevitably to the final catastrophe. It is Ahab's envy of the celestial sun which leads him to throw the quadrant to the deck: "Curse thee, thou vain toy; and cursed be all the things that cast man's eyes aloft

to that heaven, whose live vividness but scorches him, as
these old eyes are even now scorched with thy light, O
sun! Level by nature to this earth's horizon are the glances
of man's eyes; not shot from the crown of his head, as if
God had meant him to gaze on his firmament." This defiance of God as symbolized by the sun is followed almost
immediately (the chapters, "The Quadrant" and "The Candles," are consecutive) by a fiery dedication to the devil.
The corposants eerily light up the masts of the *Pequod* like
a series of candles. In a scene which partakes of the diabolical sacrament, counterpart to the quarter-deck "ceremony" at the beginning of the voyage, Ahab swears his
continued rebellion: "I now know thee, thou clear spirit [of
fire], and I now know that thy right worship is defiance. To
neither love nor reverence wilt thou be kind; and e'en for
hate thou canst but kill; and all are killed." The tip of
Ahab's harpoon, like the masts, flashes with flame, and as
Ahab thrusts it aloft shouting his defiance, and, finally, in
one mighty breath extinguishes it, the crew shrinks in fear.

Drunk with the success of his defiance and the magnitude
of his own power, Ahab moves swiftly from one act of dangerous rebellion to another. He wildly envisions himself as
the god Apollo: "Ha, ha, my ship! thou mightest well be
taken now for the sea-chariot of the sun. Ho, ho! all ye nations before my prow, I bring the sun to ye! Yoke on the
further billows; hallo! a tandem, I drive the sea!" Informed
that the thunder has turned the ship's compasses, Ahab announces that out of a bit of steel he will make a compass of
his own. And he does, with all the flourish of a devil per-
forming his diabolical magic. As the awe-struck crew steps
forward and confirms the reliability of Ahab's compass, the
Captain stands watching: "In his fiery eyes of scorn and
triumph, you then saw Ahab in all his fatal pride." Shortly
after this incident, still another mechanism for determining
the *Pequod's* course—the log and line—is destroyed: the

line snaps and the log is lost. Ahab exclaims: "I crush the quadrant, the thunder turns the needles, and now the mad sea parts the log-line. But Ahab can mend all." And he sets his crew immediately about mending the line and making a new log. As this series of incidents comes to a close, Ahab has arrogated to himself all the direction of the *Pequod.* Ahab's course is fixed—but in both a real and symbolic sense, his course is one which he in his diabolical dedication fixed himself.

Fedallah, Ahab's harpooner, is the embodiment of Ahab's demoniac subconscious and symbolizes Ahab's ultimate awareness of his dedication to evil. Ahab smuggles Fedallah and his diabolical crew aboard and keeps them mysteriously hidden until the first chase. And when Fedallah does appear it becomes clear that he is somehow "linked with Ahab's peculiar fortunes" and that there even seems to exist "some sort of a half-hinted influence." Fedallah's oppressive presence is felt more and more, particularly in those critical instances in which outraged Ahab defiantly challenges God's wisdom. When Ahab smashes the quadrant, Fedallah lurks in the background barely concealing "a sneering triumph that seemed meant for Ahab, and a fatalistic despair that seemed meant for himself." When Ahab shouts his challenge to the "clear spirit of clear fire," Fedallah is at first kneeling in front of him and finally is beneath his foot, a vital element in the diabolical oath. Although Fedallah's presence is everywhere felt, his corporeality is more and more doubted: "Such an added, gliding strangeness began to invest the thin Fedallah now; such ceaseless shudderings shook him; that the men looked dubious at him; half uncertain, as it seemed, whether indeed he were a mortal substance, or else a tremulous shadow cast upon the deck by some unseen being's body." Indeed the relationship between Ahab and Fedallah becomes so close, intertwined, and ambiguous, that they begin to seem to the crew two aspects of

the same being: "At times, for longest hours, without a single
hail, they stood far parted in the starlight; Ahab in his
scuttle, the Parsee by the main-mast; but still fixedly gazing
upon each other; as if in the Parsee Ahab saw his forethrown
shadow, in Ahab the Parsee his abandoned substance."

Ahab's gaze fixed on the Parsee and Fedallah's answering
look symbolize the instinctive, primordial recognition in
process deep within Ahab's soul. The final commitment is
not far off. Ahab *becomes* Fedallah—yet he wears the mask
of Ahab. When the Parsee prophesies Ahab's "immortality"
by listing what Ahab takes to be impossible events which
must come to pass before Ahab can die, we are witnessing
the mechanical nature of the way by which Ahab "deludes"
himself. This delusion, however, is not so much an assurance
of success as a prophetic glimpse of failure. If Ahab could—
or would—consciously decipher the cabalistic symbols of
warning which emerge from his unconscious, he would confront directly the but dimly acknowledged doom toward
which he drives.

When, just before the final, fatal chase, Ahab rejects Starbuck's plea invoking hearth and home, the gnarled captain's
feelings of helplessness are apparent; he shook "like a
blighted fruit tree" and "cast his last cindered apple to the
soil": "What is it, what nameless, inscrutable, unearthly
thing is it, what cozening, hidden lord and master, and cruel,
remorseless emperor commands me; that against all natural
lovings and longing, I so keep pushing, and crowding, and
jamming myself on all the time; recklessly making me ready
to do what in my own proper, natural heart, I durst not so
much as dare? Is Ahab, Ahab?" As this speech gathers force,
Ahab seeks to answer the profound question he raises by
placing the blame on Fate ("By heaven, man, we are turned
round and round in this world, like yonder windlass, and
Fate is the handspike"). When he stalks across the deck of
the ship to gaze down into the dark waters to find staring

back at him Fedallah's fixed eyes, he is jolted anew into self-realization. The mirror of the sea does not lie: Ahab in his dark dedication has transformed himself into his own monstrous impulse for evil—Fedallah.

Although Ahab has confronted the universe and himself with the fabulous innocence of his outraged indignation at the world's evil, he knows as he gazes down into the deep sea of his subconscious that the devil Fedallah possesses his soul and that he himself in his "fatal pride" has come to embody all of the evil he had once consigned to Moby Dick. Ahab, like Taji, is aware of his hardened heart and, like Taji, becomes his own soul's emperor—and his first imperial act is abdication.

6   *The Innocents of the* Pequod

The complexity of Ahab's labyrinthine deception proves sufficient protection from a number of brilliantly drawn Innocents. Of all these, one Bulkington, whose appearance in the novel is fleeting, is the most mysterious. He is introduced at the beginning of Ishmael's journey, in the Spouter-Inn: "He stood full six feet in height, with noble shoulders, and a chest like a coffer-dam. I have seldom seen such brawn in a man. His face was deeply brown and burnt, making his white teeth dazzling by the contrast; while in the deep shadows of his eyes floated some reminiscences that did not seem to give him much joy." At the height of the revelry in the Inn, Bulkington slips away; his shipmates miss him immediately and set off looking for him. This brief view of this remarkable sailor suggests that his role in the unfolding drama is to be important. In fact, one expects a reincarnation of Jack Chase, Captain of the foretop and a favorite of

White Jacket. But Bulkington, though he does appear again, is buried forever in a "six-inch chapter" that must serve as his "stoneless grave." Last seen (long before the end of the book), Bulkington is at the helm of the *Pequod*, steering her straight and steady into the "cold malicious waves." Ishmael explains that Bulkington, having just returned from a four-year voyage, found the land "scorching to his feet" and set out immediately to sea again on the *Pequod.*

To Ishmael, Bulkington at the helm symbolizes the ultimate courage: "Glimpses do ye seem to see of that mortally intolerable truth; that all deep, earnest thinking is but the intrepid effort of the soul to keep the open independence of her sea; while the wildest winds of heaven and earth conspire to cast her on the treacherous, slavish shore?" Bulkington, in his singular loneliness and his enviable fearlessness, rises to the role of a demigod, is etched indelibly in vivid strokes, and then disappears from the narrative forever. But he does not disappear from the imagination of the reader. There he endures, a symbol of ideal and wise frankness, deceiving neither self nor society, maintaining a courageous balance in the midst of the "malicious waves" of a treacherous world. His is the equanimity in confronting the universe as it exists that Ahab cannot achieve. Bulkington must be buried in his "six-inch chapter," for he is the one character who could have, properly developed, persuaded the monomaniac Captain from his mad pursuit.

Bulkington departs from the novel as abruptly as he enters it; Starbuck and then Pip step to the fore in roles of innocence, directing their energies of conversion not toward the wandering Ishmael but toward the lost Ahab. Starbuck is the "staid, steadfast" first mate who will not have in his boat a man unafraid of a whale. If the "welded iron of his soul" is sometimes bent by his "intelligent" superstition lured on by "domestic memories of his young Cape wife and child," he is an "honest-hearted" man whose frank fear springs from a full appraisal of the world's evil. But with all his virtues, Starbuck has a fatal flaw: "And brave as he might be, it was that sort of bravery chiefly, visible in some intrepid men, which, while generally abiding firm in the conflict with seas, or winds, or whales, or any of the ordinary irrational horrors of the world, yet cannot withstand those more terrific, because more spiritual terrors, which sometimes menace you from the concentrating brow of an enraged and mighty man." After the quarter-deck scene in which Ahab diabolically mesmerizes the crew, Starbuck reluctantly peers into his own weakened spirit: "My soul is more than matched; she's overmanned; and by a madman! Insufferable sting, that sanity should ground arms on such a field! But he drilled deep down, and blasted all my reason out of me! I think I see his impious end; but feel that I must help him to it."

Virtue divested of reason is helpless. Because Starbuck embodies "mere unaided virtue or right-mindedness," he is unable to sway Ahab from his course. Like the man who attempts to live on earth in accordance with divine or chronometrical time in *Pierre*'s Plinlimmon pamphlet (Starbuck is associated with the chronometer— ". . . be it Polar snow or torrid sun, like a patent chronometer, his interior vitality was warranted to do well in all climates"), Starbuck commits evil by his very attempt to avoid it. His final climactic failure is his inability, when the perfect opportunity presents itself, to take action against Ahab. Shortly before the final chase, Starbuck comes upon Ahab in his cabin asleep. He sees a loaded musket ready at hand: ". . . out of Starbuck's heart, at that instant when he saw the musket, there strangely evolved an evil thought; but so blunt with its neutral or good accompaniments that for the instant he hardly knew it for itself." Born of his heart rather than his reason, the "evil thought" is doomed to be banished. The crucial moment for Starbuck's spiritual courage arrives—

and he fails. He muses: "But shall this crazed old man be tamely suffered to drag a whole ship's company down to doom with him?— Yes, it would make him the wilful murderer of thirty men and more, if this ship come to any deadly harm; and will, if Ahab have his way."

But even in the knowledge that catastrophe impends, Starbuck's thoughts wander to his own soul's salvation: "Is heaven a murderer when its lightning strikes a would-be murderer in his bed, tindering sheets and skin together?— And would I be a murderer, then, if—" It is no coincidence that Starbuck thinks of his action as analogous to heaven's. He is attempting to live by divine rather than earthly law, and he weighs the doom of his thirty shipmates against the blot of "crime" on his soul—and he ironically decides that his soul must remain "spotless." In denying life's essential horror ("that horror's out of me"), Starbuck becomes reconciled to a horror that staggers the imagination. He sacrifices the entire ship to win personal salvation. He wrestles "with an angel" as he struggles to commit a "sin" whose results will be *good* compounded—and loses.

Just before the final chase begins, Starbuck makes his strongest appeal to Ahab's suppressed human sympathies. Starbuck perceives that Ahab has reached a crucial imbalance in head and heart, the intellect holding terrible and diabolical sway. The first mate therefore directs his appeal to his heart: "Oh, my Captain! my Captain! noble soul! grand old heart, after all! Why should anyone give chase to that hated fish! Away with me! let us fly these deadly waters, let us home!" Starbuck's plea is foredoomed to fail. Incapable of acting, unable to persuade, Starbuck is the personification of ineffectual Virtue. His moral righteousness but speeds on the catastrophe.

Both Starbuck and Pip are characterized by their fear, but in Pip fright leads to his ignominious leap into the sea. Abandoned by Stubb in accord with his warning, Pip is

rescued by the "merest chance." The experience is more
than harrowing: it demolishes the foundations of his being:
"The sea had jeeringly kept his finite body up, but drowned
the infinite of his soul. Not drowned entirely, though.
Rather carried down alive to wondrous depths, where
strange shapes of the unwarped primal world glided to
and fro before his passive eyes; and the miser-merman,
wisdom, revealed his hoarded heaps; and among the joyous,
heartless, ever-juvenile eternities, Pip saw the multitudinous,
God-omnipresent, coral insects, that out of the firmament
of waters heaved the colossal orbs. He saw God's foot upon
the treadle of the loom, and spoke it; and therefore his shipmates called him mad." If White Jacket's plunge into the
sea removes his jacket (his badge of innocence) but gains
for him a human identity, Pip's baptism drowns his human
identity while bestowing a higher nature. Divested of his
human reason, Pip is granted a heavenly wisdom. In the
terms of *Pierre*'s Plinlimmon pamphlet, Pip ceases to abide
by horological time and begins to live in accordance with
chronometrical time. "So man's insanity is heaven's sense;
and wandering from all mortal reason, man comes at last to
that celestial thought, which, to reason, is absurd and frantic; and weal or woe, feels then uncompromised, indifferent
as his God."

What Starbuck wins his way to through introspection and
thought, Pip discovers in sudden flash at the moment of his
greatest terror. Both nakedly view the "latent horror" of
life, life of the "unwarped primal world" where "joyous
[and] heartless . . . eternities" unite, and by the terrifying experience, both are rendered unfit for the grand tests
of *human* existence. But Pip in his madness, all heart and
no reason, comes closer than Starbuck to moving Ahab
from his fixed course. Ahab's sympathies are stirred by the
pitiful plight of Pip as he wearily searches for his lost self:
"Here, boy; Ahab's cabin shall be Pip's home henceforth,

while Ahab lives. Thou touchest my inmost centre, boy; thou art tied to me by cords woven of my heart-strings." Pip's wisdom and role are Christ-like as his love embraces the austere Captain: "They tell me, Sir, that Stubb did once desert poor little Pip, whose drowned bones now show white, for all the blackness of his living skin. But I will never desert ye, Sir, as Stubb did him. Sir, I must go with ye." Visibly shaken, Ahab answers abruptly: "If thou speakest thus to me much more, Ahab's purpose keels up in him. I tell thee no; it cannot be."

Pip's failure, like Starbuck's, is the failure of heavenly wisdom in a world that calls for earthly action. Their failure in dissuading the captain and preventing the catastrophe is caused by an imbalance of character which renders them ineffective. Bulkington, because he could have changed the course of the action in *Moby Dick,* is buried by Melville in an early chapter. Starbuck, because he refuses to sully his soul with the "sinful" acts that would prevent the catastrophe, finds his strength and courage meaningless. Pip, because his appeal though strong is not decisive and his weakness is the only source of his strength, discovers that he can but watch and wait—and love. Ahab ultimately is left alone, to work out his fate in his own mad terms.

7   I only am escaped

Ishmael and Queequeg have little to do directly with Ahab's monomania. They encounter it only as victims, not, like Starbuck and Pip, as mediators between it and Ahab's "humanities." It is Ishmael, however, who makes a series of discoveries that constitutes the "affirmation" of *Moby Dick.* This series is a recapitulation in miniature of the affirmative perceptions in Melville's previous novels. Ishmael's knowledge about human beings and their relationships, gained in his association with the savage Queequeg, parallels the knowledge gained by Tommo-Melville in his association with the savages in *Typee-Omoo;* his discovery of the guiding principle of love in his association with the crew, climaxed by the spermaceti-squeezing scene, parallels Babbalanja's discovery of Serenia, where Love rules, in *Mardi;* his immersion and recovery at the end of the novel symbolically parallels the protagonist's plunge into the sea in *White Jacket* (that "continuation" of *Redburn*).

At the beginning of *Moby Dick*, Ishmael gloomily perceives that the world is not what it professes to be. And, ironically, the first step in the restoration of Ishmael's equilibrium is the companionship he forms not with a Christian but a cannibal. In the topsy-turvy world Ishmael encounters, Christians act like savages and savages act like Christians. Although Christianity encompasses the great doctrine of human brotherhood in theory, among most Christians it never becomes practice. Yet to the simple savage Queequeg, Ishmael's bed-mate in the crowded Spouter Inn, the abstract theory has little meaning but the "practice" of comradeship has its own elaborate ritual. Queequeg, the tattooed cannibal, teaches Ishmael, the disheartened Christian, the practical meaning of Ishmael's Christianity! After Ishmael overcomes his initial fright at Queequeg's austerity and his repugnance at his cannibalistic tattooing, he begins to detect a multitude of redeeming qualities: "You cannot hide the soul. Through all his unearthly tattooings, I thought I saw the traces of a simple honest heart; and in his large, deep eyes, fiery black and bold, there seemed tokens of a spirit that would dare a thousand devils." These are the very qualities which Ishmael had despaired of ever finding in mankind.

Queequeg becomes the instrument of the restoration of

Ishmael's faith: "No more my splintered heart and maddened hand were turned against the wolfish world. This
soothing savage had redeemed it." In the innocence of the
pagan, Ishmael glimpses the glorious possibilities of man.
In their simple but close relationship, the intense character
of which is symbolized by their metaphorical marriage,
Ishmael comes to realize the spiritual possibilities of genuine comradeship. But in his search for a revivified soul,
Ishmael does not discover that the world is less wolfish or
hypocritical than he supposed, but he does discover that his
capacity for understanding and love can be expanded to
accommodate the world as it is without lessening his desire
for it to be better—and without disarming him of his knowledge of its grim realities.

When Ishmael and Queequeg, in their new-found companionship, take the boat from New Bedford to Nantucket,
the other passengers marvel "that two fellow beings should
be so companionable; as though a white man were anything
more dignified than a white-washed negro." The curiosity of
an objectionable individual offers Queequeg an opportunity,
first to demonstrate his strength in playful hostility, horrifying the man, and almost immediately afterward, when
the same individual is accidentally swept overboard, to
demonstrate his power in selfless love, rescuing the very man
he had shortly before flung recklessly into the air. In this
incident is revealed both Queequeg's major strength and his
ultimate weakness. His instinctive love which goes to extreme selfless lengths can teach Christians much they need
to know. His instinctive hostility, which flashes out as
readily as the love and with the same intensity, renders
him finally deficient—like the virtuous but fickle savages of
Typee and *Omoo*. This side of Queequeg is suggested, when
Ishmael first sees him, by the embalmed New Zealand heads
which Queequeg is selling. Like Tommo when he discovers
the heads hidden by the Typees, Ishmael shrinks with a

horror that he cannot, even with elaborate rationalization, completely dismiss.

Ishmael's voyage on the *Pequod* brings a deepening of his awareness of the plight of mankind. In the monkey-rope scene, in which Ishmael on the deck is attached by a rope to Queequeg on the captured whale, Ishmael sees into the complex interrelationship of human beings: ". . . for better or for worse, we two, for the time, were wedded; and should poor Queequeg sink to rise no more, then both usage and honor demanded, that instead of cutting the cord, it should drag me down in his wake. So, then, an elongated Siamese ligature united us. Queequeg was my own inseparable twin brother; nor could I any way get rid of the dangerous liabilities which the hempen bond entailed." Ishmael immediately perceives his predicament as symbolic of the human condition: "I saw that this situation of mine was the precise situation of every mortal that breathes; only, in most cases, he, one way or other, has this Siamese connexion with a plurality of other mortals." Human interdependence is inescapable: the only question is how best to accommodate the inevitable relationships.

The answer to this question is most elaborately dramatized a bit further on in the voyage during the spermaceti-squeezing scene. Like the Seekers in *Mardi* who find at last the land of Serenia, Ishmael discovers on the voyage of the *Pequod* the transcendent value of Love. His respect for man restored by Queequeg, Ishmael sees into the heart of things as he sits, during the latter part of the voyage, squeezing spermaceti with his comrades: "I have perceived that in all cases man must eventually lower, or at least shift, his conceit of attainable felicity; not placing it anywhere in the intellect or fancy; but in the wife, the heart, the bed, the table, the saddle, the fire-side, the country." This conclusion Ishmael reaches only after "many prolonged, repeated experiences," and when he is feeling "divinely free from all

ill-will" and even a "strange sort of insanity." Ishmael's
vision, produced by the "abounding, affectionate, friendly,
loving feeling" which sweeps over him like a wave washing
the bitterness from his soul, is not so much a new as a suddenly intensified knowledge. When Ishmael concludes his
vision with an image of "long rows of angels in paradise,
each with his hands in a jar of spermaceti," he is suggesting
intuitively the point of identity between earthly wisdom
and the divine.

As though to balance the sentiment of this scene, the try-
works episode a little later shows Ishmael achieving a
tougher kind of wisdom. One evening as he stands at the
helm of the *Pequod* and gazes into the blazing fires of the
try-works ovens, the "fiend shapes" of the fire begin to
beget "kindred visions" in his soul. As he becomes locked in
fascination and mesmerized by the hellish shapes of the
flames, he falls into a trance. To his horror he discovers that
in the brief moment that he has stood entranced by the fire,
he has turned himself about completely; he is facing away
from the compass and toward the stern of the ship—and has
nearly been the cause of the ship's destruction. "Look not
too long in the face of the fire, O man! Never dream with
thy hand on the helm!" But though the redness of the fire
that "makes all things look ghastly" in the night disappears
tomorrow—still, the sun does not hide "the millions of
miles of deserts and of griefs beneath the moon." Not all is
woe, but neither is all joy, and the man who is all one or the
other is "not true, or undeveloped." "Give not thyself up,
then, to fire, lest it invert thee, deaden thee; as for the time
it did me. There is a wisdom that is woe; but there is a woe
that is madness." Ishmael achieves the wisdom that is woe;
Ahab is driven by his woe into madness.

As Queequeg in his own person is the symbolic "vehicle"
for Ishmael's "conversion," so Queequeg's coffin serves lit-
erally as the vessel for Ishmael's final salvation. Queequeg

reaches from beyond death to grant his comrade Ishmael life. Sucked down into the sea by the whirling vortex created by the sinking *Pequod,* the coffin is spewed out again by the "upward burst" of the sea's "black bubble." Ishmael's immersion in the sea, like White Jacket's, symbolizes his final acceptance of man and the world as they are in all of their glorious possibilities and all of their inglorious imperfections. The knowledge that drove Ahab to his death thus grants renewed life to Ishmael. Like White Jacket in his plunge into the sea, Ishmael loses his old splenetic self and gains a *human* soul. He divests himself of his mask of innocence, the mask he assumes in his solitude on the opening page of *Moby Dick,* as surely as White Jacket rips off his cursed garment; and like White Jacket, he acknowledges his involvement in the human drama. The only one in the tale to achieve a balance of intellect and heart, knowledge and love, Ishmael is the single survivor. As he floats in the sea, purified and transfigured by his experience, the sharks glide by "as if with padlocks on their mouths" and the sea-hawks sail by with "sheathed beaks." Finally he is picked up by the "devious-cruising Rachel, that in her retracing search after her missing children, only found another orphan."

6

Pierre: *the flowing river in the cave of man*

In *Pierre; or, The Ambiguities* (1852), Melville turned for the first time from the sea to the land for his setting and from adventure to love for his narrative interest. He thought, at least on one level, that he was writing a conventional domestic romance, and he looked forward to recouping the losses sustained by *Mardi* and *Moby Dick*. And, in fact, *Pierre* does follow in broad outline the domestic romance, dwelling at length for narrative interest on relationships for sentimental effect. But *Pierre* never enjoyed the popularity of the novels of the domestic sentimentalists precisely because it was too intimately domestic. When Melville expected *Pierre* to be popular, he either did not realize how ambiguously he wrote or else he believed, mistakenly, that he had concealed his complex meanings from popular view. *Pierre's* public apparently recognized the drama of incest and did not like the indecent family exposure. It is ironic that Melville, in attempting to write his most orthodox book, wrote what is probably his most shocking.

The main plot-lines of *Pierre*, when extracted and set forth in isolation, are startlingly simple and melodramatic. Pierre Glendinning, apple of his mother's eye, heir to the rich country estate of Saddle Meadows, and affianced to lovely, blonde Lucy Tartan, discovers one day that a disturbing, dark beauty named Isabel Banford is his half sister, the illegitimate daughter of his father by a French girl. Pierre decides that he must not ruin his dead father's reputation and that he cannot destroy his mother's noble image of his father. To discharge his duty to his poor sister, he an-

nounces that he is married to her and takes her off to New
York to support her. This sacrificial act results in a series of
catastrophes. Pierre's mother disinherits her son, languishes
for a time, and then dies. Lucy breaks with her parents and
follows Pierre to New York, there to join him and Isabel in a
convenient but startling domestic arrangement. Lucy's
brother and Pierre's cousin (the new heir to Saddle Meadows) attempt to rescue her against her wishes; in the en-
suing feud Pierre kills his cousin. Imprisoned for his crime,
Pierre receives Isabel and Lucy in his cell. When Isabel reveals that she is Pierre's sister, Lucy falls dead. Pierre and
Isabel then drink from a vial of poison.

Were *Pierre* nothing but this somewhat ridiculous tale,
perhaps it would have been popular during its day. But
Melville subtitled the work *The Ambiguities* for good reason. Virtue and vice, right and wrong, are not so obvious as
this melodramatic plot suggests or a "popular" public would
want. Even to this day, readers are still debating the book's
real meaning.

All the critics agree that Melville manipulates the psychology of his characters with a subtlety far in advance of
his time. They all disagree as to his intentions. Debate
centers on the Plinlimmon pamphlet, the document Pierre
finds and reads as he is carrying Isabel off to New York. No
interpretation can avoid the question—is Plinlimmon's advocacy of a "virtuous expediency" rather than an "absolute"
morality Melville's truth or Melville's satire? The answer to
this question determines the theme of *Pierre*. In the many
close examinations of *Pierre*, there is still no general agreement on even the most crucial questions of interpretation.
Is Pierre's downfall brought about by a deficiency or flaw
within his character, by some weakness or evil within society, or by some subtle combination of the two? The weight
of criticism appears to support the view that the Plinlimmon
episode is satirical and that Pierre's genuine innocence

places the blame for his plight and final catastrophe on the shortcomings of society. But many of the questions this interpretation raises remain unanswered. Principal among these is the nature of an innocence that seems to catch glimpses of its hidden guilt, that seems to peer deeply into the darkness of its own "pure" motives.

1 *The young Innocent*

At the beginning of his story, Pierre Glendinning differs from almost all the other Young Seekers in Melville. Taji, Redburn, and Ishmael were common sailors, refugees from dreary, poverty-ridden households. Pierre is a young landed aristocrat, heir to a country estate of considerable size. Taji, Redburn, and Ishmael were souls already soured by the world; Pierre, as his story begins, is in a state of almost unbelievable bliss, domestically intimate with a doting mother and romantically linked to a beautiful girl in an engagement universally approved. In short, Pierre is the epitome of Happiness and Innocence, or so he seems.

But just how innocent is Pierre in the intimate relationship with his mother, Mary Glendinning? He apparently rejects her real role as mother, and at times accepts her as "Sister" (Pierre "mourned that so delicious a feeling as fraternal love had been denied him"), at other times even as mistress (Mary Glendinning glows in the "lover-like adoration of Pierre"). When Pierre addresses his mother as "Sister Mary," he is expressing a much more complex feeling than he realizes; "Nor could the fictitious title, which he so often lavished upon his mother, at all supply the absent reality [of a sister]. This emotion was most natural; and the full cause and reason of it even Pierre did not at that time entirely appreciate. For surely a gentle sister is the second best gift to a man; and it is first in point of occurrence; for the wife comes after. He who is sisterless, is as a bachelor before his time. For much that goes to make up the deliciousness of a wife, already lies in the sister." The appellation, then, is by no means innocent; for to convert a mother into a sister in whom resides the "deliciousness of a wife" suggests a latent incestuous desire.

And to live on such intimate terms as this mother and son is to live dangerously on the edge of this desire. Pierre's "lover-like adoration" is deliberately evoked by his mother's careful attention to her physical attractiveness: "With Mrs. Glendinning it was one of those spontaneous maxims, which women sometimes act upon without ever thinking of, never to appear in the presence of her son in any dishabille that was not eminently becoming. . . . as in the admiring love and graceful devotion of Pierre lay now her highest joy in life; so she omitted no slightest trifle which could possibly contribute to the preservation of so sweet and flattering a thing." This extraordinary love, however, not "limited in duration by that climax which is so fatal to ordinary love . . . . *seemed* almost to realize here below the sweet dreams of those religious enthusiasts, who paint to us a Paradise to come." (Italics added.) The disparity between what *is* and what *seems* constitutes the essence of Pierre's ambiguities.

If the innocence of Pierre's relationship with his mother is open to question, so, too, is the depth of his ebullient happiness in the prospect of his imminent marriage to Lucy Tartan. Lucy is beauty personified. She makes the viewer wonder "that in a world so full of vice and misery as ours, there should yet shine forth this visible semblance of the heavens." She is noiseless and insubstantial: "Thus far she hath floated as stilly through this life, as thistle-down floats over meadows." The term "angelic" is applied to her so often

as to cast some doubt on her earthly origins. Pierre's engagement to this ethereal creature has been maneuvered, as he
vaguely realizes, by his and Lucy's mother, and even by
the "naïve" Lucy herself; the announcement of the engagement has been precipitated by Lucy's two brothers. But
Pierre has thought, "I'm entirely willing to be caught, when
the bait is set in Paradise, and the bait is such an angel." So
he has assured himself. But that he needs such assurance
suggests a conflict in his deepest feelings. In the opening
"love" scene of the book, already there are curious con-
straints: "Then would Pierre burst forth in some screaming
shout of joy; and the striped tigers of his chestnut eyes
leaped in their lashed cages with a fierce delight. Lucy
shrank from him in extreme love; for the extremest top of
love, is Fear and Wonder." Again and again Melville emphasizes through situation and metaphor that Pierre's robust
love and strength of passion are far too vigorous for Lucy's
fragile ethereality, as symbolized particularly by her snow-
white, "holy" bedroom. And already in this initial "love
idyl," Lucy is disturbed by remembrance of Pierre's story of
a "dark-eyed, lustrous, imploring, mournful face."

For even before Pierre has discovered the convenient ex-
cuse of his familial relationship, he has been so haunted by
the "mystically" pale face of Isabel that he has confided in
Lucy his misgivings. When she expresses to him her un-
easiness ("Ah, Pierre, sometimes I have thought,—never will
I wed with my best Pierre, until the riddle of that face be
known"), he immediately regrets the confidence: "Cursed
be the hour I acted on the thought, that Love hath no re-
serves." Intrusion of the face has instantly destroyed the
magic of the afternoon for both Lucy and Pierre. Pierre's
response to the unknown face is a puzzle. If he unconsciously
recognizes in the anonymous Isabel a resemblance to the
youthful "chair-portrait" of his father, his excited response

is charged with a thrill of anticipation inexplicable in terms of mere recognition.

A concluding episode which ends the afternoon outing of the two "lovers" makes clear that Pierre's unconscious attraction to Isabel's dark but powerful beauty is founded on a deeply suppressed revulsion at his "beloved" Lucy's ethereal loveliness. After Pierre takes Lucy home, she asks him to fetch her portfolio of drawings from her bedroom. Pierre's moment in Lucy's room bestows a terrifying glimpse into his own ambiguous passions. "The carpet seemed as holy ground. Every chair seemed sanctified by some departed saint." As Pierre moves across the room, he glimpses in a mirror an image of Lucy's bed, and the experience is traumatic: "For one swift instant, he seemed to see in that one glance the two separate beds—the real one and the reflected one—and an unbidden, most miserable presentiment thereupon stole into him." The image which stays in his mind is the "spotless bed" and "a snow-white roll" beside the pillow; Pierre longs "to unroll the sacred secrets of that snow-white, ruffled thing." When he returns to Lucy with her portfolio, he exclaims, "Ah, thou holy angel, Lucy!" Although Pierre's love for Lucy seems superficially intensified, his "miserable presentiment" suggests that he glimpses the naked truth that life with Lucy, though full of holy passions, would bring no fulfillment of earthly ones. Lucy is angelic—and sexless.

Ultimately, then, Pierre, at the beginning, is not far different from Taji, Redburn, or Ishmael. And after the discovery of his half sister Isabel and the decision to take flight with her, Pierre falls into the role of these Young Seekers who reject the world they inherit and set out in search of a new. Unlike Redburn, White Jacket, and Ishmael, however, Pierre never becomes reconciled to the world as it is. His quest is ceaseless, like Taji's, and ends only with his death, like Ahab's. Pierre dons the mask of innocence and engages in a Titanic struggle with the evil of this world. And like Taji and Ahab, he finds himself finally and horribly committed to an evil greater than that he had first recognized and defied.

Pierre is so haunted by the strange face he has glimpsed and so prepared, by intuition and presentiment, for high romance that it takes no more than an unverified letter, anonymously and mysteriously delivered, to sway him forever from the main purposes of his life. After he reads the letter in which Isabel Banford declares herself daughter of his father, sister to himself, Pierre not only accepts the new role of brother with high passion but plots his course with overwhelming determination. Pierre vows—"Henceforth I will know nothing but Truth; glad Truth, or sad Truth; I will know what *is*, and do what my deepest angel dictates." Like Ahab, who swears to Starbuck that he will strike through the "pasteboard masks" of the world, Pierre swears, "I tear all veils; henceforth I will see the hidden things; and live right out in my own hidden life!" The response is far more emotionally charged than a mere unverified letter could call forth, and the reason is clear. Pierre intuitively but only half-consciously detects in the unfolding situation a way to the fulfillment of his unspeakable desires while masquerading them, to himself and to the world, as pure and noble impulses.

2   A loathed identity

In preparing himself for his new role of brother to his half-sister Isabel, Pierre suffers a series of shocks as he gradually recognizes the many deceptions which surrounded his innocent youth. The father loved by both the son and the mother turns out to be far different from the sacred image worshiped by them. In his "affair" with the French girl, mother of Isabel, Pierre's father proved himself heir to ignoble weaknesses of the flesh, a man capable of infidelity to the bonds of marriage, and, crowning all, capable of concealing his guilt behind a mask of domestic bliss and public eminence. This terrible, new view of his father necessitates an alteration in his long-held view of his mother. The image of the "lovely, immaculate mother" fades as Pierre, confronted by the truth about the unfaithfulness of his father, instinctively realizes that Mary Glendinning "would crumble into nothing before it." The great moral stamina he had always assumed to be a part of his mother's angelic character, he recognizes finally as fiction. Pierre's intuitive knowledge of his mother's reaction is confirmed as he observes how coldly, unmercifully, unforgivingly—even casually—she condemns that "vile fellow Ned" and Delly Ulver and her infant, inhabitants of the Glendinning estate, whose situation ironically parallels that of Pierre's father and the mother of Isabel.

The idyllic, innocent world of his youth crumbling about him, hastened in part by his desire to see it fall, Pierre rushes to Isabel more certain than ever of the path of his duty. He is more elated than he knows in the discovery of his mother's incapacity for forgiveness or understanding. This discovery seems to cloak with righteousness his own obscure but thrilling longings for Isabel. "Pierre, though charged with the fire of all divineness, his containing thing was made of clay." Melville himself grows wary about the revelations of Pierre's inner character and feels it necessary to offer an explanation. In an aside to the reader, he says: "How shall I steal yet further into Pierre, and show how this heavenly fire was helped to be contained in him, by mere contingent things, and things that he knew not. But I shall follow the endless, winding way,—the flowing river in the cave of man; careless whither I be led, reckless where I land." The ironic truth is that the flame of Pierre's "heavenly fire" of righteousness is fed by Isabel's alluring attractiveness: "womanly beauty, and not womanly ugliness, invited him to champion the right." In feeling and heeding impulses he was barely conscious of, and in being inspired by motives he did not clearly understand, Pierre is not unique among those presumably fired by the heavenly fire. Melville confesses, "I am more frank with Pierre than the best men are with themselves." That "flowing river in the cave of man" which Melville explores so deeply in *Pierre* flows through us all: Sigmund Freud was later to call it the unconscious, the hidden receptacle of our suppressed desires.

Confronted by the dilemma of discovering the "righteous" way out of a predicament charged with immense possibilities for evil, Pierre reasons his way tortuously (and more deviously than he knows) toward a novel solution. Pierre's psychology becomes the central drama of the book as he wrestles with the multitude of conflicting impulses besetting him. Pierre dimly understands that his affection for Isabel far transcends the feelings of a brother for a sister: he "felt that never, never would he be able to embrace Isabel with the mere brotherly embrace; while the thought of any other caress, which took hold of any domesticness, was entirely vacant from his uncontaminated soul, for it had never consciously intruded there." *Consciously,* perhaps not; but, the implication is clear—*un*consciously, yes. This is the central ambiguity in this book of ambiguities. *Consciously* Isabel becomes "transfigured in the highest heaven of uncorrupted Love"; *unconsciously* she becomes the desired object of Pierre's deepest physical passion.

As Pierre's heart has been frozen by the frigid whiteness and spotless purity of Lucy, so it has been melted by the warm darkness of Isabel. If Lucy is unalloyed holy angel, Isabel is of a more complex substance: her face, "hovering

between Tartarean misery and Paradisiac beauty," is "compounded . . . of hell and heaven." On that memorable first
encounter that was to leave so lasting an impression, Isabel
is associated with darkness: "Her unadorned and modest
dress is black; fitting close up to her neck, and clasping it
with a plain, velvet border." And her dark, olive cheek is
without a blush." On their first meeting as "brother and
sister," Isabel falls into Pierre's arms: "He felt a faint struggling within his clasp; her head drooped against him; his
whole form was bathed in the flowing glossiness of her long
and unimprisoned hair." From this moment to his death,
when he lies entangled in Isabel's tresses—"arbored . . . in
ebon vines"—Pierre is fascinated by the mysterious darkness
of her long black hair—which both lures and ensnares.

Pierre formulates a number of "grand resolutions" that
are contradictory. There must be a "public acknowledgment
of Isabel" and, at the same time, a "charitable withholding
of her existence" from his own mother. He must "screen" his
father's honorable memory from reproach," and yet there
must be "open vindication" of his "fraternalness to Isabel."
Confronting himself with these mutually exclusive goals,
with a deliberateness far greater than he knows, he drives
himself to the point of madness. He must work himself up
emotionally to the supreme conviction that to go to Isabel
is to follow Dante and Shakespeare in the *Inferno* and
Hamlet, to follow Duty and Virtue, to follow, indeed, the
way of God; while to stay with his mother and Lucy is to
deny Dante and Shakespeare, to commit Evil, to end, finally,
in Hell. In the agony of decision, Pierre conveniently discovers that he cannot live with the "cowardly" Pierre. But
there is ambiguity in the self-recognition as Pierre peers into
his own soul. What, indeed, is the identity Pierre loathes?
"The cheeks of his soul collapsed in him: he dashed himself
in blind fury and swift madness against the wall, and fell
dabbling in the vomit of his loathed identity." It is significant

10

that Pierre finds his solution only the morning following this peak of emotional fury, apparently after night and sleep have opened his unconscious for unholy communion with his soul. He awakes with his course determined but his "real" motive still veiled: he will proclaim to the world that he and Isabel are wed, thereby discharging his "brotherly" obligation without destroying his father's name or his mother's faith. The greatest "victim," he assures himself, in this act of "unequaled renunciation" will be himself. But Melville immediately tells the reader that there are other "persuasions and potencies than those direct ones" which have "unconsciously left their ineffaceable impressions on him, and perhaps without his privity" have "mainly contributed to his resolve"—"magnetic" Isabel herself, with her "bewildering eyes and marvelous story."

When Pierre embraces Isabel and whispers to her the plan of marriage and flight he has formulated, both she and Pierre reach a new depth in the understanding of their real feelings. Isabel looks at Pierre with the "inexpressible strangeness of an intense love, new and inexplicable." And over the face of Pierre shoots "a terrible self-revelation." Their response is immediate and passionate: "He imprinted repeated burning kisses upon her; pressed hard her hand; would not let go her sweet and awful passiveness." And Melville draws the curtain on the guilty love scene in a metaphorical and highly suggestive language: "Then they changed; they coiled together, and entangledly stood mute." The "loathed identity" which had before driven Pierre toward madness has become in this scene a "terrible self-revelation." As Isabel and Pierre "coil together," there can be no doubt that they cast aside their masks of innocence, confront openly and directly for the first time their physical attraction to each other, and indulge their passions. They enact anew the old, old roles of Adam and Eve in the Fall:

surely entangled in their "coil" is the ancient Garden's enduring serpent.

3   From a green foliaged tree to a blasted trunk

Pierre's struggle bestows on him a heightened moral awareness: what he discovers behind society's masks dismays him.
"In the joyous young times, ere his great grief came upon
him, all the objects which surrounded him were conceal-
ingly deceptive." Now they stand revealed for what they
are and the revelations shake the foundations of his being:
"Not only was the long-cherished image of his father now
transfigured before him from a green foliaged tree into a
blasted trunk, but every other image in his mind attested
the universality of that electral light which had darted into
his soul. Not even his lovely, immaculate mother, remained
entirely untouched, unaltered by the shock."
    Throughout his youth his father had been for Pierre the
sustaining image of his family faith. Now the father,
stripped of his awesome cloak of respectability, is discovered guilty of compounding a sin of the flesh by concealing it. The ambiguities of the nature of Pierre's father are
suggested by the two antithetical portraits, one made in his
bachelorhood, the other as the head of the family at Saddle
Meadows. Pierre owns the early portrait, given him by an
old maiden aunt, and he has placed it in a private closet of
his room: it reveals a "brisk, unentangled, young bachelor,
gayly ranging up and down in the world; light-hearted, and
a very little blandish perhaps; and charged to the lips with
the first uncloying morning fullness and freshness of life."
This picture of Pierre's father is "namelessly unpleasant and

repelling" to Pierre's mother. She emphatically prefers the later portrait as one which conveys correctly "his features in detail, and more especially their truest, and finest, and noblest combined expression." This portrait is of a "middle-aged, married man, and seem[s] to possess all the nameless and slightly portly tranquilities, incident to that condition when a felicitous one."

Pierre's new knowledge of his father is paralleled by a fresh insight into his mother. He finally comes to understand that "Infinite Haughtiness had first fashioned her; and then the haughty world had further molded her; nor had a haughty Ritual omitted to finish her." Pierre muses, "Now, do I remember that in her most caressing love, there ever gleamed some scaly, glittering folds of pride." Pierre's intuition that his mother could not morally assimilate the knowledge he holds is confirmed by her display of ethical rigidity in the discussion with the Reverend Falsgrave, her minister and suitor, about the adultery case at Saddle Meadows. When finally he makes his fateful decision and announces to his mother his "marriage," she replies: "My dark soul prophesied something dark. If already thou hast not found other lodgment, and other table than this house supplies, then seek it straight. Beneath my roof, and at my table, he who was once Pierre Glendinning no more puts himself." Mary Glendinning's pride will never permit her to reverse her sentence, and she is to disinherit Pierre, leave Saddle Meadows to Pierre's cousin, and go to her death never realizing that Pierre's confession of marriage was the desperate means to conceal from her an infidelity whose knowledge would destroy the most intimate illusions of her life.

Pierre's cousin is the third great jolt in Pierre's awakening to reality. Glendinning Stanly had been in boyhood one of Pierre's most intimate friends. "At the age of ten, they had furnished an example of the truth, that the friendship of fine-hearted, generous boys, nurtured amid the romance-engendering comforts and elegancies of life, sometimes transcends the bounds of mere boyishness, and revels for a while in the empyrean of a love which only comes short, by one degree, of the sweetest sentiment entertained between the sexes." Though in maturity the friendship of Pierre and Glen has grown less ardent, it has not died, and as Pierre leaves Saddle Meadows in his new social status and with his numerous newly-acquired dependents (including Delly Ulver and her illegitimate child), it is his hope to accept Glen's long-standing offer of a charming house—an offer made at a time when Pierre's marriage with Lucy appeared imminent. Upon his arrival in New York City with his retinue of distraught females, Pierre discovers the house bolted tight against his admission. And when he goes to his cousin's splendid establishment, Pierre must force his way in, only to be denied recognition by his cousin. Pierre hardly recognizes his cousin: "The dandy and the man; strength and effeminacy; courage and indolence, were so strangely blended in this superb-eyed youth, that at first sight, it seemed impossible to decide whether there was any genuine mettle in him, or not." Glen's pretense not to know his cousin enrages Pierre—but Pierre's only course is to vent his anger and depart.

This final estrangement cuts off Pierre's last possible resource—except himself. His dead father has failed him; his living mother has disinherited him; his closest friend has denied him. He stands at the moment of his greatest responsibility absolutely alone. And all that he has done is in the name of Virtue. As he is indirectly the cause of his mother's death, so he deals the deathblow directly to his once beloved cousin. By this time Glen Stanly has inherited Saddle Meadows and is seeking to remove Lucy Tartan from Pierre's New York establishment. Pierre does not conceal his hate: " 'Tis speechless sweet to murder thee!" And with this

"crime," Pierre's fate is sealed: "Spatterings of his own kindred blood were upon the pavement; his own hand had
extinguished his house in slaughtering the only unoutlawed
human being by the name of Glendinning."

Discovery of the world's evil proves too great a burden
for Pierre. He cannot come to terms with the terrible
knowledge he has gained. And he cannot reconcile himself
to his own deepest knowledge of his desires. The masks
worn by father, mother, and cousin differ from Pierre's only
in the quality of the deception they conceal: theirs is a
petty and shamefully trivial wickedness, while Pierre's sin is
measured on a heroic scale: his mask conceals as much
from himself as it does from the world.

4   *Chronometricals and horologicals*

There was a Serenia in *Mardi* and there were maskless or
"self-unmasked" characters in *White Jacket* and *Moby Dick*
(Jack Chase, White Jacket himself, Ishmael); similarly in
Pierre there appear some hints for the ideal character. In
this novel, however, Melville does not attempt to recreate
the society or to rely on mere delineation of character, but
boldly takes to pamphleteering. During the flight to New
York, Pierre finds in his coach a leaflet by one Plotinus
Plinlimmon entitled "Chronometricals and Horologicals,"
whose primary argument is that the same relation exists between chronometrical (or Greenwich) time and horological
(or local) time as exists between heavenly wisdom and
earthly wisdom. That the two are not always the same does
not mean that one must be wrong or that they are even
opposed: ". . . it follows not from this, that God's truth is
one thing and man's truth another; but—as above hinted,

and as will be further elucidated in subsequent lectures—by their very contradictions they are made to correspond." As men are not angels and somewhat less than perfect, they may best adapt their lives to the local (or earthly) time. If they attempt to live solely by heavenly time, they are doomed. Pierre's situation seems to be the precise case in point when Plinlimmon writes: ". . . almost invariably, with inferior beings, the absolute effort to live in this world according to the strict letter of the chronometricals is, somehow, apt to involve those inferior beings eventually in strange, *unique* follies and sins, unimagined before."

In short, the man who attempts to live like an angel may well end up unwittingly, or half-wittingly, or wholeheartedly, in the role of the devil—like Taji in *Mardi*, or Ahab in *Moby Dick*, or, indeed, like Pierre in all of his ambiguities. All of these individuals bring about their own deaths by attempting to live in accord with an absolute perfection. As Plinlimmon says (delineating in the process the character of these "righteous" Titans): "What man who carries a heavenly soul in him, has not groaned to perceive, that unless he committed a sort of suicide as to the practical things of this world, he never can hope to regulate his earthly conduct by that same heavenly soul? And yet by an infallible instinct he knows that that monitor can not be wrong in itself." That the ideal is unattainable on earth renders it no less useful as a proper guide, provided one make the necessary concessions—for the sake of life itself—to "the practical things of this world."

The heavenly ideal which cannot practically be pursued on earth consists of such advice as "to turn the left cheek if the right be smitten" or to "give *all* that thou hast to the poor." Such advice is ultimately impossible for imperfect man to follow. On the other hand, the earthly ideal is within the capabilities of man: ". . . if a man gives with a certain self-considerate generosity to the poor; abstains from doing

downright ill to any man; does his convenient best in a
general way to do good to his whole race; takes watchful
loving care of his wife and children, relatives, and friends;
is perfectly tolerant to all other men's opinions, whatever
they may be; is an honest dealer, an honest citizen, and all
that; and more especially if he believes that there is a God
for infidels, as well as for believers, and acts upon that
belief"—then he is living a life of "virtuous expediency"
which is the "highest desirable or attainable earthly ex-
cellence for the mass of men." Plinlimmon emphasizes that
his theory of ethics does not embrace all wickedness by
excusing some: "This chronometrical conceit does by no
means involve the justification of all acts which wicked
men may perform. For in their wickedness downright
wicked men sin as much against their own horologes, as
against the heavenly chronometer. That this is so, their
spontaneous liability to remorse does plainly evince." And
Plinlimmon concludes his pamphlet: "I hold up a practi-
cable virtue to the vicious; and interfere not with the eternal
truth, that sooner or later, in all cases, downright vice is
downright woe."

Plinlimmon's pamphlet is in reality a philosophical ex-
pansion of that insight which White Jacket had into the
discrepancy between heavenly and practical wisdom when
he saw the efficient "murderous" cannoneer indulging in
genuine prayer. But whereas White Jacket instantly understands what he sees, Pierre never comprehends what he
reads. He continues his attempt to live chronometrically
while his "unique" sins multiply and his follies increase.
Later, when Pierre glimpses Plotinus Plinlimmon, he looks
for the pamphlet he had carelessly cast aside and is unable
to find it. All the time he is looking for it, it is on his very
person trapped in the lining of his coat, not two inches from
his hand. Melville poses the question: "Could [Pierre] . . .
have carried about with him in his mind the thorough un-

derstanding of the book, and yet not be aware that he so understood it?" Pierre would naturally suppress the understanding just as, previously, he had suppressed his insight into his real motives in devising his "pious imposture" of a marriage to Isabel.

Although Pierre is never to meet the author of the pamphlet, he is to come to know some of Plinlimmon's followers when he takes up his residence at the Bohemian Church of the Apostles and the "Grand Master" is to be pointed out to him from a distance. Plinlimmon's tower quarters are so located as to make his window visible from Pierre's room. Pierre watches there a "remarkable face of repose,—repose neither divine nor human, nor any thing made up of either or both—but a repose separate and apart—a repose of a face by itself." The "blue-eyed, mystic-mild face" begins to haunt Pierre: "When in his moods of peculiar depression and despair; when dark thoughts of his miserable condition would steal over him; and black doubts as to the integrity of his unprecedented course in life would most malignantly suggest themselves; when a thought of the vanity of his deep book would glidingly intrude; if glancing at his closet-window that mystic-mild face met Pierre's; under any of these influences the effect was surprising, and not to be adequately detailed in any possible words." The face seems to say: "Vain! vain! vain! . . . Fool! fool! fool! . . . Quit! quit! quit! . . . *Ass! ass! ass!*" At these times the face seems to peer into Pierre's very soul: "What was most terrible was the idea that by some magical means or other the face had got hold of his secret. 'Ay,' shuddered Pierre, 'the face knows that Isabel is not my wife! And that seems the reason it leers.'" Plinlimmon's extraordinary face functions symbolically, much as his misplaced pamphlet, to suggest Pierre's glimpse into and revulsion at his own dark motives, and his attempt to suppress a knowledge he only obscurely possesses.

Two of Plinlimmon's apparent followers suggest the genuine complexity of the ethics of "virtuous expediency." The Reverend Falsgrave is not a declared adherent, but it seems clear that he is intended as a portrait of the Plinlimmon-like man. But Falsgrave is far from the ideal: he is a caricature of the philosophy carried to an extreme of equivocal inaction. Falsgrave is introduced into the action when Pierre is closely observing his mother formulating a decision disposing of the case of adultery on the estate. His position as minister renders his judgment significant. His face is "radiant with a courtly, but mild benevolence" and he is "peculiarly insinuating, without the least appearance of craftiness or affectation." He still has the "beauty, grace, and strength" of youth and has already acquired the "mildness" and "wisdom" of age. Falsgrave assumes the role of mediator in the discussion of the local adultery case, cautioning Mrs. Glendinning against her hot and brittle indignation while gently rebuking Pierre for his too-generous indulgence. When Mrs. Glendinning quotes, "The sins of the father shall be visited upon the children to the third generation," in justification for punishment of the illegitimate child, Falsgrave asserts: "But Madam, that does not mean, that the community is in any way to take the infamy of the children into their own voluntary hands." When Pierre pointedly asks, "And what was that [our blessed Saviour] so mildly said to the adulteress," Falsgrave after a long ambiguous preamble concludes: "Millions of circumstances modify all moral questions; so that though conscience may possibly dictate freely in any known special case; yet, by one universal maxim, to embrace all moral contingencies,—this is not only impossible, but the attempt, to me, seems foolish." When Pierre asks bluntly whether the commandment to "Honor thy father and mother" admitted ever of any exceptions, again Falsgrave replies: "That is another question in morals absolutely incapable of

a definite answer, which shall be universally applicable." At
each answer Falsgrave's "exquisitely cut cameo brooch"
shows forth from the folds of his clothing, revealing a representation of "the allegorical union of the serpent and dove."

When Pierre visits Falsgrave late at night to find out what
the minister and Pierre's mother have determined to do with
the adulteress, Falsgrave tells Pierre: "She is to depart the
neighborhood; why, her own parents want her not." Pierre
is incensed, but he does not blame the clergyman: "I think I
begin to see how thy profession is unavoidably entangled by
all fleshly alliances, and can not move with godly freedom
in a world of benefices." The next day, when Falsgrave calls
on Mrs. Glendinning to inform her of Pierre's peculiar behavior, he discovers her in a collapsed state, furious and
frustrated at Pierre's news that he has married a "slut."
Falsgrave assumes a posture of "the profoundest deference"
which is "almost cringing" as he confesses his inability to
console: "Permit me to withdraw from thee, leaving my best
prayers for thee, that thou mayst know some peace, ere this
now shut-out son goes down." Mrs. Glendinning orders him
to leave: "Begone! and let me not hear thy soft, mincing
voice, which is an infamy to a man!" Though Falsgrave appears at first to follow the Plinlimmon philosophy, he ultimately is proved, like Starbuck in *Moby Dick*, incapable
of action. He remains too meditative, too compromising, and
too disengaged.

If Falsgrave seems always to be too coolly in control of his
basic human passions, *Pierre*'s confessed follower of Plinlimmon, Charlie Millthorpe, seems always too much at the
mercy of his outsized heart. Millthorpe, whose father once
tilled Glendinning land and whose boyhood was spent in
amiable companionship with Pierre, turns up in New York,
first to help Pierre and his "wife" settle in the strange quarters known as the Church of the Apostles, and later to pay
off Pierre's debtor in a time of personal economic crisis.

Pierre remembers Charlie as a handsome boy "but little vigorous in mind": "Yet was Charlie Millthorpe as affectionate and dutiful a boy as ever boasted of his brain, and knew not that he possessed a far more excellent and angelical thing in the possession of a generous heart." After experiencing one of Millthorpe's innocently-motivated, generous deeds, Pierre muses: "Now, by heaven! the god that made Millthorpe was both a better and a greater than the god that made Napoleon or Byron—Plus head, minus heart— Pah! the brains grow maggoty without a heart; but the heart's the preserving salt itself, and can keep sweet without the head." Millthorpe is as unbalanced in faculty as Falsgrave, possessing in abundance that which had paled under too great a restraint in the minister. Although Pierre himself would like to believe that his fate is brought about by his cultivation of the heart, his mind is too keen and is burdened by too many flashes of insight into his hidden motives for him ever to convince himself deep within of his assumed innocence. Pierre even demonstrates that he understands Plinlimmon more thoroughly than the declared disciple. Pierre muses: "Though in all human probability Plotinus well understood Millthorpe, yet Millthorpe could hardly yet have wound himself into Plotinus;—though indeed Plotinus . . . might . . . have tacitly pretended to Millthorpe, that he (Millthorpe) had thoroughly wriggled himself into his (Plotinus') innermost soul." Clearly Pierre knows more of Plinlimmon and his pamphlet than he will openly confess to himself.

5   *That cunning purpleness*

In his attempt to avoid the inevitable consequences of his father's sin, Pierre precipitates catastrophe. He takes on himself, publicly, the entire burden of an evil not his, yet conceals from himself a genuine guilt that works from deep within. His act of heroic "renunciation" (which he knows is really "fulfillment") results in incest, murder, and death. From the time that he first sees Isabel and is drawn by her dark beauty, his soul's cool innocence is compounded with hot desire. From the time that he receives the letter revealing the blood relationship, his "chronometrical" actions constitute the commission of a "suicide as to the practical things of this world." Pierre's "innocence" results in his mother's death; his own, Isabel's, and Lucy's disgrace; the murder of his cousin, Glen Stanly; and, finally, the death by shock of Lucy and the death by suicide of Isabel and himself. And, fate's final irony for Pierre, his grandiose act of innocence is precisely that which leads to his greatest sin.

In a symbolic dream, shortly before his death, Pierre once again glimpses the truth of his situation. In the vision he sees, near his ancestral home, Saddle Meadows, the Mount of Titans (a mountain once christened the Delectable Mountain by an admirer of Bunyan). From a distance the peak is a beautiful, inviting purple, but this "purple promise" turns out to be an illusion: "Stark desolation; ruin, merciless and ceaseless; chills and gloom,—all here lived a hidden life, curtained by that cunning purpleness." On one of the paths of the mountain is "Enceladus the Titan, the most potent of all the giants, writhing from out the imprisoning earth." The significance of the dream is clear, but Pierre will not openly confront its meaning. The apparently noble intent has ended in terrible devastation for the simple reason that Pierre's "containing thing" is made of clay. Like Taji and Ahab, he has sought, absolutely and without compromise, to transcend evil and has ended by becoming its votary and finally its victim.

7

Israel Potter: *survival in the desert*

Israel Potter: His Fifty Years of Exile (1855), a slender biographical narrative tracing the fortunes and misfortunes of a soldier in the Revolutionary War and after, seems a strange successor to the magnificent success of *Moby Dick* and the magnificent failure of *Pierre.* Whatever the virtues of the two preceding novels, they had not popularized their author, and perhaps Melville was seeking an art form that would restore his earlier reputation of the days of *Typee* and *Omoo.* In *Israel Potter* he found a story of high adventure, and he preserved, as he asserts, "almost in a reprint, Israel Potter's autobiographical story."

Though *Israel Potter* seems lost in the shadows of its two Titanic predecessors, nevertheless there were great potentialities, both in the story and in a number of the characters which, no doubt, initially attracted Melville's mind; hence the book has a position of some consequence in Melville's work. Melville felt in no way bound by the limitations imposed by the original narrative. He felt free to modify, change, alter. He developed at length the characters that interested him (such as Benjamin Franklin), and he inserted historical figures (such as John Paul Jones) for the sake of increasing suspense, prolonging adventure, and illustrating theme. Though the basic body of narrative was borrowed, Melville breathed his own, original life into it. He allowed his moral and allegorical imagination full play. For example, when he described John Paul Jones quietly and secretly maneuvering his ship near an enemy British vessel, he comments: "So easily may the deadliest foe—so he be dexterous—slide, undreamed of, into human harbours or hearts. And not awakened conscience, but mere prudence, restrain such, if they vanish again without doing harm." The imagination involved in this observation is not far removed from that which dived deep and wondrously into Pierre and his ambiguities. It is not an imagination which has compromised itself to produce a mere potboiler.

1 *Wondrous adventures*

Born in the hill-country of Berkshire, Massachusetts, in pre-Revolutionary days, Israel Potter manages to turn up in the vicinity of most of the important events of his time, as well as in the presence of many of the important men. He initially leaves home, however, because his father will not approve the mate he has selected; his wanderlust is confirmed when he discovers the girl faithless and married to another. This early experience launches him on a life of wandering even before the Revolutionary War has begun; like all of Melville's young Seekers, Israel goes to sea: "A hermitage in the forest is the refuge of the narrow-minded misanthrope; a hammock on the ocean is the asylum for the generous distressed. The ocean brims with natural griefs and tragedies; and into that watery immensity of terror, man's private grief is lost like a drop." Israel dissipates his private grief in the hard struggle for survival—whether fleeing a burning ship or hunting the huge leviathan.

Beginning with the Battle of Bunker Hill where he was wounded, Israel's tale is never short on high adventure: he is assigned to the brigantine *Washington* which is captured by the British; he is shipped off to England, where he escapes to make his way to London; he finds various employ-

ment, at one time as gardener to the king which makes
possible a highly improbable conversation with George III;
he falls in with a group of "friends of America" (among
them Horne Tooke) who dispatch him on a secret errand
across the channel to Benjamin Franklin in Paris, where he
meets John Paul Jones; he returns to London, risks capture,
has a number of hairbreadth escapes, and finally, through a
fortunate junction of miraculous chance and endeavor, he
ends up sailing on the *Ranger* with John Paul Jones; as a
favorite of Jones's, he participates in the vengeful but daring firing of Whitehaven, the encounter with the British
ship *Drake,* and, later, the desperate struggle between
Jones's *Bon Homme Richard* and the British *Serapis;*
through a freak accident in a sea-battle, Israel finds himself once more on a British ship bound for Falmouth; in
England, he witnesses the imprisonment of Ethan Allen,
escapes again and makes his way to London, where, by
strange quirks of fortune, he disappears into the "London
deserts" for some forty-five years, returning at last to his
native land to view once more the scenes of his youth—and
to die.

Throughout his adventures, wandering for more than
forty years in the "wild wilderness of the world's extremest
hardships and ills," Israel Potter maintains a cool head in
fortune and misfortune, never deliberately misrepresenting
his situation or the world's to himself or others. As we learn
early in his history, Israel, "however brave-hearted, and
even much of a dare-devil upon a pinch, seems nevertheless
to have evinced, throughout many parts of his career, a singular patience and mildness." He is not a man of virtuous extremes but an individual of balance. When he finds himself
a prisoner-of-war early in the fighting, he gives himself up to
neither despair nor defiance, but "keeps his eye on the main
chance." There is a strong, basic sense of reality in him that
enables him always to come to practical terms with any

situation in which he finds himself. In short Israel, "with much of the gentleness of the dove, is not wholly without the wisdom of the serpent."

As the white-haired, eighty-year-old Israel Potter finally finds his way back with his youngest son to view the country of his youth, he sits gazing over the area where he had once fought his country's wars. Here "he had received that slit upon the chest, which afterward, in the affair with the *Serapis,* being traversed by a cutlass wound, made him now the bescarred bearer of a cross." Like Christ, Israel has patiently borne the cross thrust upon him by a world in conflict, a world that has demanded much and granted little. Unlike Christ, Israel has, through ingenuity born of his intimate knowledge of evil, endured.

2 History revisited

King George III, Horne Tooke, Benjamin Franklin, John Paul Jones, and Ethan Allen parade into and out of Israel's presence, or he theirs, with little in the way of preparation. They are flat characters, of course, curiously like the pictures in the history books, but they emerge with a difference, as one might expect from Melville. And they appear not just for the excitement of their presence but to enable Melville to probe the national character as well as the verdicts of history. The meaning of *Israel Potter* is invested in large measure in the dramatization of these historical figures.

When Israel first finds himself a fugitive in England fleeing the authorities, moving from place to place as he attempts to make a living and preserve his anonymity, he is told by a friend that he will find the greatest safety in the King's Gardens at Kew: "It struck the poor exile as curious, that the very den of the British lion, the private grounds of the British king, should be commended to a refugee as his securest asylum." Not only does this vantage point give Israel a glimpse of the "lonely figure" of the king on his meditative walks, but at one point they engage in a highly improbable but extremely interesting conversation. The king tells Israel that he is rumored to be a spy and offers him service in the army. Although Israel refuses, the king generously and secretly affords him the protection of his grounds. If the king does not win Israel's services, he does command Israel's high regard: "Israel now thought that it could not be the warm heart of the king, but the cold heads of his lords in council, that persuaded him so tyrannically to persecute America." One might have guessed that Melville would approve discovery of some good where history had discovered such stupid and monstrous evil. Although the judgment appeared in the original *Israel Potter,* Melville pointed it up by rewriting and emphasizing it.

After a number of adventures in England, Israel falls in with another famous figure of history, one of the many individuals of the country who were "patriotic and gifted men, who not only recommended conciliatory measures, but likewise denounced the war as monstrous": Horne Tooke, author of *Diversions of Purley,* later to suffer imprisonment for his sympathetic help of the Colonies. Israel turns up at just the right moment to aid the plans hatched by John Woodcock, Horne Tooke, and James Bridges—plans which involve secret and crucial communication with Benjamin Franklin in Paris. In the midst of these impressive figures, Israel recounts the history of his adventures (for his hosts must discover first whether he is trustworthy); and he notes "the expressive, enthusiastic, candid countenance of Horne Tooke—then in the first honest ardour of his political career." Israel by his account puts to rest any doubts about his loyalties and wins the role of messenger, with the secret document hidden in the heel of his shoe.

Having discovered some virtues among his country's enemies, Israel next finds some complexities in his country's servants. In Paris to deliver his message, Israel looks with no small amount of awe upon the famous and now aged Dr. Benjamin Franklin: "the living lime and dust of the sage was frescoed with defensive bloom of his soul." Israel gazes on the man in his study: "It was a goodly sight to see this serene, cool, and ripe old philosopher, who by sharp inquisition of man in the street, and then long meditating upon him, surrounded by all those queer old implements, charts, and books, had grown at last so wondrous wise." Israel's encounter with the good "Doctor" is in reality a prolonged probe into the nature of that wisdom.

The first lesson Franklin teaches Israel is the need to keep a balance between suspicion and common sense. Israel reveals that as he was approaching Franklin's quarters he encountered a bootblack who wanted to polish his boots; Israel consented but then, suspicious that the bootblack was after the message in his heel, knocked over the man's box and fled from his presence. Franklin immediately chides Israel for his behavior: "An indiscriminate distrust of human nature is the worst consequence of a miserable condition, whether brought about by innocence or guilt. And though want of suspicion more than want of sense, sometimes leads a man into harm, yet too much suspicion is as bad as too little sense." Franklin does not argue (as Melville's satanic confidence man is to do later) for unqualified trust in human nature but for a balanced, common-sense view. And Israel is persuaded that he can best correct his error by paying the bootblack for his losses.

As Israel is going to bed in Franklin's residence, the sage appears in his room to remove the brandy, the cologne, and

the sugar before they can be used and added to the bill;
and the good Doctor later arranges for the chambermaid, a
"young French lass" with "bloom on her cheek," to "waive
her visits of ceremony" to Israel's room—and all of these
"services" are rendered for Israel's comfort, benefit, and
good. "Oh, confound all this wisdom!" Israel finally exclaims: "Somehow, the old gentleman has an amazing sly
look—a sort of wild slyness—about him, seems to me. His
wisdom seems a sort of sly, too."

Melville devotes one entire chapter to probing Franklin's
intricate character. There was "a touch of primeval oriental-
ness in Benjamin Franklin. . . . The diplomatist and the
shepherd are blended; a union not without warrant; the
apostolic serpent and dove. A tanned Machiavelli in tents."
For his closest kin, Melville selects Jacob and Hobbes:
"three labyrinth-minded, but plain-spoken Broadbrims, at
once politicians and philosophers; keen observers of the
main chance; prudent courtiers; practical Magians in linsey-
woolsey." Franklin had "carefully weighed the world" and
"could act any part in it." He was a "jack of all trades,
master of each and mastered by none" and he was "the
type and genius of his land." That is, he was "everything
but a poet." In short, Franklin's character is much like
Israel Potter's, but brought to mature ripeness. He blends,
like Potter, the serpent's wisdom and the dove's gentleness
in proportions which assure survival and provide for a life
devoted to the practical service of mankind.

One of the services Franklin performs for Israel is to
bring him together with John Paul Jones: the two share the
room which the accommodating sage has so generously made
barren of worldly comforts. At the outset Jones, discovering
Israel to be a sailor, demands to know whether his shipmates
talked much of John Paul Jones—"with a look as of a parading Sioux demanding homage to his gewgaws." As Israel
watches Jones undress in their shared bedroom, he observes

on Jones's arm a "tattooing such as is seen only on thorough-bred savages—deep blue, elaborate, labyrinthine, cabalistic." This primitive design is complemented, ironically, by the "civilised" decoration of Jones's hand, "muffled in ruffles" from his "laced coat-sleeve" and "ornamented with several Parisian rings." Melville cannot resist pointing up the symbolic significance in the appealing paradox: "So at midnight, the heart of the metropolis of modern civilisation was secretly trod by this jaunty barbarian in broadcloth . . . ; showing that brooches and finger-rings, not less than nose-rings and tattooing, are tokens of the primeval savageness which ever slumbers in human kind, civilised or uncivilised."

Although Melville poses the question as to "whether Paul Jones was a knave or a hero, or a union of both," he refuses to give a direct answer; but he does assert that fortune played an immense role in the formation of Jones's reputation for courage and fortitude—"In a word, luck—that's the word—shortly threw in Paul's way the great action of his life: . . . the unparalleled deathlock with the *Serapis*." As Franklin, with his "sly" wisdom, may be the national genius, so Jones, with his frank savagery, may be the national spirit —"intrepid, unprincipled, reckless, predatory, with boundless ambition, civilised in externals but a savage at heart, America is, or may yet be, the Paul Jones of nations."

Near the end of his Revolutionary War adventures, Israel encounters Ethan Allen. Again a prisoner in England, he comes upon the scene of the "caged" Ethan Allen: "Unshaven, beard and hair matted, and profuse as a cornfield beaten down by hail-storms, his whole marred aspect was that of some wild beast." A "Samson among the philistines," Ethan Ticonderoga Allen heartily insists on being the Christian captive of the pagans. He exclaims, "You Turks never saw a Christian before. Stare on!" And when he is told he will hang like a thief, he cries out, "If I am, the great Jehovah and the Continental Congress shall avenge me;

while I, for my part, shall show you, even on the tree, how a Christian gentleman can die."

Melville pauses in his narrative to explore the depths of Allen's character. The Titanic Vermonter is no simple individual: he "seems to have been a curious combination of a Hercules, a Joe Miller, a Bayard, and a Tom Hyer; had a person like the Belgian giants, mountain music in him like a Swiss; a heart plump as Coeur de Lion's." Though a son of Vermont, Allen has none of the New England reserve: "He was frank, bluff, companionable as a Pagan, convivial, a Roman, hearty as a harvest." Indeed, he emerges as a symbol not of the region he comes from but of the American West: "His spirit was essentially Western; and herein is his peculiar Americanism; for the Western Spirit is, or will yet be (for no other is, or can be) the true American one."

The prototype of John Paul Jones and Ethan Allen exists in the savages of *Typee,* those Polynesians who were so attractive in their vigor and virtue, yet frightening in their heedless strength and thoughtless, casual cruelty. Like Ahab, Jones and Allen cannot compromise but must strike out in blind and righteous wrath. And like Ahab, they face their fate with exhilaration and defiance. There is a warning for America in these hero-portraits. Wild beast, pagan, Ethan Allen is essentially Western in spirit, and this spirit is (or will be) the essential American spirit; when America's spirit has become Western, she will be "intrepid, unprincipled, reckless, predatory, with boundless ambition, civilised in externals but a savage at heart"—in short, America will become the "Paul Jones of nations." And America might, like Ahab, go in defiance to her doom.

But for the time, the national genius is Benjamin Franklin —"homely sage and household Plato." And Israel Potter fashions himself after the cunning sage rather than the reckless savage. And Israel Potter, like Franklin, survives to a ripe old age.

3 *Vanity and clay*

Melville cannot for long refrain from discovering symbols and ferreting out metaphysical hints. One of the most vivid passages in all of his work appears near the end of *Israel Potter*, when Israel, wandering just outside London, comes upon a great brickyard where "hordes of the poorest wretches are employed." Israel takes a job in the pit where a "muddy mixture" is readied for placing in the brick moulds which other workmen bear from the pit to the kilns: as Israel slaps the doughy mud into the moulds, he seems "some gravedigger, or churchyard man, tucking away dead little innocents in their coffins on one side, and cunningly disinterring them again to resurrectionists stationed on the other." Before long Israel discovers himself partaking of the "reckless sort of half-jolly despair" expressed by all the workmen: "What signifies who we be—dukes or ditchers? . . . all is vanity and clay."

The image seems to take possession of Melville's imagination as he envisions the plight of all mankind through Israel's experience in the brickyard: "brick is no bad name for any son of Adam; Eden was but a brickyard; what is a mortal but a few luckless shovelfuls of clay, moulded in a mould, laid out on a sheet to dry, and ere long quickened into his queer caprices by the sun?" Clearly Melville begins to soar on the wings of his metaphor as it expands to explain the universe: "Are not men built into communities just like bricks into a wall? Consider the great wall of China: ponder the great populace of Pekin. As man serves bricks, so God him, building him up by billions into edifices of his purposes." But only man in the mass may be compared to the bricks: "Man attains not to the nobility of a brick, unless taken in the aggregate."

Even bricks, however, have their differences, brought about by their positions in the kiln. Israel often takes "a peep into the low vaulted ways at the base, where the flaming faggots had crackled." The bricks are divided into three types: "The furnace-bricks were haggard, with the immediate blistering of the fire—the midmost ones were ruddy with a genial and tempered glow—the summit ones were pale with the languor of too exclusive an exemption from the burden of the blaze." The implications for human nature are clear. If the fire represents evil or misfortune—or both—the individual man is shaped by his fate in the world (the kiln). If too close to or distant from the fire he is rendered useless—too discolored and grotesque (like Taji or Ahab) or too pale and languorous (like Bartleby or Benito Cereno). But neither burned in the fire nor innocent of it, some men (like Jack Chase—or Israel) achieve that enviable balance between blackness and paleness, that ruddy glow of health and equanimity that is an assertion of life, not a defiance of it nor a withdrawal from it.

But Israel is in the brickyards only long enough to allow Melville his metaphysical caprice. His small wages in his pocket, Israel soon makes his way to the "City of Dis," where, for some forty years, he wanders in the "London deserts." From the depths of some inner resource, Israel finds the stoicism to endure a "fate, uncommon even to luckless humanity—a fate whose crowning qualities were its remoteness from relief and its depth of obscurity—London, adversity, and the sea, three Armageddons, which, at one and the same time, slay and secrete their victims." But Israel survives, and in surviving every conceivable form of misery and poverty, he never sinks "below the mud, to actual beggary."

Melville passes over these years of exile and wandering in a few pages to portray his hero in his last years voyaging with the "spared Benjamin of his old age" to "the Promised

Land"—America. There he discovers not a single token of the time of his youth: even his parents' home has given way to the plough. But misfortune continues to accumulate. "Repulsed in efforts after a pension by certain caprices of law," his scars prove "his only medals." Even a gesture to preserve an account of his fortunes for the future proves futile. He fades "out of being" and "his name out of memory."

Israel Potter must take his place in Melville's gallery of Young Seekers, the exiled or fatherless young men who go out into the world, discover its grim and bitter terms, comply and endure. All of these young men are baptized into the devious and complex ways of the world: the baptism symbolizes their acknowledgment of their essential humanity, their ultimate acceptance of a share in the common human fate. White Jacket and Ishmael plummet into the sea; Clarel disappears in the throng on the *Via Crucis* in Jerusalem; Israel plunges into London and adversity. But they all ascend and endure, shed of their deceptive innocence, but with a profound wisdom of complicity that affirms a frank confrontation of the self and the world.

8

Tales and sketches: withdrawals and reconciliations

If one may judge by Melville's total work it seems a fair conclusion that he found the short forms of fiction too restricting for his particular needs. As suggested by *Mardi* and confirmed by *Moby Dick*, Melville's genius needed a broad canvas, a vast expanse, to accommodate his complex vision. But there was one period during his life when Melville turned to short works for the magazines, apparently in an attempt to make money. *The Piazza Tales*, the only collection which appeared during Melville's lifetime, was published in 1856, and contains the two best "short" stories of Melville—"Benito Cereno" and "Bartleby." Another collection containing ten short works, *The Apple-Tree Table and Other Sketches*, was published in 1922. One additional work, "The Temples," which survived only in manuscript form, was added to these other works to make up the *Complete Stories of Herman Melville*, published in 1949. These pieces, most of which were published in periodicals from 1850 to 1856, resemble the informal essay more than the modern short story in both tone and technique. But many of these sketches not only help illuminate Melville's themes but also have considerable merit of their own.

1 *"Benito Cereno"*

"Benito Cereno" is one of the most brilliant technical performances among Melville's works, maintaining almost to the end a constantly increasing suspense matched only by the three-day chase of the white whale at the conclusion of *Moby Dick*. The story itself is quite simple, but Melville has caught and sharpened the high drama of the tale. An American Captain, Amasa Delano, aboard his *Bachelor's Delight* in the Chilean harbor of St. Maria in 1799, notices the erratic behavior of another ship, the *San Dominick*, when it enters the bay. Assuming that the strange ship has suffered some misfortune and needs assistance, Captain Delano decides to board her and offer aid. The bulk of the narrative is devoted to Captain Delano's visit on the *San Dominick*, his sometimes cordial, sometimes rude reception by its ailing captain, Benito Cereno, his detailed observation of the strange and puzzling behavior of the large number of unrestricted Negroes aboard, his initial admiration for the Captain's attentive aide, the Negro Babo, and his subsequent annoyance with him because of his refusal to leave Captain Delano alone with his master for a single moment. It is not until Captain Delano is preparing to return to his ship and Captain Benito Cereno suddenly leaps into the boat beside him that the mystery is entirely cleared up. The Negroes, led by the "devoted" aide, Babo, had revolted and held the whites aboard ship in subjection. They have practiced their nearly successful deception in the hope that an opportunity will arise to capture Delano's ship also. In the following fight, Captain Delano succeeds in saving Benito and recapturing his ship for him. Melville concludes the story with some long extracts from the depositions at the subsequent trial of the Negroes—documents which summarize the history of the *San Dominick* before it sailed into the Chilean bay. A postscript relates the disposition of the Negroes at the trial and the final fate of Benito. The matter-of-fact legal style of the depositions, contrasting severely with the preceding highly-dramatic style, shows Melville in perfect command of his technique: the mystery has aroused a curiosity which only the "facts" of the testimony will satisfy.

The suspense evoked by "Benito Cereno" is compounded not only of a puzzling series of events aboard the *San Dominick* but also of Captain Delano's alternating suspicion and understanding. At some point in the story, the reader's suspicions rise above those of the American Captain's and refuse to be dissipated by the intricate reasoning with which he destroys his own doubts. The initial question—what will happen?—is gradually shifted: when will Captain Delano finally understand that something is amiss aboard the *San Dominick?* Gradually the American Captain is impressed on the reader's engrossed consciousness as a character of almost superhuman innocence.

For Melville's drama of evil emerges in the old familiar patterns. And Captain Delano is his maskless man, a man frank and sincere in his basic nature, quick with his help for others, kind and forgiving out of a spontaneously generous heart—but not so naïve in his understanding of the human scene as to be unable, when convinced of the necessity, to cope with evil. His is a practical virtue, neither too much nor too little of this world. At least so it turns out. For the whole length of the story, however, the issue is uncertain as Delano's good nature seems to render him incapable of distinguishing innocence from its disguise.

Captain Amasa Delano, from Duxbury, Massachusetts, is Melville's Western Man, with all of his most noble traits. He is endowed with a "singularly undistrustful good nature, not liable, except on extraordinary and repeated incentives, and hardly then, to indulge in personal alarms, any way involving the imputation of malign evil in man." Melville poses a question which he declines at the outset to answer: "Whether, in view of what humanity is capable, such a trait implies, along with a benevolent heart, more than ordinary quickness and accuracy of intellectual perception, may be left to the wise to determine." As always in Melville, the crucial question revolves about the balance of *heart* and *mind.* An imbalance, as in Ahab or Billy Budd, courts disaster. A perfect balance, as in Jack Chase, achieves the ideal. Captain Delano may seem at first to suffer from an excess of the one and a deficiency of the other—but in the showdown, when action is crucial, he acts.

It is Captain Delano's basic good nature and generous heart which impel him when he first sights the crippled ship to offer his assistance, and it is these same noble traits which force him to forgive so easily the apparently ungrateful and even rude recipients of his aid. Numerous small incidents momentarily arouse the suspicions of Captain Delano, but he invariably and ingeniously lulls the suspicions to rest. Even when Captain Benito Cereno is shaved, at his Negro's reminder, during Delano's visit in the middle of the day, and trembles so violently that the "servant" Babo draws blood, the serene American Captain cannot yet sustain his suspicions. He reflects—"But then, what could be the object of enacting this play of the barber before him? At last, regarding the notion as a whimsy, insensibly suggested, perhaps, by the theatrical aspect of Don Benito in his harlequin ensign, Captain Delano speedily banished it." Captain Delano is constantly seeking a rational explanation for the evil he fleetingly imagines, and when he can find none, he dismisses the suspicion as "whimsy."

In the exciting climax of the story, when first Don Benito Cereno and next Babo leap into Captain Delano's boat before it can part from the crippled ship, Delano can still not sense the presence of evil, and for a moment it appears that he will never awaken to the distraught state of affairs aboard the *San Dominick.* But finally he spots Babo in the boat with a dagger at his master's heart: "That moment, across the long-benighted mind of Captain Delano, a flash of revelation swept, illuminating, in unanticipated clearness, his host's whole mysterious demeanor, with every enigmatic event of the day, as well as the entire past voyage of the *San*

Dominick." Captain Delano's insight has the speed and scope of a sudden vision as he sees in a flash behind the multitudinous masks of innocence which have so long and dangerously betrayed him: "Captain Delano, now with scales dropped from his eyes, saw the negroes, not in misrule, not in tumult, not as if frantically concerned for Don Benito, but with mask torn away, flourishing hatchets and knives, in ferocious piratical revolt." As the discarding of the "masks" confirms his insight, Captain Delano acts—and acts swiftly and positively. Though reluctant to recognize evil, he is not slow to confront it; though hesitant in naming it, he does not hesitate to cope with it. Unlike either Ahab or Billy Budd, Captain Delano can deal with evil in a practical and effective manner, for in him mind and heart are held in balance. His great and generous heart, although it leads him near to disaster, does not push him over the edge. He releases Don Benito, binds Babo, picks up the other Spanish sailors who have leaped from their captivity, and, when he returns to his ship, dispatches a whaling boat in successful pursuit of the fleeing *San Dominick.* By this immediate and courageous action Captain Delano demonstrates that his notable generosity is kept within "human" bounds by a strong, instinctive sense of realism.

If Captain Delano is the maskless man of the tale, Benito Cereno is the subtly masked man, presenting one face to society, another to himself—neither of which, as he perhaps recognizes subconsciously, is the true Don Benito. In his occasional and gloomy glimpses into his own dark interior, he is like Pierre peering at times into his own deep soul; in his unwillingness to confront evil and his final withdrawal to a monastery, he is like Billy Budd responding whimsically as a child to the world's sin. Benito Cereno contrasts markedly with Amasa Delano, captain from the New World of America. His ship is no *Bachelor's Delight* (like Delano's) but the stately reminder of the past, the *San Domi-*

nick. Don Benito himself is a Spanish Catholic, both his country and his religion steeped in compelling traditions. In his weakness in the face of danger and in his final withdrawal from life, Don Benito seems to be the representative of a proud but nearly exhausted civilization, one on the brink of disintegration and decay. His inability to cope with the Negroes is not so much a failure of intellect or strength as a failure of will. Though the victim of black evil, Don Benito seems himself to emanate a darkness of his own.

Don Benito's outermost mask, removed only by his leap into Captain Delano's boat, is forced upon him by his captors. Beneath this mask lies the mask of innocence. When Captain Delano confesses that he at first believed, when Don Benito leaped, that Benito was signaling the launching of a plot against Delano and his crew, Don Benito replies: "You were with me all day; stood with me, sat with me, talked with me, looked at me, ate with me, drank with me; and yet, your last act was to clutch for a monster, not only an innocent man, but the most pitiable of all men. To such degree may malign machinations and deceptions impose." Innocent of the plot imagined by Captain Delano—Don Benito certainly was. But he is not, as he says, an innocent man; indeed, the experience brings to him an acute sense of his heritage of guilt. In Babo, who appears symbolically as his double (they are of the same age, have many similar characteristics), Don Benito vividly perceives his own—and man's—evil, and the knowledge undoes him.

His irrational fear, compounded in part of an insane hate, causes him when he is rescued by Captain Delano to refuse to come on deck of the *Bachelor's Delight* until the securely bound Babo is removed from sight, and he refuses ever after, even at the trial, to endure the presence of the Negro. He carefully notes in his deposition the reversal of the barbarism, the attack on the blacks (after they have been captured and shackled) by the Spanish sailors—a

number were killed, others saved by Captain Delano just
as the razor was aimed at the throat, the dagger at the
heart. This reversal impresses clearly on Don Benito the
universality of the savage impulse. And in the closing lines
of the story, he reveals his inability to accept the human
fate. When Captain Delano cries out to Don Benito to
forget—"See, yon bright sun has forgotten it all, and the
blue sea, and the blue sky; these have turned over new
leaves"—Don Benito quietly replies: "Because they have no
memory . . . because they are not human." Captain Delano asks Don Benito the cause of his dejection, and receives
in simple reply: "The negro." In his withdrawal and subsequent death, Don Benito deliberately severs his link in the
common human chain: he refuses any longer to bear the
responsibility of his *humanhood*.

Among the rebelling Negroes, two provide the necessary
leadership—Babo the intellect, Atufal the brute strength. It
is Babo who not only has masterminded the mutiny but also
has conceived the fantastic plot of deceiving Captain Delano as to the true state of affairs aboard the *San Dominick*.
Babo is a colored confidence man, a bit more sinister, perhaps, but reveling like the common racketeer in an ingenious and complicated plot fiendishly calculated to hurt as
well as to fleece. Babo obviously enjoys evil for itself alone.
This perverted joy is most clearly demonstrated in the relish
with which he murders Don Benito's friend, Don Alexandro
Aranda, the owner of the slaves on board, and mounts his
bleached skeleton in place of the figure of Christopher Co-
lumbus as the *San Dominick*'s figurehead. With this constant reminder of his cruelty on conspicuous display, Babo
"teases" the remnant of the Spanish crew and Don Benito
about the whiteness of the skeleton. One by one, he asks
each sailor whether he cannot affirm, from the whiteness of
the bones, that they belong to a white man. This is but one
of several small incidents which testify to the depth of

Babo's "negro slave" resentment against the "master" white race.

Babo's silent accomplice, the magnificently built Atufal, is another reminder of the seething rebelliousness of the black man. Once a chief of his tribe in Africa, he has had thrust upon him the indignities of slavery by men physically inferior who, ironically, espouse a religion of charity and love. Though the cruelties of the Negroes are extreme, they are not without precedents among white men, and they well up spontaneously from a confusion of fear and hate only dimly (if at all) understood by the perpetrators. But Babo and his followers are clever enough to understand that evil is most likely to succeed when it masquerades as innocence: they are as diligent in conceiving their naïve drama of deception as they are in executing their acts of violence.

In "Benito Cereno" Melville uses the drama of the masks to generate suspense. The deceptions in this story in a real sense *are* the story, for the deceptions capture the imagination of author and reader. The fate of the characters at the end is in part a dramatic reflection of their attitudes. Captain Delano, the maskless man, endures, and will continue his direct and frank confrontation of life. The clever Babo, once deprived of his ingenious mask, refuses to speak a word either at his trial or on any other occasion; but his severed head, "that hive of subtlety," is displayed in public where it meets, "unabashed, the gaze of the whites." And Benito Cereno, three months after the trial, is borne from his monastery on a bier as he makes the ultimate withdrawal from the human scene. Captain Delano welcomes life; Benito Cereno welcomes death; Babo seems to scoff defiantly at both.

12

2 *"Bartleby the Scrivener"*

Among Melville's remaining tales, "Bartleby" must be given
a prominent position. It is as impressive as it is simple. The
narrator of the story, a Wall Street lawyer, takes into his
business a scrivener named Bartleby. The entire story is
constructed about Bartleby's progressive withdrawal from
life. Bartleby's unusual nature is first hinted at when he is
asked by his employer to help examine some copied documents and replies, "I would prefer not to." More and more
frequently Bartleby baffles his boss by replying in this
manner to requests for his assistance. Finally, he refuses to
do copying or anything else, and stands silently staring out
of his window at the "dead brick wall." Bartleby's awkward
presence, day and night, in the Wall Street office becomes
so annoying to his employer that the latter betakes himself
to new offices elsewhere—but his conscience troubles him as
he continues to feel a responsibility for the now ghostly
Bartleby. When the scrivener is removed by the police from
the Wall Street quarters to the Tombs, he is visited by his
former employer, but refuses to heed pleas to eat or partici-
pate in any way in the usual human activities. It is the
employer who finds him one day totally withdrawn from
the human scene—in death. After a brief postscript relating Bartleby's former position in the Dead Letter Office
in Washington, the narrator sighs, "Ah, Bartleby! Ah, humanity."

When "Benito Cereno" and "Bartleby" are read in succession, the similarities between the "title" characters appear
striking. Both set out to encounter life, seem to find its demands too great, and begin a gradual withdrawal which
ends ultimately in death. Both are clearly sympathetic characters, their origins somewhat shrouded in mystery, the

cause of their deaths not entirely clear. If Benito Cereno has felt too intimately the impact of an evil with which he cannot cope, Bartleby, first in the handling of the terrible "dead letters" and later in the endless copying of law documents, has had a vision of life's futility (if not, indeed, hostility) which he cannot overcome. The static, enduring, and dependable elements of non-life (the monastery, the blank wall) seem preferable to the rushing flux of competitive life. And finally the tomb seems best of all; for both Don Benito and Bartleby appear not only to welcome but even to seek death.

In contrast with Bartleby, his employer and only friend has made an apparently effortless compromise with life. He confesses as he begins his story, "I am a man who, from his youth upwards, has been filled with a profound conviction that the easiest way of life is the best." Although he describes himself as "unambitious," he takes care to boast just a little of his connection with John Jacob Astor (he loves to repeat the name because it "hath a rounded and orbicular sound to it, and rings like unto bullion") and he emphasizes his cool-headedness: "I seldom lose my temper; much more seldom indulge in dangerous indignation at wrongs and outrages." In short, this moderately successful Wall Street lawyer is a congenial masked-man who is aware of the mask and just a bit cynical about it. But his profound sympathies for Bartleby (and, in his closing sigh, for all humanity) demonstrate that his cynicism is kept well within bounds, as does, too, his toleration of his other clerks, the all too human, dyspeptic, and frequently quarrelsome Turkey, Nippers, and Ginger Nut. Their continuous, terrible struggle with physical life, with its failures and triumphs, its alternating brightness and darkness, content and discontent, stands in humorous but meaningful contrast with Bartleby's emotionless, silent, and ultimate withdrawal.

3 *"The Encantadas"*

The most unusual of all Melville's short works is "The Encantadas," a series of some ten sketches of the Pacific island
group known on the maps as Galapagos. These sketches
are wrought out of an imagination fascinated by the volcanic,
barren, melancholy islands which have a paradoxical but
compelling beauty of their own. Descriptions of the desolation of these islands recur throughout the sketches, as does
the single metaphor—hell—that seems fitting: "In many
places the coast is rock-bound, or, more properly, clinker-
bound; tumbled masses of blackish or greenish stuff like
the dross of an iron-furnace, forming dark clefts and caves
here and there, into which a ceaseless sea pours a fury of
foam. . . . In no world but a fallen one could such lands
exist."

Not the least of the terrors on these hellish islands are
the strange living creatures which reside there—particularly
the "huge antediluvian-looking" tortoises, "mystic creatures"
who, when they emerge from their "unutterable solitudes"
seem "newly crawled forth from beneath the foundations of
the world." Though they seem figures of "unmitigated
gloom," they have their other, their bright, side. Melville
moves easily from tortoise to man: "Enjoy the bright, keep
it turned up perpetually if you can, but be honest, and don't
deny the black. Neither should he, who cannot turn the
tortoise from its natural position so as to hide the darker
and expose his livelier aspect, like a great October pumpkin
in the sun, for that cause declare the creature to be one total
inky blot. The tortoise is both black and bright."

In addition to containing vivid descriptions of inhuman,
eerie landscapes and strange, other-worldly creatures, "The
Encantadas" presents a number of brief narratives concern-

ing various individuals whose terrible fate it was to become
inhabitants at one time or another of these islands. One of
the islands, Charles's Isle, was taken over as a gift from
Peru by a Creole adventurer after he had helped the country
in its revolt against Spain. Setting himself up as king, he
was soon overthrown by the very rascals he had assembled
as his subjects, and Charles's Isle became notorious for its
"*Riotocracy*, which gloried in having no law but lawless-
ness."

Melville relates also the story of the Chola widow, one
Hunilla, who with her husband and brother are left on Nor-
folk Isle by a ship with promises to return in due time.
The ship does not return, the two men are drowned in a
fishing accident, and Hunilla is left alone to wait—and survive if she can on her forsaken island. She does survive, but
the experience proves so horrible that even Melville cannot
describe all that happens. Apparently the unspeakable incidents involve visits to Hunilla's island by whale-boats. Melville comments: "Events, not books, should be forbid. But
in all things man sows upon the wind, which bloweth just
there whither it listeth; for ill or good, man cannot know.
Often ill comes from the good, as good from ill."

Melville's last inserted narrative in "The Encantadas" con-
cerns the hermit Oberlus, who takes over Hood's Isle as his
evil kingdom: "So warped and crooked was his strange
nature, that the very handle of his hoe seemed gradually
to have shrunk and twisted in his grasp. . . . It was his
mysterious custom upon a first encounter with a stranger
ever to present his back; possibly, because that was his
better side, since it revealed the least." In the account of
this misanthrope's machinations against his fellow man,
Melville describes how he reduces the "ranging Cow-Boys
of the sea" who fall into his power to the status of brute
animals: ". . . rotted down from manhood by their hopeless
misery on the isle; wonted to cringe in all things to their

lord, himself the worst of slaves; these wretches were now
become wholly corrupted to his hands. He used them as
creatures of an inferior race; in short, he gaffles his four
animals, and makes murderers of them; out of cowards
fitly manufacturing bravos." After detailing the various evil
schemes which simmer and bubble out of the head of
this Fedallah-Claggart-like creature, Melville relates that
Oberlus is ultimately thrown into a South American jail
which presents "both within and without the grimmest aspect." Melville concludes: "And here, for a long time, Oberlus
was seen; the central figure of a mongrel and assassin band;
a creature whom it is religion to detest, since it is philan-
thropy to hate a misanthrope."

4 "The Bell-Tower"

"The Bell-Tower," a story remarkably Hawthorne-like, is
cast in the form of a legend purporting to explain the history
of a mouldering stump of an Italian tower. The story relates
the fate of one Bannadonna, celebrated architect of the
tower and designer of the unique bell which was to grace the
belfry. The townspeople are a bit upset when Bannadonna
clashes with one of his workmen, but they do not see the
human "splinter" that drops into the molten mass to become
the bell's flaw. The people become more disturbed when
Bannadonna works so long and mysteriously over an ingenious device which is to ring the bell. In actuality, Bannadonna is laboring to create for this purpose an "iron slave,"
Tolus by name, who is to have the excellences of "all God-
made creatures."

Melville is careful to define precisely Bannadonna's motives and methods in creating his diabolical servant. The

architect is a "practical materialist," devoted to neither al-
chemy nor theosophy: "In short, to solve nature, to steal
into her, to intrigue beyond her, to procure some one else
to bind her to his hand;—these, one and all, had not been
his objects; but, asking no favors from any element or any
being, of himself, to rival her, outstrip her, and rule her. He
stooped to conquer. With him, common sense was theurgy;
machinery, miracle; Prometheus, the heroic name for ma-
chinist; man, the true God." Like Ahab in pursuing Moby
Dick, Bannadonna meets death where he had expected triumph. As he stoops, absorbed in correcting some defect in
the design of his bell, the monster of his creation starts on
its appointed rounds to strike the hour and strikes instead
the proud artist. At Bannadonna's funeral, as a live bell
ringer strikes the bell, it breaks and crashes to the ground.

Melville concludes: "So the blind slave obeyed its blinder
lord; but, in obedience, slew him. So the creator was killed
by the creature. So the bell was too heavy for the tower. So
the bell's main weakness was where man's blood had flawed
it. And so pride went before the fall." Benito Cereno,
Bartleby, and Bannadonna have in common the fact that
they designed their own deaths, Don Benito and Bartleby
by their withdrawal from life, Bannadonna by his attempt
to triumph over life. Like Taji, Ahab, and Pierre, Bannadonna sought a superhuman perfection and found death
instead. The machine he deifies turns into his own destroying devil.

5 *"Cock-A-Doodle-Doo!"*

One of Melville's most unusual stories is "Cock-A-Doodle-
Doo! or The Crowing of the Noble Cock Benevantano." The

plot is quite simple: at the opening of the story, the narrator
is plunged into cynicism and despair about the world and
about his own affairs; but upon hearing the noble cock crow,
he swings to the opposite extreme as he feels a "pure over-
flow of self-reliance and a sense of universal security"; the
narrator pursues the cock and discovers that it belongs to a
poverty-stricken and starving family whose plight is transfigured—"irradiated," "glorified"—by the magnificent crowing of the majestic cock; finally, the narrator witnesses the
death of the family accompanied by the exultant crowing
of the cock—"He seemed bent upon crowing the souls of
the children out of their wasted bodies." In the midst of
his triumphant crowing, the cock himself drops dead.

The cock's crow is not the "vain-glorious crow of some
young sophomorean cock, who knew not the world," but the
"crow of a cock who had fought the world and got the better
of it and was resolved to crow, though the earth should
heave and the heavens should fall." Repeatedly we are told
that the crow is an "all-glorious and defiant crow." In short
the cock symbolizes the impractical, all-embracing idealist
who cries out foolishly his joyful gibberish in the very face
of poverty, misery, and death. The defiant cock is a comic
version of Taji, Ahab, and Pierre, sharing their inability to
confront the evil of the universe realistically and to come to
practical terms with it.

In the early passages of "Cock-A-Doodle-Doo!"—before
the appearance of the cock, when the narrator is still "full
of hypoes"—appear some of Melville's best descriptions of
the world's complexly interwoven texture of good and evil,
life and death. The narrator walks out into the countryside
and finds that it looks "underdone, its raw juices squirting
out all round." Buttoning out the "squitchy air," the narrator walks stubbornly on: "All around me were tokens of a
divided empire. The old grass and the new grass were striving together. In the low wet swales the verdure peeped out

in vivid green; beyond, on the mountains, lay light patches of snow, strangely relieved against their russet sides; all the humped hills looked like brindled kine in the shivers. The woods were strewn with dry dead boughs, snapped off by the riotous winds of March, while the young trees skirting the woods were just beginning to show the first yellowish tinge of the nascent spray." What would necessarily come from a direct confrontation of this "divided empire," from the perception of a unifying significance within nature's divisiveness, within the tortured struggle of life out of death, is an honest optimism. The noble cock neither confronts the world as it is nor projects an honest spiritual vision. His bravado is as flashy and unrealistic as his own brilliant plumage.

6 The bright and the dark

A number of Melville's stories are variations on the theme of reconciliation. "Jimmy Rose" tells the story of a rich man's fall from eminence, as he loses first his wealth and then his "friends," but the entire point of the tale is that the unfortunate man does not withdraw from life but persists in ferreting out, sometimes in the meanest of ways, his fair share. Although in his misery he is at first tempted to become a misanthrope and withdraw, like Shakespeare's Timon, from the human scene, he resists the temptation: "Perhaps at bottom Jimmy was too thoroughly good and kind to be made from any cause a man-hater. And doubtless it at last seemed irreligious to Jimmy even to shun mankind." In still another story, "The Happy Failure," an old man discovers happiness only in the absolute failure of a fantastic machine he has invented. Obsessed with the "universal drift of the mass of humanity toward utter oblivion," the old man attempts through his invention to invest himself with immortality. His failure impresses him with the futility of his motive, and, rid of his distorted ambition, he discovers true happiness for the first time. The old man advises his nephew: "Boy, take my advice, and never try to invent anything but —happiness. . . . Boy, I'm glad I've failed. I say, boy, failure has made a good old man of me. It was horrible at first, but I'm glad I've failed. Praise be to God for the failure." The old man's final years are now filled with "peaceful days of autumnal content."

Similar in theme to "The Happy Failure" is "The Fiddler." The narrator is a poet who is suffering the agony of adverse reviews and looking forward to oblivion, an "intolerable fate." His attitude is gradually transfigured as he becomes acquainted with Hautboy, once famous as a child prodigy on the violin, who in adulthood has lost his fame and fortune but not his genius. Hautboy does not withdraw from life, nor does he don the mask of unrewarded, unrecognized genius (as the narrator, at first, is about to do). Instead, "good sense and good humor" join to enable him to live a life of fullness: "It was plain that while Hautboy saw the world pretty much as it was, yet he did not theoretically espouse its bright side nor its dark side. Rejecting all solutions he but acknowledged facts. What was sad in the world he did not superficially gainsay; what was glad in it he did not cynically slur; and all which was to him personally enjoyable, he gratefully took to his heart. It was plain, then—so it seemed at that moment, at least—that his extraordinary cheerfulness did not arise either from deficiency of feeling or thought."

Unlike the foolish cheerfulness of the noble cock of "Cock-A-Doodle-Doo!" Hautboy's good spirits are founded on realism, on a clear look at the world as it is. Espousing neither the bright side nor the dark side of the world, recognizing both the sad and the joyful, Hautboy is one of those few men who in their frankness and wisdom bring into rare balance the admirable traits of the Melvillean maskless man.

9

The Confidence-Man: *a comic masquerade*

Critics have found *The Confidence-Man: His Masquerade* (1857) more difficult to classify than any other of Melville's books. Melville himself refers to the narrative as "our comedy," and at one point signals his reader that he is passing "from the comedy of thought to that of action." He creates an unusual thematic setting by reducing the dimensions of his characters and by curtailing the scale of their actions. The shallowness of the confidence man, unfitting him for the profound pathos or even tragedy of *Moby Dick* or *Pierre*, prepares him eminently for the role of the comic racketeer, the city slicker, hornswoggling and bamboozling the country (and city) yokels. Certainly we do not cry, and perhaps we don't even laugh, but surely we smile, if a little grimly, as the confidence man swindles victim after victim in the course of his adventures, relying all too frequently on the innate weaknesses in human nature—the desire to get something for nothing, the willingness to traffic in the misery of others. But the confidence man exploits generous and noble impulses, too, and this apparent mockery of unquestionable values gives the book a complexity and at times an ambiguity that cause many readers to abandon it in bewilderment.

Although recent criticism tends to elevate *The Confidence-Man* to a rather high position in Melville's work, the original view still prevails that the book is the deeply-pessimistic product of a disillusioned, embittered man. Running through most of the critical commentary is the uncomfortable if unconfessed feeling that the novel is radically different in character from the work that came before and after. The explanation has been most persistently sought in personal, biographical terms. There remains, however, the possibility that Melville was simply seeking a new form—satire or the comic allegory—in which to embody afresh his old vision of man and the world.

1 Speeds the daedal boat

On the first of April (significant in American folklore as Fool's Day) the steamboat *Fidèle* leaves St. Louis on its way to New Orleans. Assembled on the boat are all of the various kinds of that "multiform pilgrim species, man." The steamboat and the river it sails upon have a unique national significance: "Here reigned the dashing and all-fusing spirit of the West, whose type is the Mississippi itself, which, uniting the streams of the most distant and opposite zones, pours them along, helter-skelter, in one cosmopolitan and confident tide." *Cosmopolitan* and *confident*—these are terms that come in for close scrutiny on the journey down the great river, virtues of the New World which in excess may easily become vices. The device of the steamboat sailing down the Mississippi offers something more than a means for bringing together for brief periods of time the various types of humankind. The slow but steady flow of the river, the constant coming and going of the people, the stopping and starting of the boat in its long journey—all suggest not only the flux of life but also the world of fantasy, the world of dream. Melville's style in key transitional passages suggests the dreamlike drift of this witty and biting analysis of the American—or human—condition: "The sky slides into blue, the bluffs into bloom; the rapid Mississippi expands; runs sparkling and gurgling, all over in eddies; one magnified wake of a seventy-four. The sun comes out, a golden huzzar, from his tent, flashing his helm on the world. All things, warmed in the landscape, leap. Speeds the daedal boat as a dream." The reader becomes increasingly aware that the rhythmical flow of the swindling masquerade not only has the unreal quality of dream but even the unsettling impact of the comic nightmare. It is as though the repressed spiritual history of America (or of mankind) escapes from the unconscious and insists on realistic recognition.

One after another in the flow of action, a number of individuals assume center stage. There appears in the book's opening chapter a deaf-mute who writes maxims about charity on his slate for the curious public. Almost immediately afterwards appears a Negro cripple, Black Guinea, who makes a grotesque music while he begs for pennies. Next comes a man in mourning under the name of John Ringman whose tale of misfortune is designed to elicit not merely pity but money as well. Another man, appearing in a gray coat and white tie as a professional do-gooder with a business approach to charity, collects a contribution from a clergyman for the Seminole Widow and Orphan Asylum, demonstrates the invalid's easy chair of his own invention, and proposes a scheme for the World's Charity whereby there would be levied "one grand benevolence tax upon all mankind" and the missions would be "quickened" by the "Wall Street spirit." Next appears John Truman carrying a "ledger-like volume" and selling shares in the Black Rapids Coal Company; he tops his series of dubious deals by collecting from an old miser a large sum on the simple promise of trebling it for him. The constant argument of all these individuals throughout is that suspicion and pessimism are evil, and an optimistic confidence, particularly in the speaker as an individual, is the greatest of virtues.

Next appears the herb doctor, selling to the sick and injured, the uncomfortable and the miserable, either his Samaritan Pain Dissuader or his Omni-Balsamic Reinvigorator. The latter he sells to the same pain-ridden miser from whom earlier John Truman had extracted money upon promise of multiplying it. Following the herb doctor comes a representative of the Philosophical Intelligence Office, identified by a brass plate suspended from a chain around his neck. He successfully dissuades a disillusioned Missourian from replacing his boy worker with a machine (the Missourian had concluded that "boyhood is a natural state of rascality"), and takes his money by promising to produce a boy in whom confidence can be placed. Next a cosmopolitan, draped in vivid if grotesque colors, appears to argue against Indian depravity, as against human depravity, and to contend that the notorious Indian hater and killer, Colonel John Moredock, really possessed a kind heart—like an "inviting oyster in a forbidding shell." As Francis Goodman, this cosmopolitan strikes up a "friendship" with one Charles Arnold Noble, but the relationship is almost destroyed when Goodman confesses that he needs money. Protesting quickly that it was all a joke, Goodman succeeds in re-establishing the friendship, if only precariously. Goodman again tries his tactics for accumulating easy money on a "mystic," Mark Winsome, and his practical disciple, Egbert, but discovers that their mystical view of friendship, though highly idealistic, is grounded in a thoroughly shrewd knowledge of mankind. He cannot separate them from their money, and, indeed, concludes his interview by handing over some of his own.

Descending several steps on the philosophical ladder, the cosmopolitan next talks the barber (who had appeared in the book's opening chapter with "no trust" in mankind) into a confidence in human beings and out of the price of his haircut. The last we see of this cosmopolitan, he has demonstrated to an old man, beset by a multitude of suspicions, that the Bible, omitting the "apocryphal" Apocrypha, supports and encourages a supreme faith in "confidence" ("Jehovah shall be thy confidence"), and he is leading the old man, whose sight is failing, to his stateroom. After all of the old gentleman's numerous precautions, such as the purchase of a money belt and the search for a life preserver, he ironically places himself in the devious hands of this "man-charmer," this master racketeer. The episode (and the book) concludes ominously: "Something further may follow of this Masquerade." And, indeed, the reader feels, something undoubtedly will.

2   *The Devil and his legions*

One does not read far into *The Confidence-Man*, with its maze of plot and multitude of characters, without a growing suspicion that there is a subtle relationship among all the successive "protagonists." Indeed, one concludes the book convinced that one has witnessed the title character, the confidence man, in a series of guises. The confidence man glides out of one guise and into another in such a slick manner as to put even that infamous snake of Eden to shame. Endowed with the gift of the chameleon, the crafty confidence man seems able to assume innumerable appearances as they are called forth by a constantly shifting moral or immoral situation. But the changes in costume are not haphazardly assumed. There is a scheme in the changing shapes of this man of many faces. The central figures in the successive chapters of *The Confidence-Man* are:

I (Chapter 1) The deaf-mute, promoting biblical charity.

II (Chapters 2-3) Black Guinea the cripple, begging for money.

III (Chapters 4-5) The man with a weed, in mourning, John Ringman, soliciting aid from strangers.

IV (Chapters 6-8) The man in a gray coat and white tie, representing the Seminole Widow and Orphan Asylum and promoting World's Charity.

V (Chapters 9-15) The man with a book, John Truman, president of the Black Rapids Coal Company, encouraging speculative investments.

VI (Chapters 16-21) The herb-doctor, promoting his Omni-Balsamic Reinvigorator and Samaritan Pain Dissuader.

VII (Chapters 22-23) The man with a brass plate, representing the Philosophical Intelligence Office, promoting faith in the goodness of man.

VIII (Chapters 24-45) The cosmopolitan, promoting trust in and love of one's fellow man on all levels, from the exalted philosophical to the mundane practical.

Meaning in *The Confidence-Man* exists on three interlocking levels—the realistic western narrative, the symbolic American satire, and the universal allegory. Reading the book on one level only, many critics have condemned it for failure to achieve something it did not attempt. The story presents a constantly shifting and widely various group of people traveling on a steamboat down the Mississippi; but, though the story is studded with a number of convincing episodes and brilliantly vivid characters, its realism is weakened, both by the symbolism, which makes the meaning of the narrative peculiarly applicable to America, and, even more, by the insistent allegory of universal significance. If Melville was protraying an "action" on a boat gliding down the great, continental river, he was also, through symbolism, presenting some rather acute criticism of his native land,

and, above all, making some comprehensive observations through allegory about the nature of man and evil.

The first individual to claim our attention on the steamboat *Fidèle* is the deaf-mute, a man in "cream-colors": "His cheek was fair, his chin downy, his hair flaxen, his hat a white fur one, with a long fleecy nap." This man appears to be "evenly pursuing the path of duty, lead it through solitudes or cities," and he bears an "aspect . . . singularly innocent" as he stands about writing on his slate, "charity thinketh no evil," "charity suffereth long, and is kind," "charity endureth all things," "charity believeth all things," "charity never faileth." To the crowds on the steamboat, who have been reading a poster offering a "reward for the capture of a mysterious impostor, supposed to have recently arrived from the East," and who observe the boat's barber hang out his routine and expected "No Trust" sign, the deaf-mute might well seem a "simpleton." He does not, however, intrude himself, but after displaying his biblical quotations, he retires inconspicuously to the foot of a ladder and rests: ". . . though he might not have a long way to go, yet he seemed already to have come from a very long distance," from "some far country beyond the prairies." The deaf-mute submits finally to his weariness: "Gradually overtaken by slumber, his flaxen head drooped, his whole lamb-like figure relaxed, and, half reclining against the ladder's foot, lay motionless, as some sugar-snow in March, which, softly stealing down over night, with its white placidity startles the brown farmer peering out from his threshold at daybreak."

This singular figure is distinguished from all the other individuals in *The Confidence-Man* by his utter innocence, or naïveté, as symbolized by his innumerable associations with whiteness, and by his action: Unlike all of the succeeding "protagonists," the mute does not practice a con game, he does not fleece any of the passengers on the *Fidèle*. In short, the mute is Christ bringing the essence of the Christian ethical message to the world. This identification is suggested by innumerable symbolic clues, not the least of which is the final position by the stairs leading upward: the way to heaven, salvation, is through Christ.

Details such as the flaxen hair which suggest the eunuch, or sterility, indicate the major and recurring theme on which Melville is about to embark in the *Fidèle:* the inapplicability to this world of heaven's law. This theme or its variation appears in all of Melville's work—in *White Jacket*, for example, in the vignette of the "murderous" but praying cannoneer; and in *Pierre* in the Plinlimmon pamphlet's distinction between chronometrical and horological time (or ethics). Like *Pierre*, *The Confidence-Man* is major treatment of the theme, but the literary form is comic, not melodramatic or tragic.

As the first chapter of *The Confidence-Man* conveys the heavenly ethic which is to be humanly tested, the next two chapters reveal the reason the law of heaven will be found drastically inadequate. As the first figure to appear is Christ, the second is the Devil: the first white, the next black: ". . . a grotesque negro cripple, in towcloth attire and an old coal-sifter of a tambourine in his hand." This beggar has "something wrong with his legs" and is "cut down to the stature of a Newfoundland dog." When asked where he sleeps, "Black Guinea" answers, in the "good baker's oven." The questioner exclaims, "In an oven? Whose, pray? What baker, I should like to know, bakes such black bread in his oven, alongside of his nice white rolls, too." Black Guinea smiles and points to the sun. On the symbolic level this brief exchange raises once again one of Melville's favorite metaphysical problems: why does God permit the existence of evil?

Black Guinea makes his way by the "game of charity": the devil quotes scripture for his own purpose. The crippled

Negro, unable to attract sufficient attention, begins to catch pennies in his mouth as they are thrown to him by the passengers. But shortly the people, spurred on by a cynical, one-legged man who voices his doubts about Black Guinea's honesty, begin to believe that he is an impostor. But as a young Episcopal clergyman and a militant Methodist come to Black Guinea's aid, the one-legged cynic retreats, suggestively shouting: "You flock of fools, under this captain of fools, in this ship of fools." Meantime, the innocent and tender clergyman asks Black Guinea who on board might vouch for his identity. The Negro cripple ironically replies with a list of the very guises (a "good ge'mman wid a weed, and a ge'mman in a gray coat and white tie" etc.) of the confidence man: the devil does indeed know his legions, those who are busy upon earth doing his bidding in tempting man.

The confidence man (or the devil) appears in six costumes during the voyage down the great river. Each time he appears, he makes a different kind of appeal, working a different racket in a new field. In the first two guises, the one a man with "a long weed on his hat," the other a man "in gray coat and white tie," the confidence man's varied grays contrast sharply with Christ's whiteness and the devil's blackness. In the first disguise the confidence man, promoting himself as a child of misfortune, makes his appeal through his personal plight; in the second, promoting grandiose charitable schemes, he makes his appeal through the world's suffering. Having prepared the way for his next role, the confidence man appears as a "ruddy-cheeked man in a tasselled travelling-cap, carrying under his arm a ledger-like volume"; as president and transfer agent of the Black Rapids Coal Company, the confidence man makes a bold appeal to the desire for money. Next appearing "in a snuff-colored surtout," the confidence man presents himself as the herb doctor and makes his devilish appeal to the human desire for youth, health, vigor. Confronted finally by a cynic, the confidence man appears as a "round-backed, baker-kneed man, in a mean five-dollar suit, wearing, collar-wise by a chain, a small brass plate, inscribed P.I.O." This man, wearing a "canine deprecation" and "seeming to wag his very coat-tails behind him, shabby though they were," is a strong reminder of the dog-like Black Guinea. As representative of the Philosophical Intelligence Office he makes his appeal to the secret yearning that man contains to find his own kind basically good.

In his final appearance, the confidence man becomes, through his brilliant colors and dress, the sum of all his other appearances: ". . . the stranger sported a vesture barred with various hues, that of the cochineal predominating, in style participating of a Highland plaid, Emir's robe, and French blouse; from its plaited sort of front peeped glimpses of a flowered regatta-shirt, while, for the rest, white trowsers of ample duck flowed over maroon-colored slippers, and a jaunty smoking-cap of regal purple crowned him off at top." In this finery, the confidence man announces the universality of his nature: "A cosmopolitan, a catholic man; who, being such, ties himself to no narrow tailor or teacher, but federates, in heart as in costume, something of the various gallantries of men under various suns. Oh, one roams not over the gallant globe in vain. Bred by it, is a fraternal and fusing feeling." The confidence man remains in this guise for the remainder of the voyage (about one-half the book), and makes his sophisticated appeal to the human desire to find stability, permanency, and mutual trust in human relationships.

In succession the confidence man appeals to the basic human desires: the desire to comfort grief, to alleviate suffering, to gain money, to have health, to discover goodness, and, finally, the desire for love. His victims attempt to place their faith in alms-giving, in organized charity, in business, in nature, in philosophy, and, finally, in friendship. In each guise, the confidence man is able to gull his victims by exploiting or manipulating their desire and faith. Throughout, it is demonstrated over and over again, in a constantly shifting context, that Christ's heavenly doctrine of charity (love) is unworkable, at least in any absolute sense, among human beings on earth—primarily because it does not take into account the very real presence of evil.

3   *The pilgrim species, man*

On the *Fidèle*, as on Chaucer's pilgrimage to Canterbury, appear a great variety of human types, enough, indeed, to satisfy the lust for experimentation of any number of devils: "Natives of all sorts, and foreigners; men of business and men of pleasure; parlor men and back woodsmen; farm-hunters and fame-hunters; heiress-hunters, gold-hunters, buffalo-hunters, bee-hunters, happiness-hunters, truth-hunters, and still keener hunters after all these hunters. Fine ladies in slippers, and moccasined squaws; Northern speculators and Eastern philosophers; English, Irish, German, Scotch, Danes; Santa Fe traders in striped blankets, and Broadway bucks in cravats of cloth of gold; fine-looking Kentucky boatmen, and Japanese looking Mississippi cotton-planters; Quakers in full drab, and United States soldiers in full regimentals; slaves, black, mulatto, quadroon; modish young Spanish Creoles, and old-fashioned French Jews; Mormons and Papists; Dives and Lazarus; jesters and mourners, teetotallers and convivialists, deacons and black-legs; hard-shell Baptists and clay-eaters; grinning negroes, and Sioux chiefs solemn as high-priests. In short, a piebald parliament, an Anacharsis Cloots congress of all kinds of that

multiform pilgrim species, man." The *Fidèle* should, indeed, be just the devil's dish—and such it proves. He is able
to find easy victims aplenty among all these pilgrims, and,
too, he is able to find some that are tough enough to incite
him to the exhilarating exercise of his most subtle wiles.

The victims of the confidence man are ultimately victims
of their own weaknesses and evil impulses. They suffer some
imbalance of head and heart that makes them vulnerable.
The two religious men who come to the aid of the crippled
Black Guinea are deficient: the Episcopal clergyman with
his naïve faith is lacking in common sense (he is taken in
later, too, by the fantastic charity schemes of the confidence
man appearing as the man in the gray coat); and the militant Methodist demonstrates by his impulsive militancy his
lack of understanding of the very faith he would defend so
vigorously. Henry Roberts, "forwarding merchant, of Wheel-
ing, Pennsylvania," is gulled twice, first by the tale of woe
told by the man with the weed, and next by the stock
scheme of the Black Rapids Coal Company represented by
the man with the book. Roberts may be the average man of
both generous and greedy impulses whose mediocre faculties are insufficiently developed to cope with the devil. A
sophomore "collegian," student of Tacitus, who hears the
same tale of woe told Roberts, does not succumb, but he
falls harder than Roberts for the Black Rapids Coal Company scheme of quick and easy money. In contrast to the
collegian, who seems all greediness, the man with the gold
sleeve buttons seems all goodness. Indeed it is his natural
goodness that is contrasted so sharply with the confidence
man's "righteousness." But this man's goodness, though genuine, does not prove sufficient guard against a cheat. As the
confidence man relates his schemes for world charity, this
"singularly good-hearted" man remains "proof to such elo-
quence; though not . . . to such pleadings." Though he listens with "pleasant incredulity" and bestows a look of "half

humor, half pity" on the confidence man, he hands over a donation—"charitable to the last, if only to the dreams of enthusiasm." Though this man is intelligent enough to see that these charitable schemes won't work, his unalloyed natural goodness will not allow him to perceive the wicked motive behind their promotion.

As the naturally good man seems a push-over for the devil, so too does a "charitable lady," "a plump and pleasant person, whose aspect seems to hint that, if she have any weak point, it must be anything rather than her excellent heart." Having just reread Chapter 13 of I Corinthians, containing the passages on charity with which the deaf-mute opened the journey down the Mississippi, she makes fair game for the confidence man soliciting for his charitable causes. In the absence of faculties which would provide a balance, her big heart allows her to be duped. Like this lady with too much heart, a miser with a heart too small proves an easy victim. He is gulled twice, first by the lure of wealth promised by a simple scheme to treble his money and next by the lure of health promised by the "natural" medicine made of herbs. As the charitable lady thinks too much of others, the miser thinks too much of himself. Another traveler proves a harder nut to crack, but the confidence man as the herb doctor finally claims him as victim. A chronically sick man, "visited, but not warmed, by the sun—a plant whose hour seems over, while buds are blowing and seeds are astir," he at first takes a cynical view of all the claims the herb doctor makes for his medicine, but at last out of a desperate yearning for hope—even the smallest—he buys the herb doctor's vials. The desire to be cured of the "misery of weakness" is so strong as to break through his rigid defense against false hope and quackery.

Two victims of the confidence man share the honor with him of appearing in the list of character references that Black Guinea, or Satan, presented near the opening of the book: "a ge'mman as is a sodjer" and "a ge'mman in a yaller west." These two individuals are con men in their own right, plying their trade on the *Fidèle*. They are already devotees of the devil, and the confidence man recognizes in each of them a fundamental kinship. The "soldier of fortune" is presenting himself to his fellow travelers as a crippled veteran of the Mexican wars and is begging alms. But he confides to the confidence man, with an occasional and startling hyena-like laugh, that his crippled condition was brought about by a series of accidents and mistakes, in which his only fault was not having friends to help him. When the confidence man replies that he does not believe this fantastic tale of woe, the "soldier" confesses that he is not surprised: "Hardly anybody believes my story, and so to most I tell a different one." A bystander who has heard the soldier's two stories exclaims, "he belongs to the Devil's regiment," but the confidence man defends his own: "The vice of the unfortunate is pardonable." The confidence man inspects the soldier's legs and significantly notes that he has "much such a case as the negro's,"—Black Guinea's. Discovering this clear connection with the devil, the confidence man asserts he will do the "friendly thing" and give the soldier the same liniment he has given the crippled Negro (Satan). The soldier responds to this generous gesture by insisting on paying for what was given and on buying more of the medicine, and he thanks the confidence man for treating him "like a good Christian." The entire scene is implicit with the irony of one con man gulling another, of the devil practicing his tricks on one of his own.

The confidence man does not have so easy a time, however, with the other individual who had turned up amidst his own guises on Black Guinea's list. This man, later to identify himself as one Charles Noble, appears in a "violet vest" which sends up "sunset hues to a countenance betokening a kind of bilious habit." He seeks out the confidence man in order to relate the story of Colonel John Moredock, "Indian-hater," a frontiersman in Illinois, who, when his entire family was massacred by Indians, devoted himself coldly and earnestly to a prolonged period of vengeance, obsessively and methodically killing Indians. Just as he could not believe the hard-luck tale of the soldier of fortune, so the confidence man cannot believe in Indian-hating. In the chat after the tale of the Indian-hater, the confidence man (identifying himself as Francis Goodman) and Charles Noble agree that they cannot understand misanthropy because in all their experience of mankind, it has been "worthy one's best love." Declaring that they have found "friendship at first sight," they settle down to drink and exchange confidences. As the conversation ranges from wine to Shakespeare, the confidence man slyly manages to ply his companion with an excess of drinks, preparing him for an experiment. The experiment is a simple one: the confidence man will attempt to borrow fifty dollars.

The results are more complex. In a "metamorphosis more surprising than any in Ovid," Charles Noble exclaims, "go to the devil, sir! Beggar, impostor!" At this moment of exposure, Noble's true character lies revealed: "While speaking or rather hissing those words, the boon companion underwent much such a change as one reads of in fairy-books. Out of old materials sprang a new creature. Cadmus glided into the snake." The confidence man clearly sees that he is, as before, dealing with one of his own. He hastens to perform a ritual of necromancy which works a "successful charm" and restores the transformed Noble to his former "friendly" self. The two lie profusely as they assure each other that they had been acting parts. After a further brief discussion of the hypothetical case of Charlemont, a wealthy man who, when he lost his wealth, disappeared until he had regained it in order to save his friends from the embarrassment of cutting off a poor acquaintance, Charles Noble retires from view, befuddled by the liquor and confused by the confidence man's slick talk. Although he does not take money from Charles Noble, the confidence man demonstrates quite clearly that he can control his "friend" at his own pleasure. He agrees that Noble ought to go rest ("sleep it off"), and says in parting: "go, go—I understand you exactly. I will see you tomorrow." The understanding is, indeed, the deep understanding the devil has of his own. The confidence man possesses much more than the mere money of Charles Noble.

4 Cynics, Titans, and Yankees

In vivid contrast with these congenial con men are a number of ruggedly honest individuals characterized by their intuitive perception of evil and their primitive response to it. They all realize the undesirability and, indeed, impossibility of living on earth by an absolute application of the heavenly law of "charity." And they all possess an awareness of the shortcomings of human nature acute enough to permit them to perceive the quackery of the confidence man.

The first of these characters is the wooden-legged man who attempts to expose the Negro cripple, Black Guinea. This cynic is first introduced as a "limping, gimlet-eyed, sour-faced person" who begins to "croak" that Black Guinea's deformity is a "sham, got up for financial purposes." When the militant Methodist pleads for charity, the wooden-legged man exclaims: "To where it belongs with your charity! to heaven with it! . . . here on earth, true charity dotes, and false charity plots. Who betrays a fool with a kiss, the charitable fool has the charity to believe is in love with him, and the charitable knave on the stand gives charitable testimony for his comrade in the box." This maimed man realizes that on earth, if one would not be duped, he must mix wisdom with charity, mind with heart ("When you find me a virtuous jockey, I will find you a benevolent man"). When the confidence man reappears as the man in the gray coat promoting grandiose charitable schemes, and he and the gullible, young Episcopal clergyman assert that Black Guinea must have been innocent because his pains were so great for so paltry a reward, the wooden-legged man cries out: "You two green-horns! Money, you think, is the sole motive to pains and hazard, deception and deviltry, in this world. How much money did the devil make by gulling Eve?" With this perceptive comment, the cynic disappears from the pages of the novel. Although he has not been gulled by being parted from his money, he has been duped in a larger sense, for he is without a sense of humor or a sense of the joy of living which might balance the bitterness springing from his recognition of the ubiquity and complexity of evil. His acute and obsessive cynicism has isolated him from mankind: the devil has, indeed, done his work.

This character (in a sense the same) reappears later as the "invalid Titan in homespun" who carries a heavy walking stick and leads a "puny girl, walking in moccasins, not improbably his child, but evidently of alien maternity, perhaps Creole, or even Comanche," who seems "a little Cassandra, in nervousness." This striking pair is accosted almost immediately by the confidence man, appearing now as the herb doctor, who sees in the ailing frontiersman a possible sucker for his quack medicine. As the Titan is bent over in pain, "slanting his tall stature like a mainmast yielding to the gale, or Adam to the thunder," the confidence man sees him as an easy victim of false hope. But when the herb doctor claims that his medicine "kills pain without feeling," the Titan exclaims, "You lie! Some pains cannot be eased but by producing insensibility, and cannot be cured but by producing death." Ignoring this remark and its effect on

the bystanders, the herb doctor continues glibly to claim
miraculous cures from his medicine. The Titan, "with a countenance lividly epileptic with hypochondriac mania," strikes
the herb doctor a heavy blow, shouting, "Profane fiddler on
heart-strings! Snake!" The herb doctor does not pursue the
Titan as he leaves but cites his own meekness to the bystanders as proof of his innocence. There can be little doubt
that the confidence man may claim the Titan as his victim,
for though he does not extract money from him, he does incite him to violence: the Titan's blow is evidence of a more
profound gulling than the Titan's money ever could be. Like
the Indian-haters of Charles Noble's tale, the Titan responds
to evil on an instinctive level and in an obsessed manner.
Unable to cope with it by cunning, he resorts to force, becoming what he would destroy.

The Missouri bachelor is a reincarnation of the cynic and
the Titan. "Sporting a shaggy spencer of the cloth called
bear-skin; a high-peaked cap of raccoon-skin, the long bushy
tail switching over behind; raw-hide leggings; grim stubble
chin" and carrying "a double-barrelled gun in hand," this
colorful figure turns up to challenge the herb-doctor's confidence in "natur" and his "yarbs." Upon hearing the frontiersman's philosophy of distrust, founded upon his observations of the "natural" rascality of the boys who have
worked for him, the herb doctor presents his usual arguments
and finds them of no avail. He then resorts to a new guise,
appearing as a representative of the Philosophical Intelligence Office, and argues more successfully on new grounds.
Although the Missouri bachelor claims that "St. Augustine
on Original Sin is [his] text-book," and although he asserts
firmly, "polite boys or saucy boys, white boys or black boys,
smart boys or lazy boys, Caucasian boys or Mongol boys—
all are rascals," he allows himself finally to be won over by
an argument based on analogy: "The petty vices of boys are
like the innocent kicks of colts," and their essential goodness,

like their beards, will become evident as they grow to manhood. The bachelor deposits with the confidence man a sum
of money for the future delivery of a "sound boy." But the
moment he is gulled, he begins to have second thoughts
about his departed companion: "Analogically, he [the bach-
elor] couples the slanting cut of the equivocator's coat-tails
with the sinister cast in his eye; he weighs slyboot's sleek
speech in the light imparted by the oblique import of the
smooth slope of his worn boot-heels; the insinuator's un-
dulating flunkyisms dovetail into those of the flunky beast
that windeth his way on his belly." By the time the bachelor
has realized that he has been taken in by the devil, the confidence man appears again—as the cosmopolitan. In this
new guise the confidence man almost regains the bachelor's
confidence, but ironically the bachelor mistakes him for a
fellow misanthrope. With this error, the confidence man departs, "leaving the discomfited misanthrope to the solitude
he [holds] so sapient."

Thus, directly or indirectly, the confidence man is successful, even with the most mistrustful, in his gulling of mankind.
He meets his match, however, in the mystic, Mark Winsome,
and his disciple, Egbert, who turn the tables and gull the
devil. Like the wooden-legged cynic and the invalid Titan,
Winsome and Egbert recognize the confidence man for the
devil he is, but they resort to wiles rather than force and
save themselves a gulling by besting the devil at his own
con game. Winsome and Egbert alone on the *Fidèle* understand the nature of evil sufficiently to be able to cope with
it without getting hurt or duped. At the conclusion of the
encounter, the confidence man, instead of extracting money,
hands over a shilling to Egbert—an act symbolizing the
devil's recognition of his own defeat.

Mark Winsome has the "look of plain propriety of a Puritan sort, with a kind of farmer dignity" and has "that look
of youthfulness in maturity, peculiar sometimes to habitual

health of body, the original gift of nature, or in part the effect or reward of steady temperance of the passions." Most marked in Winsome, however, are "shrewdness and mythiness, strangely jumbled"; he seems "some kind of cross between a Yankee peddler and a Tartar priest." Winsome first accosts the confidence man to warn him against the charlatanism of Charles Noble, but he recognizes right away that the cosmopolitan is no innocent victim of petty trickery. When the confidence man begins to speak of the "latent benignity of that beautiful creature, the rattlesnake," he becomes so intent on what he is saying that he begins "to wreath his form and sidelong crest his head, till he all but [seems] the creature described." Winsome observes this revealing metamorphosis "with little surprise, apparently, though with much contemplativeness of a mystical sort." This scene, indeed, is a scene of recognition, and all of Winsome's subsequent actions are determined by his discovery that he is dealing with the devil. Realizing that he will need all his wits, he not only refuses the offer of wine but so suppresses his emotions that he becomes "purely and coldly radiant as a prism." When a disheveled, dirty man interrupts their conversation, the confidence man calls the beggar his "friend" and willingly pays a shilling for his "transcendental" tract. The mystic realizes at once that this pathetic figure has been conjured up by the devil to aid in the softening up of a potential victim and, assuming "an expression of keen Yankee cuteness," refuses to contribute, claiming the man is a "cunning vagabond" who is "playing the madman."

Winsome introduces Egbert, his disciple, as the man who puts his theory into practice, asserting, "any philosophy that, being in operation contradictory to the ways of the world, tends to produce a character at odds with it, such a philosophy must necessarily be but a cheat and a dream." Winsome repeatedly claims that his philosophy is practical, a "serviceable knowledge" which recognizes "that mouth and purse must be filled." He does not propose a "soft Utopianism" nor does he support a doctrine that will lead to the "mad house [or] the poor-house." When Winsome withdraws, Egbert proves, on a practical level in a test of wits, that he is equal to the subtle deceptions of his antagonist. Indeed, after the confidence man fails to gull him by the elaborate pretense of friendship, Egbert takes the situation in hand and relates the long story of China Aster to demonstrate the paradoxical instance of a man ruined by the "generosity" of his friends, or, as China Aster's tombstone related—"ruined by allowing himself to be persuaded, against his better sense, into the free indulgence of confidence, and an ardently bright view of life." The confidence man protests that China Aster's "bright view" was "but a cheerful trust that, if he but kept up a braver heart, worked hard, and ever hoped for the best, all at last would go well"—a trust which is precisely that which the confidence man has been promoting and exploiting on the *Fidèle* (and which, incidentally, seems to be the popular and peculiarly American myth). When the confidence man ironically accuses the Winsome philosophy of being "inhuman," gives Egbert a shilling, and stalks off in "grand scorn," he is acknowledging his single major defeat on the *Fidèle*.

If Winsome and Egbert really do at times seem inhuman in their dealings with the confidence man, it is because they know that they cannot share human sympathies with the non-human—with the devil himself. Further, their identity as Emerson and Thoreau, or the ideal and practical sides of Emerson, is not so important ultimately as their relation with other Melvillean characters, and particularly with Babbalanja of *Mardi* and Plinlimmon of *Pierre*. Winsome's "incoherencies" are remarkably like Babbalanja's mutterings when possessed by his devil Azzageddi; and as Babbalanja found and accepted some kind of reconciliation of the ideal and the practical in the society of Serenia, so Winsome does not let his mystic vision obscure his steady view of this world and its practical demands. His disciple Egbert is living proof of the reconciliation of the ideal and the actual which his philosophy achieves. Like Plinlimmon in *Pierre*, though not with his terminology, Winsome distinguishes between "chronometric" and "horological" ethics and advises man, while on earth, to abide not by heaven's law but earth's. Actually, Winsome (through his essay on friendship and through its application in Egbert's story of China Aster) goes farther than Plinlimmon in reconciling the apparent contradictions in the two codes of behavior: the "friendship celestial" may indeed exist on earth, but it must not be called upon to fill terrestrial functions, or catastrophe (as with China Aster) will result. Winsome thus demonstrates what Plinlimmon states but does not show: that heavenly and earthly "law," though different, are not necessarily opposed or incompatible.

The gulled devil turns from Winsome and Egbert to an easy victim, to that barber who was introduced in the first chapter of the book as he put a "No Trust" sign up to begin his business day. The devil as the cosmopolitan has no real difficulty in maneuvering the barber into taking down his sign by the simple trick of promising to make up any losses. The confidence man then walks away without paying for his services, the barber realizing too late that he has been the victim of a "man-charmer"—an ingenious term suggesting that the confidence man's success stems from the evil (or snake) in man's make-up. Having come full circle in his gulling of the barber, the confidence man claims one more victim before we lose him, to our distress, in the crowd. This last victim, "a clean, comely old man, his head snowy as the marble, and a countenance like that which imagination ascribes to good Simeon," is first portrayed studying a Bible under a "solar lamp" whose shade is adorned by pictures of

14

a flaming "horned altar" and a "robed man, his head en-
circled by a halo." Clearly this individual is Christian, related spiritually to that white-clad proponent of charity, the
mute who (like the barber) appeared in the first chapter.
After establishing that they are agreed in their charitable
trust of mankind, the confidence man again resorts to his
tricks and conjures up a boy-assistant who reveals the old
man's almost hysterical distrust by selling him a traveler's
patent lock, a money-belt, and a counterfeit detector. Armed
with these tokens of "confidence," together with a life-pre-
server (which "seems so perfect—sounds so very hollow"),
the old man is "kindly led" away by the cosmopolitan. The
simple Christian who, even when he experiences it directly,
cannot comprehend the inapplicability in any absolute sense
of the divine law to the human situation proves an easy dupe
for the devil. The confidence man turns off the solar lamp and
leads the old man away in the dark. And the book concludes:
"Something further may follow of this Masquerade." The
action cannot end, for the devil is still among us, testing his
tricks as we travel on the *Fidèle*. Indeed, he may very well be
in the chair across from us as we close *The Confidence-Man*
and look about with a slight feeling of discomfort and expectation.

10
Clarel: *cross bearers all*

Melville's four-part poem, *Clarel: A Poem and Pilgrimage in the Holy Land*, was published privately in 1876 with funds, as the dedication confesses, supplied by Melville's kinsman, Peter Gansevoort. This was the only really significant appearance of Melville in print from the publication of *The Confidence-Man* in 1857 to his death in 1891. Three volumes of lyric poems did appear, at widely separated intervals, but these volumes made hardly a ripple on the still surface of his life; while *Billy Budd*, which he finished in 1891, was not published until 1924.

The imaginative and intellectual force of *Clarel* proves, however, that Melville had not exhausted his creative powers. It would seem more likely that he had used up his material, which he himself had largely restricted to the experiences of his youth. It would seem, too, that he had either exhausted or lost the sympathies of those closest to him for his work. His wife exclaimed of *Clarel* in one of her private letters of 1876: "If ever this dreadful *incubus* of a *book* (I call it so because it has undermined all our happiness) gets off Herman's shoulders I do hope he may be in better mental health." Just as this remark reveals the complexity of a relationship we can never fully understand, so too Melville's casual description of *Clarel* in an 1884 letter suggests an attitude toward his work quite difficult to comprehend: "a metrical affair, a pilgrimage or what not, of several thousand lines, eminently adapted for unpopularity."

Melville had used his early voyages and journeys in his

major fictional works; so too he availed himself of the experience gained on his extended pilgrimage in the Holy Land (1856-57) for his one full-length narrative-philosophical poem. Some ten years separate the taking of the trip and the publication of the poem. But when he turned to its composition, he did not have to rely entirely on memory. Melville had kept a journal where he jotted down miscellaneous observations and meditations which later on could serve to renew and refresh memories and impressions, just as he had on his 1849 trip to England to arrange for the publication of *White Jacket.* The journal does not, however, expose to view Melville's internal struggles during this critical period of his life (his family had sent him abroad to prevent what seemed to be an approaching nervous collapse); rather it presents a daily account, limited for the most part to barren facts and cryptic notations. In England, which he visited on his way to Constantinople, Melville recorded a day with Hawthorne as follows: "*Wednesday Nov 12* at Southport. An agreeable day. Took a long walk by the sea. Sands & grass. Wild & desolate. A strong wind. Good talk." There is little here to satisfy curiosity about the Melville-Hawthorne relationship, but we can guess that the bare details of the setting—*wild, desolate, strong wind*—could recall much to Melville's mind when he thumbed through these pages and contemplated creation of the parallel Clarel-Vine relationship in his long narrative poem. We can determine much more fully what the "good talk" along the sandy, windy seacoast was about from the fictional *Clarel* than from the factual journal.

Clarel opens:

In chamber low and scored by time,
Masonry old, late washed with lime—
Much like a tomb new-cut in stone;
Elbow on knee, and brow sustained

All motionless on sidelong hand,
A student sits, and broods alone.

This rhythm and rhyme, with only slight variation, are main-
tained for some six hundred pages. Only the supremely un-
critical and enthusiastic admirer of Melville can read *Clarel*
without tiring of the monotonous, rhyming iambic tetrameter
and yearning for a return to the vigorous, unrestrained but
subtly disciplined style of *Moby Dick*. Indeed, there are those
who persuasively argue that there is more poetry in the prose
of *Moby Dick* than in the metrics of *Clarel*. But for all its
defects of form, *Clarel* has a fascination peculiarly its own
which the critics have been slow in affirming. Their hesitance
may have been caused by the poem's formidable length.
Though no longer an entirely forgotten or completely neglected work, *Clarel* has not yet taken its proper, prominent
position in the Melville canon.

1   *The Young Seeker*

In *Clarel* there appears again a familiar Melvillean figure—
the Young Seeker. Clarel is an American student-tourist
beset by questions and doubts; he hopes on his tour of the
Holy land to resolve them and, in the resolution, discover
intellectual peace. The narrative which provides the frame
for the poem's weighty philosophy is remarkably frail and
frequently melodramatic. In Part I, "Jerusalem," Clarel,
touring the Holy City chances to meet the dark and attractive Ruth—daughter of an American Jew, Nathan, who had
returned with his family to live out his life in the land and the
faith of his ancestors. A single glimpse of Ruth is enough to
win Clarel's heart:

She looked a legate to insure
That Paradise is possible
Now as hereafter. 'Twas the grace
Of Nature's dawn: an Eve-like face. . . .
A dove, she seemed, a temple dove,
Born in the temple or its grove.

The reader of Melville, and especially of *Pierre*, will detect in this description a foreshadowing of deprivation in the very promise of paradise. In exploring the nature of Clarel's feelings toward Ruth, Melville recreates his classic situation:

Clarel, bereft while still but young,
Mother or sister had not known.

Ruth and her mother assume these roles for Clarel. And in the very midst of the love affair appears an obstacle only vaguely explained by concern for the difficulties Ruth's father is having in a new land:

Clarel, when in her [Ruth's] presence, strove
The unrest to hide which still could blend
With all the endearings of their love.

Clarel's restlessness bears a startling resemblance to Pierre's in his courting of Lucy.

When Ruth's father, Nathan, is killed by marauding Arabs, Ruth and her mother must, in accordance with Jewish custom, go into prolonged seclusion for mourning, during which time Clarel is unable to visit them. As he waits for this period of time to pass, Clarel decides to join a caravan making a trip through the wilderness to Bethlehem and back—

                    . . . Lot's land,
And sea, and Judah's utmost drought

Fain would he view, and mark their tone:
And prove if, unredeemed by John,
John's wilderness augmented doubt.

The remainder of the poem is devoted largely to interminable philosophical conversations which take place on the
tour. In Part II, "The Wilderness," Clarel and his companions traverse the desert and view the Dead Sea, where
one of the party dies; in Part II, "Mar Saba," the caravan
stops at a monastery of that name high in the mountains,
where another "pilgrim" dies; and in Part IV, "Bethlehem,"
the group tours Christ's birthplace. At the very end of this
final book, Clarel returns to Jerusalem to discover both
Ruth and her mother dead—from fever, or grief, or perhaps
both.

Stricken with grief, Clarel cries out against the Jews,
whose faith, he claims, kept him from Ruth's side during
her period of mourning:

And ye—your tribe—'twas ye denied
Me access to this virgin's side
In bitter trial: take my curse!—
O blind, blind, barren universe!
Now am I like a bough torn down,
And I must wither, cloud or sun!—
Had I been near, this had not been.

Although in his first bitterness and sorrow Clarel wants to
die ("Take me, take me, Death! / Where Ruth is gone, me
thither whirl, / Where'er it be!"), his passion gradually sub-
sides into a dirge of love:

Stay, Death. Not mine the Christus-wand
Wherewith to charge thee and command:
I plead. Most gently hold the hand
Of her thou leadest far away;

Fear thou to let her naked feet
Tread ashes—but let mosses sweet
Her footing tempt, where'er ye stray.

When Clarel last sees Ruth, in his vision of his dead friends in procession, she has become remote and transformed:

But Ruth—ah, how estranged in face.
He knew her by no earthly grace:
Nor might he reach to her in place.

Clarel's final act is to search· for a faith to sustain him: "Where, where now He who helpeth us, The Comforter?— Tell, Erebus!"

This narrative skeleton seems quite unpromising, and, indeed, it proves almost irrelevant (like the narrative in *Mardi*) to the poem's real content—the philosophical and religious debates carried on by various of the poem's numerous characters. Many of these emerge in familiar Melvillean roles. The real drama of the poem lies outside the central action in the constantly shifting, alternately relaxed and tense interrelationships of these several characters. There is Derwent, the talkative English clergyman, who wears the mask of congenial optimism to shield his religious doubts from the world and himself. There is Vine, brilliant and attractive, whose mask is not meant to deceive so much as to isolate him from his fellow man. There are the rebellious Titans, Nehemiah, Mortmain, and Ungar, the first a religious fanatic bent on converting the wicked world, the latter two, fanatics of despair whose eyes are open only to man's abundant capacity for evil. And there is Rolfe, the finest example of Melville's maskless man, who sees the world as it is and confronts it directly with physical and mental poise. All of these characters vie for Clarel's emotional and intellectual allegiance, and it is the "messmate of the elements"—Rolfe—who finally wins.

2   Confidence man and recluse

The English Clergyman, Derwent, is the petty deceiver, the
poem's confidence man, whose transactions are not in coin
but in an "easy" religious faith. When he is introduced in
the Chaucer-like "prologue" of Part II, he is described as
one who kept up with changing fashions in ideas:

Thought's last adopted style he showed;
Abreast kept with the age, the year,
And each bright optimistic mind

As the journey progresses, it becomes clear that the chief
content of Derwent's congenial religion is his omnipresent
optimism, a trait which he affably attributes to Christ:

I do avow He still doth seem
Pontiff of optimists supreme!

Such constant and apparently shallow optimism is bound to
irk Derwent's earnest companions, unsettled yet in belief,
seeking truth not ease. Mortmain, the bitter Swede, accuses
Derwent of "Trying to cheerfulise Christ's moan."
    In his search for an adherent of a philosophy of depth
and genuine profundity, the student Clarel does not take
long to penetrate Derwent's smiling surfaces. Derwent's "easy
skim / Never had satisfied throughout." In an interview
between the two (in a canto significantly entitled "In Confidence"), Clarel frankly expresses his doubts intensified
by the "din of clashed belief" he has discovered in Palestine,
and by the "strife intestine" at home, where "The very pews
are each a sect." Derwent's reply reveals that he himself
has not resolved the doubts uttered by Clarel, but that he

has simply cast them aside. He asserts that he makes a "clean breast" as he advises:

Have Faith, which, even from the myth,
Draws something to be useful with:
In any form some truths will hold;
Employ the present-sanctioned mould.

Derwent advises a faith of easy expediency if not of opportunism. His defense of his hypocrisy—his pretending to believe what he does not really believe—is based on his total rejection of the intellect in the fear that it leads to discomfort. He says to Clarel:

My fellow-creature, do you know
That what most satisfies the head
Least solaces the heart? Less light
Than warmth needs earthly wight.
Christ built a hearth: the flame is dead
We'll say, extinct; but lingers yet,
Enlodged in stone, the hoarded heat.
Why not nurse that? Would rive the door
And let the sleet in?

As Derwent cannot achieve a balance between head and heart, he rejects the intellect and takes the way of easy comfort. He confesses that once he, like Clarel, had been in uneasy intellectual turmoil:

                    All your ado
In youth was mine; your swarm I knew
Of buzzing doubts. But is it good
Such gnats to fight? or well to brood
In selfish introverted search,
Leaving the poor world in the lurch?
Not so did Christ.

Derwent, with the slick and easy prattle of the confidence
man, makes over Christ in his own image. Christ, says Derwent, lived too in a "troubled era" and faced the same
"problem gray," and his solution was like Derwent's:

Then heed Him, heed His eldership:
In all respects did Christ indeed
Credit the Jews' crab-apple creed
Whereto He yet conformed? or so
But use it, graft it with His slip
From Paradise?

Assured that his picture of Christ as the conformer and
compromiser is persuasive, Derwent exclaims:

Be not extreme. Midway is best.
Herein 'tis never as by Nile—
From waste to garden but a stile.
Betwixt rejection and belief,
Shadings there are—degrees, in brief.

Derwent's middle way is not the balance of head and heart
but the comfortable suspension between "rejection and belief."
    Derwent assures Clarel that the student's intellectual
quest is "obsolete, no more the mode." And he condemns
Rolfe and Vine, too, for the same old-fashioned doubts—they
are "much like prints from plates but old." When Clarel
cites Job, and pleads—

Own, own with me and spare to feign,
Doubt bleeds, nor Faith is free from pain!

Derwent grows flustered, averts his face, and exclaims:

            Alas, too deep you dive.
But hear me yet for little space:

This shaft you sink shall strike no bloom:
The surface, ah, heaven keeps *that* green;
Green sunny: nature's active scene,
For man appointed, man's true home.

In spite of himself, Derwent has briefly "spared to feign,"
has momentarily removed his mask, and has thus revealed
that his cheerful optimism is an uneasy deceit rather than a
solid faith, that it derives from denying or ignoring reality
rather than achieving a balanced view which recognizes
both bright and black.

As Derwent is, appropriately, most fully revealed in the
canto entitled "In Confidence," so Vine is significantly introduced in a canto called "The Recluse," in which his cool,
aloof nature is deeply probed:

> Vine's manner shy
> A clog, a hindrance might imply;
> A lack of parlour-wont. But grace
> Which is in substance deep and grain
> May, peradventure, well pass by
> The polish of veneer. No trace
> Of passion's soil or lucre's stain,
> Though life was now half-ferried o'er.

Although past middle-age, Vine shows no sign of earthly
struggle, no human scars. But he is no saint:

> What cooled the current? Under cheer
> Of opulent softness, reigned austere
> Control of self. Flesh, but scarce pride,
> Was curbed: desire was mortified;
> But less indeed by moral sway
> Than doubt if happiness thro' clay
> Be reachable.

Vine's withdrawal is not a shrinking of the self but rather an
assertion of pride, an aloofness from the human scene, an

expression of superiority akin to White Jacket's in donning his garment of purity:

> Like to the nunnery's denizen
> His virgin soul communed with men
> But thro' the wicket.

Melville dives deep into Vine's motives only to surface with new enigmas:

> Was it clear
> This coyness bordered not on fear—
> Fear or an apprehensive sense?
> Not wholly seemed it diffidence
> Recluse. Nor less did strangely wind
> Ambiguous elfishness behind
> All that: an Ariel unknown.

Whatever the cause or motive, Vine lives in an impenetrable isolation:

> Thronged streets astir
> To Vine but ampler cloisters were.

Vine is clearly related not only to White Jacket (before the loss of the coat) but also to Bartleby the scrivener, whose withdrawal from the human scene extends finally to death, and to Benito Cereno, the Spanish Captain, who, in horror at the evil he had witnessed, retired to a real cloister and, then, like Bartleby, made the ultimate withdrawal. But though Vine appears to inhabit a cloister, Melville modifies the metaphor:

> No monk he was, allow;
> But gleamed the richer for the shade
> About him, as in sombre glade
> Of Virgil's wood the Sibyl's Golden Bough.

During the course of the long journey through the wilderness to the Dead Sea, Clarel and Vine are to fumble with an intimacy that strikes a discord for both. On one crucial occasion, Clarel seeks out Vine and finds him, as usual, apart and alone and radiant with innocence:

> Pure as the rain
> Which diamondeth with lucid grain
> The white swan in the April hours
> Floating between two sunny showers
> Upon the lake, while buds unroll;
> So pure, so virginal in shrine
> Of true unworldliness looked Vine.

Drawn instinctively toward this "unworldliness," this "clear sweet ether of the soul," Clarel feels a "thrill / Of personal longing":

> Thought he, How pleasant in another
> Such sallies, or in thee, if said
> After confidings that should wed
> Our souls in one:—Ah, call me *brother!*—
> So feminine his passionate mood
> Which, long as hungering unfed,
> All else rejected or withstood.

During this entire episode, Clarel's strong feelings are coursing through subterranean depths while the conversation meanders and rambles on superficially.

Finally the student lets fall "some inklings" of his emotions, and Vine, all restraint and reserve again, retreats immediately into the shadows of his spiritual isolation as if to say:

> Why, on this vernal bank to-day,
> Why bring oblations of thy pain
> To one who hath his share? here fain

Would lap him in a chance reprieve?
Lives none can help ye; that believe.
Art thou the first soul tried by doubt?
Shalt prove the last? Go, live it out.

But Vine has also detected, Clarel senses, the student's personal longing, and seems to say:

But for thy fonder dream of love
In man toward man—the soul's caress—
The negatives of flesh should prove
Analogies of non-cordialness
In spirit.

Stung by these imaginary rebukes, Clarel pulls back into
himself and suppresses his feelings, as he accuses himself:

How findest place within thy heart
For such solicitudes apart
From Ruth?

Vine's aloof purity turns out to be an incapacity for close
human companionship, an inability to share spiritually with
others the doubts and affirmations of life. He wears the
mask of shy purity to conceal his deficiency of sympathy
for the common human condition.

3   Titans and rebels

Three characters in *Clarel*, Nehemiah, Ungar, and Mortmain, are unrelenting critics of man and his evil, and each
has his individual obsession—or monomania. Clarel in his
search hears each of them, and with the greatest sympathy,

but ultimately he turns from them all as somehow, someway deficient.

In Book I, Nehemiah, the wandering prophet, steps out of the crowded streets of Jerusalem into Clarel's path to be his guide. He seems half saint, half madman,

> Giving those years on death which verge
> Fondly to that enthusiast part
> Oft coming of a stricken heart
> Unselfish, which finds solace so.

His mission is both simple and impossible:

> Passages, presages he knew:
> Zion restore, connect the Jew,
> Reseat him here, the waste bedew;
> Then Christ returneth: so it ran.
> No founded mission chartered him;
> Single in person as in plan,
> Absorbed he ranged, in method dim,
> A flitting tract-dispensing man.

Haunting the streets of Jerusalem, Nehemiah converts no one but is tolerated by all. His mad faith seems to grant him a heavenly innocence which shines forth for all to see:

> For, say what cynic will or can,
> Man sinless is revered by man
> Thro' all the forms which creeds may lend.

Nehemiah's wild prophecies are strangely fulfilled for himself, at the end of Book II of *Clarel*, in the wilderness by the Dead Sea. During a night of illness, his "throbbing brain o'erwrought by travel," Nehemiah beholds in his dreams a vision of the New Jerusalem for which he had so frequently yearned, and he hears a "great voice":

Pain is no more, no more is death;
I wipe away all tears: Come, ye,
Enter, it is eternity.

Yielding to the beckoning voice, Nehemiah gives up the
ghost.

If Nehemiah is an extreme of simplicity, all heart and
little mind, Ungar, the Titan who steps to center stage in
Book IV of *Clarel*, is an extreme of complexity, mostly intellect with little heart. Though "sprung from Romish race,"
he himself

       had spared to feed
On any one elected creed
Or rite, though much he might recall
In annals bearing upon all;
And, in this land named of Behest,
A wandering Ishmael from the West.

Ungar emerges as the scourge of mankind, prophesying
(as Rolfe tells him) a "dark extreme" which wells up from a
monomaniacal view of the colossal and inevitable evil of
man's nature. Nehemiah prophesies the advent of another
world; Ungar prophesies the doom of this. The grand social
experiment in the New World will prove but one thing:

Be sure 'twill yield to one and all
New confirmation of the fall
Of Adam.

Ungar presents a frightening vision of the possible future of
America, with "Myriads playing pygmy parts— / Debased
into equality":

Dead level of rank commonplace:
An Anglo-Saxon China, see,

May on your vast plains shame the race
In the Dark Ages of Democracy.

Ungar offers no hope of a way out of his dark prophecies,
but instead finds constant confirmation of them. He cries
out in defiance to the stumbling, seeking world:

What incantation shall make less
The ever-upbubbling wickedness!

Clarel listens to Ungar's misanthropic thrusts with great
care, but at last reasons his way to the correct questions—
and doubts:

If man in truth be what you say,
And such the prospects for the clay,
And outlook of the future—cease!
What's left us but the senses' sway;
Sinner, sin out life's petty lease:
We are not worth the saving.

But between Nehemiah's mad prophecies of Book I and
Ungar's dark predictions of Book IV appears *Clarel's* Titanic
rebel and master despairer, Mortmain. The first we see this
bitter Swede he is pronouncing his outraged judgment:

Man's vicious: snaffle him with kings;
Or, if kings cease to curb, devise
Severer bit.

Like Taji, Ahab, and Pierre, Mortmain's search is for an
unrealizable ideal:

That uncreated Good
He sought, whose absence is the cause
Of creeds and atheists, mobs and laws.
Precocities of heart outran
The immaturities of brain.

And like all the other Titanic rebels in Melville, Mortmain
discovers himself committed to a greater evil than the one
he would destroy. Melville's comments might well stand as
inscription for all his greatest sinners:

Yea, ponder well the historic page:
Of all who, fired with noble rage,
Have warred for right without reprieve,
How many spanned the wings immense
Of Satan's muster, or could cheat
His cunning tactics of retreat
And ambuscade?

It is Mortmain who, in a ritualistic gesture of self degra-
dation, scoops a handful of the "Sodom waters dead" to sip
the bitter "gall." And it is Mortmain who seats himself on
a camel's skull by the Dead Sea to meditate on the wickedness of the "Cities Five / Engulfed." The catastrophe was not
entirely caused by "carnal harlotry":

'Tis *thou* who servedst Mammon's hate
Or greed through forms which holy are—
Black slaver steering by a star,
'Tis *thou*—and all like thee in state
Who knew the world, yet varnished it;
Who traded on the coast of crime
Though landing not; who did outwit
Justice, his brother, and the time—
These, chiefly these, to doom submit.
But who the manifold may tell?
And sins there be inscrutable,
Unutterable.

These "crimes of the spirit" constitute the real wickedness
of mankind, and Mortmain seems to refer obliquely to his
own sins of despair and bitterness at the close of this mono-
logue. Although lucid in his perception of the guilt of

humanity, Mortmain seems unable to accept his own heritage of responsibility for that guilt, as he is unwilling to
recognize his own complicity. Like Nehemiah, though without his religious fanaticism and simple innocence, Mortmain
is unable to make his peace with the world's evil and is
doomed to die. As the caravan leaves Nehemiah by the
Dead Sea, it departs from the Mar Saba monastery without
Mortmain. Always isolated in life, the Swede remains apart
in death, for the monks bury him just outside the "conse-
crated" walls. In neither life nor death can he remove the
galling garment—his white jacket of aloneness.

4   *Genial heart and brain austere*

There are a number of minor characters in *Clarel* who appear briefly on the scene and then go on their way, many of
them admirable individuals who confront the world with
frankness and even gaiety. One of the strangest relationships in all of Melville's fiction is that which develops, without a word passing from one to the other, between Clarel
and the deformed youth, Celio, in Jerusalem. Celio is an
inhabitant of a Franciscan monastery, but, like Clarel, his
mind has opened to doubt and he cannot close it. In fact,
it is the torture of doubt in the open face of Celio that
draws Clarel to him in their few chance encounters in the
streets of Jerusalem; but, in one of the poem's minor tragedies, Celio dies before Clarel is able to strike up a friendship. One of Clarel's last acts before leaving Jerusalem on
his journey through the wilderness is to visit and meditate
at Celio's graveside, ironically found "among the fellowships
/ Of Rome's legitimate dead." Clarel feels a strong and
binding sympathy for a fellow victim of doubt. Other simi-

lar characters in *Clarel* are fortunately more happy, endowed with a more youthful heart. In Book II, the Smyr-
niote, one Glaucon by name, assumes the role of devotee to
merriment; he is "like a land of springs . . . he gushes so
with song." In Book III, it is first a joyful Cypriote, and next
a carefree Lesbian who abandon themselves to fun and
frolic. And in the last book of the poem a Lyonese, who
turns out, to Clarel's amazement, to be a Jew, advocates a
life of greater devotion to the pleasures; he exclaims to
Clarel:

. . . . You of the West,
What devil has your hearts possessed,
You can't enjoy?

But the most admirable character of the poem, maintaining a perfect balance between heart and intellect, and perhaps the fullest portrait of the maskless man in all of Melville, is Rolfe. One must go back to *White Jacket*'s Jack
Chase for a similar man. When Rolfe is first introduced he
is endowed with all of the finest Melvillean traits—

One read his superscription clear—
A genial heart, a brain austere—

And "though given to study," he is no "scholastic Partisan"
but a "messmate of the elements." He looks like a "trapper
or Pioneer." But above all, there is not the slightest deception in his make-up:

And yet, more bronzed in face than mind,
Sensitive still and frankly kind—
Too frank, too unreserved, may be,
And indiscreet in honesty.

In the progress of the poem an intellectual-spiritual struggle
develops between Rolfe and Vine for Clarel's mind and

soul. Rather early in the journey, at a time when Clarel is
drawn toward Vine, he thinks he detects inconsistencies in
Rolfe—

Clarel recalled each prior word
Of Rolfe which scarcely kept accord,
As seemed, with much dropped latterly

But later, Clarel seems intuitively to discover a core of
higher consistency in Rolfe. As he views Rolfe from a distance on one of their stops in the wilderness:

. . . . . . Then and there
Clarel first noted in his air
A gleam of oneness more than Vine's—

Rolfe gradually wins the admiration of Clarel, in spite of
the student's frequent dismay at his frankness. When Rolfe
says of the genial priest, Derwent—

Things all diverse he would unite:
His idol's an hermaphrodite

Clarel shrinks, but as quickly masters his "distaste":

. . . . . for still the hue
Rolfe kept of candour undefaced,
Quoting pure nature at his need,
As 'twere the Venerable Bede:
An Adam in his natural ways.

But in the face of his utter frankness, Rolfe can still be puzzling. His mind is not rigidly fixed upon one discovered
truth. He is capable of ardently defending Catholicism, arguing its ascendancy over Protestantism, and crying out at
America—

'Tis the New World that mannered me,
Yes, gave me this vile liberty
To reverence naught, not even herself.

But, later, Clarel is startled to discover the same Rolfe "involving all creeds in one fold / Of doubt" as he recognizes and recites the origin and counterpart of Christian ritual in pagan rites and customs, not only in Greece but also in "mid Pacific, where life's thrill / Is primal." These positions are not, of course, really contradictory, and may logically be held, as Clarel comes to understand, side by side, in a mind "Poised at self-centre and mature" such as Rolfe's. When a "crabbed scorpion" startles the group, Rolfe maintains his equanimity as he addresses it:

O small epitome of devil,
Wert thou an ox couldst thou thus sway?
No, disproportionate is evil
In influence. *Evil*, do I say?
But speak not evil of the evil:
Evil and good they braided play
Into one cord.

Rolfe's great virtue lies in his balance. He, too, can doubt, and can ponder long his doubts, but without abandoning himself to despair and death. But if he is capable of following, without monomania, the intricate paths of the intellect, he is also capable of making his way, without being duped, through the labyrinths of the heart. His is the ideal maskless nature—"a genial heart, a brain austere." He is "frankly kind"—a phrase which combines the fine features of both the mind and the heart: frankness is the mind's ultimate wisdom, and kindness the heart's final truth. Rolfe can acknowledge the rightness of the dark views of Mortmain and Ungar without assuming their despair. He can understand the value of Vine's solitude without joining him in retreat.

And he can comprehend Derwent's commitment to optimism without condoning his hypocrisy. Between a shallow optimism and a deep-plunging pessimism, between foolish hope and dark despair, Rolfe does indeed remain "poised at self-centre and mature."

5   Via Crucis

Amidst his numerous companions, and particularly through the example of Rolfe, Clarel finds his way not to a resolution of his disturbing doubts but to a position of poise and equanimity. Near the beginning of Book IV, as the party leaves Mar Saba for Bethlehem, he muses:

> What may man know?
> (Here pondered Clarel;) let him rule—
> Pull down, build up, creed, system, school,
> And reason's endless battle wage,
> Make and remake his verbiage—
> But solve the world! Scarce that he'll do:
> Too wild it is, too wonderful.
> Since *this* world, then, can baffle so—
> Our natural harbour—it were strange
> If *that* alleged, which is afar,
> Should not confound us when we range
> In revery where its problems are—

And when Clarel's greatest personal crisis arrives, in his discovery of the death of his beloved Ruth and her mother, his initial blind and furious grief is followed by a gradual reconciliation brought about in part by the age-old Christian ritual of Easter in the Holy Land. Clarel is last seen joining the throng of humanity, of every faith and creed, which

streams along the *Via Crucis,* the lane in Jerusalem along
which, tradition tells, Jesus once carried his cross:

As 'twere a frieze, behold the train!
Bowed water-carriers; Jews with staves,
Infirm gray monks; overloaded slaves;
Turk soldiers—young, with home-sick eyes;
A Bey, bereaved through luxuries;
Strangers and exiles; Moslem dames
Long-veiled in monumental white,
Dumb from the mounds which memory claims;
A half-starved vagrant Edomite;
Sore-footed Arab girls, which toil
Depressed under heap of garden-spoil;
The patient ass with panniered urn;
Sour camels humped by heaven and man,
Whose languid necks through habit turn
For ease—for ease they hardly gain.
In varied forms of fate they wend—
Or man or animal, 'tis one:
Cross-bearers all, alike they trend
And follow, slowly follow on.

The picture of the toiling, confused struggle of humanity
en masse, captured in these lines, recalls the jumbled and
crowded scene of travelers on the Mississippi steamboat
Fidèle in the opening pages of *The Confidence-Man;* but on
the *Via Crucis* emphasis is on the burden and the agony:
"Sluggish, life's wonted stream flows on."
    And here, on this street thronged with life, Clarel finds
his way out of his self-torment:

        But, lagging after, who is he
Called early every hope to test,
And now, at close of rarer quest,
Finds so much more the heavier tree?
From slopes whence even Echo's gone,

Wending, he murmurs in low tone:
'They wire the world—far under sea
They talk; but never comes to me
A message from beneath the stone.'

Clarel, at the "close of rarer quest," has found not what he
sought but "so much more the heavier tree." Shouldering his
cross, Clarel joins the pressing crowd and "vanishes in the
obscurer town." Clarel's plunge into the stream of humanity
on this obscure street, like White Jacket's plunge into the sea
or Ishmael's immersion in the whirlpool of the fated *Pequod*,
is an act of affirmation, a baptism into the world, a final acceptance of man's heritage and man's fate.

In his Epilogue, Melville gives his last word to cautious
hope. These last lines of *Clarel* are not so much an acceptance of Faith as an affirmation of the necessity of the heart.
From "Luther's day" to "Darwin's year," the struggle between Despair and Faith has intensified: as Despair
"scrawls undeterred his bitter pasquinade," Faith

Inscribes even on her shards of broken urns
The sign o' the cross—*the spirit above the dust!*

The battle between "ape and angel," "chimes and knell,"
"star and clod" shall run for ever, says Melville—"if there
be no God." Melville does not accept faith to the exclusion
of doubt, but rather he advises Clarel (and surely himself)
to reconcile heart (where faith and hope reside) and mind
(where live doubt and despair), and to hold them in a balance of sanity. As Clarel's entire quest has been the quest
of doubt, the search for wisdom, he must be reminded of
what he has neglected—the issues of the heart:

Then keep thy heart, though yet but ill-resigned—
Clarel, thy heart, the issues there but mind.

This is the advice that, heeded, could have saved Taji, Ahab, Pierre, and Mortmain from catastrophe and death. Melville concludes—

That like the crocus budding through the snow—
That like a swimmer rising from the deep—
That like a burning secret which doth go
Even from the bosom that would hoard and keep;
Emerge thou mayst from the last whelming sea,
And prove that death but routs life into victory.

"Emerge thou *mayst*," not "Emerge thou *will*." Though a remarkably eloquent conclusion, these last lines are not Melville's final reconciliation to a conventional Christian faith, but a plea for a balance of doubt with faith, a plea for the exclusion of the extremes of insane despair and foolish hope. Melville's final wisdom for Clarel is—"Though yet but ill-resigned," still "keep thy heart."

In his embracement of the brotherhood of humanity, from Jew to Moslem, Edomite to Arab, on the *Via Crucis,* Clarel is clearly meeting the issues of the heart: he takes the way of the cross—he acknowledges his complicity and takes up his human burden. His final knowledge is that all men, if they are to accept their humanity and remain human, must become not dying Christs but living cross-bearers; not uncompromising and suicidal Tajis, but balanced and living Babbalanjas; not defiant or destructive Ahabs and Pierres, but renewed and humanized White Jackets and Ishmaels; not withdrawing, death-seeking Bartlebys and Cerenos, but involved, life-living Delanos and Rolfes; not primitively innocent Billy Budds, but intricately wise Captain Veres.

11

Billy Budd: *the catastrophe of innocence*

On the manuscript of *Billy Budd* appeared the notation in Melville's hand that he had begun the story in 1888, started revision in 1889, and completed the work in 1891—the year of his death. For this final embodiment of his imaginative vision, Melville turned once again to the sea. But as though to avoid the gulf of time separating his old age from his youth at sea, Melville liberated his imagination from his own experience and turned to history: the turbulent period at the end of the eighteenth century, during the French-English Napoleonic wars, just after the Great Mutiny at Nore and its stern suppression by the alarmed British. The action of Melville's story is simple: Aboard a British ship during this period comes the primitively innocent sailor, Billy Budd, whose fate it is to force the ship's captain to the gravest decision of his career. The evil master-at-arms, Claggart, falsely accuses Billy of involvement in a conspiracy to mutiny; Billy, so astounded by the accusation that his speech is reduced to a stutter, strikes Claggart a blow that results in his death. Captain Vere, though he recognizes Billy's innocence, realizes that Billy must hang for his "crime" or the whole British fleet might become involved in new mutinies that would disrupt the order of the state. Captain Vere makes his decision: the innocent Billy hangs.

At first glance it might seem that Billy has much in common with Melville's "ideal" maskless men, the Jack Chases and Rolfes (the story opens with a generous dedication to Chase). And indeed he does, for his virtues of friendliness and frankness are theirs. But there is a practical or earthly wisdom in such individuals as Jack Chase and Rolfe, White Jacket and Ishmael, which is missing in Budd, and this vital deficiency makes him more akin to Taji, Ahab, Pierre, Mortmain—the Titanic Innocents who war with the world's evil and lose. It is this deficiency which renders Billy Budd incapable of comprehending much less coping with evil.

Criticism of *Billy Budd* has ranged as widely in its interpretation as has that great mass of writing on *Moby Dick*. Some critics have seen a retelling of the story of Christ that constitutes Melville's "testament of acceptance" after all the years of doubt and defiance. Others, interpreting it primarily as satire and irony, have seen a subtle diabolism at work throughout the story. Some have read the story as a commentary on the impersonality and essential brutality of the modern state, exacting death penalties of the innocent. Still others have found the tale an affirmation of the need, even at the risk of injustice, for society to protect itself and to assure order for the general welfare. It is not easy to sift the truth from all this conflicting comment, but an understanding of Melville's themes in his other works will help to clarify his meaning in *Billy Budd*.

1   A radical innocence

Almost invariably Melville has described his Titanic heroes as stricken Christs, but with none has the analogy been so complete as with Billy Budd. From beginning to end, Christ is the dominant metaphor of the story. When Billy is brought aboard the H.M.S. *Indomitable* in 1797, shortly after the Great Mutiny which had rocked the British fleet, he is the epitome of innocence. Asked the routine questions— where was he born, who was his father—he replies, significantly, "God knows, Sir." His reputation, borne out by his behavior aboard ship, is that of a peacemaker, one who can miraculously transfigure hate and hostility into admiration and love. When Billy stands falsely accused before his Captain and cannot speak, his expression is "a crucifixion to behold." And when he kills his accuser with one blow, his Captain mutters, "Struck dead by an angel of God." Billy's last words before he hangs are—"God bless Captain Vere." And even after his death (or ascension), his "legend" lives on, and the spar from which he was hanged becomes sacred: "to [sailors] a chip of it was as a piece of the Cross."

But Billy is much more complex than simply a duplicate of Christ. Christ-like, yes, but also like Adam—Adam before the Fall: "Billy in many respects was little more than a sort of upright barbarian, much such perhaps as Adam presumably might have been ere the urbane Serpent wriggled himself into his company." Captain Vere congratulates his officers on gaining in Billy "such a fine specimen of the genus homo who, in the nude might have posed for a statue of young Adam before the fall." In his character and his appearance, Billy is an Adam as well as a Christ. The main import of this figure is that it emphasizes Billy's ignorance of evil: unlike Christ's, Billy's innocence is compounded, like Adam's before he ate the fruit, of his lack of knowledge of good and evil, and not of a profound insight into the nature of the world and man.

In fact, throughout the tale Billy's ignorance and naïveté are so emphasized as the main components of his innocence that he seems, like an animal, deprived almost entirely of a moral faculty. Melville uses a number of metaphors to suggest the nature of Billy's innocence and the quality of his intelligence. Billy is a "sort of upright barbarian." His attitude toward death, containing no trace of the irrational fears of the "civilized," is like that of the "barbarous" tribes: "a barbarian Billy radically was." And Billy is child-like: ". . .

yet a child's utter innocence is but its blank ignorance, and the innocence more or less wanes as intelligence waxes. But in Billy Budd intelligence such as it was, had advanced, while yet his simple-mindedness remained for the most part unaffected." Without knowledge of evil gained through experience, Billy is also deprived of any "intuitive knowledge of the bad." Not without reason Billy goes on board by the name of Baby Budd. Billy has little or no self-consciousness —"or about as much as we may reasonably impute to a dog of St. Bernard's breed." Melville returns to this startling figure in describing Billy's reaction to Captain Vere's intricate remarks to the drumhead court trying Billy: the reasoning caused Billy "to turn a wistful interrogative look towards the speaker, a look in its dumb expressiveness not unlike that which a dog of generous breed might turn upon his master seeking in his face some elucidation of a previous gesture ambiguous to the canine intelligence."

Barbarian, child, dog— Christ and Adam—Billy Budd is indeed a strange mixture of many ingredients, perhaps a "simple-minded" but certainly a complex character. And increasing the complexity is Billy's "flaw," his "occasional liability to a vocal defect." Both as emblem and as fact, this "flaw" assumes a leading role in Billy's tragedy: "In this particular Billy was a striking instance that the arch interferer, the envious marplot of Eden still has more or less to do with every human consignment to this planet of earth. In every case, one way or another he is sure to slip in his little card, as much as to remind us—I too have a hand here." Billy's stammer is emblematic of his human imperfection, a symbol of the necessity for his adhering to the human condition because of his inborn incapacity to attain the divine.

Billy's stutter is not so much the cause of his catastrophe as its trigger. Billy by his very nature is hopelessly unfitted for existence in the world of men. He is naïve in his dedication to becoming so shipshape that he will never earn verbal reproof; he is immature in his fretting about his failure; and he is gullible in his persistence in believing, even when disabused by the cynical Dansker, in the kind disposition of the master-at-arms, John Claggart. Through his incapacity to understand the significance or consequences of evil, he fails to report to his officers the vaguely mutinous plan broached to him in secret. And when he stands falsely accused of inciting mutiny by the "friendly" John Claggart, Billy Budd can still neither comprehend nor cope with evil. He is struck dumb and cannot speak. And since he cannot speak he acts, and the only act he knows—barbarian-, child-, animal-like —is a blow. The Christ-like Billy, incapable of angelically turning the other cheek, answers with a solidly human— even Satanic—fist.

Billy's blow on Claggart symbolizes man's—perhaps America's—naïve attempt to obliterate natural depravity by a simple act of violence. And ironically, the act arises out of that very depravity (Billy's stutter, remember, is the "little card" of Satan) which it would destroy. The smallest denial from Billy's lips would have been enough for the already convinced Captain. But Billy's stammer would not let him speak and Billy's nature could not prevent him from violence. Like Ahab, Billy's only response to evil is to lash out and annihilate it. And like Ahab, Billy becomes inextricably entangled in the very evil which he would destroy.

2 A natural depravity

The Master-at-Arms, John Claggart, like Billy, is the last of a long line of similar Melvillean characters, but has, like Billy, his individuality. Claggart is the accomplished hypocrite. Like the missionaries in *Typee* and *Omoo*, like Red-

burn's captain and White Jacket's officers, like Derwent in
Clarel, like society generally in Melville, Claggart wears the
congenial mask of respectability to conceal from the world
his true nature. Claggart may be best described as a cross
between Fedallah, with his infinite capacity for the grossest
of evils, and the Confidence Man, with his cunning and craft
in the pettiest of crimes. The mask with which Claggart confronts his superiors is persuasive. His responsible position,
master-at-arms, a "sort of chief of police," has been be-
stowed upon him by his officers because of his "constitu-
tional sobriety, his ingratiating deference to superiors, together with a peculiar ferreting genius" and a "certain
austere patriotism."

Nothing less than "natural depravity" itself is the real mo-
tivating force within Claggart. This natural depravity has
the quality but not the universality of Calvin's. It has nothing to do with the brutish or the sordid or the sensual, but
is "dominated by intellectuality" and an overruling pride
which transcends "vices or small sins." The person born
with this "natural depravity" may appear "subject to the
law of reason"—but "toward the accomplishment of an aim
which in wantonness of malignity would seem to partake of
the insane, he will direct a cool judgment sagacious and
sound." Curiously enough, the master-at-arms is one of the
two individuals on the *Indomitable* "intellectually capable
of adequately appreciating the moral phenomenon presented in Billy Budd"—and the appreciation is galling. In a
passage which imparts to the relationship a fascinating psychological complexity, Melville speculates that, Claggart
being "well moulded" himself, it was probably Billy's "significant personal beauty" which aroused simultaneously Claggart's "envy and antipathy." But on the symbolic level Claggart's plot against Billy is one act in the eternal drama of
the war between good and evil, innocence and guilt.

Claggart at first devises small schemes to keep Billy, in

spite of his resolve to conform, in constant "petty" trouble. The first major encounter of the two is in a minor incident involving spilled soup. By accident Billy spills his soup-pan when Claggart happens to be passing the mess, and the "greasy liquid" rolls across the path of the master-at-arms. This small event, charged symbolically with psychological subtlety, comes to assume gigantic proportions in the minds of both. Claggart's quick but calculated exclamation— "Handsome is as handsome did"—disarms Billy (if the un-armed can be disarmed) by convincing him that Claggart is his friend. But the reply, too subtle for the victim or his companions, is ironic. In Claggart's distorted but keen intel-lect, the spilled soup is interpreted as "the sly escape of a spontaneous feeling on Billy's part more or less answering to the antipathy of his own." And Claggart welcomes this "justification" for shifting from trivial to significant plotting against Billy.

The scheme for entangling Billy in a mutinous conspiracy succeeds in appearances only, but that success is sufficient for Claggart's main purpose—the destruction of Billy. Nei-ther Captain Vere nor his officers could be convinced of Billy's guilt in a conspiracy, but they know of his guilt in kill-ing a superior officer—an individual "mutiny" extremely se-rious in war-time— and they must render judgment within the knowledge of the clear consequences of Billy's act on the crew. So Claggart's scheme succeeds not because of its cleverness but because of Billy's weakness at the crucial mo-ment of the accusation, his substitution of primitive violence for civilized reason. But Claggart's success necessitates his own death. As he lies sprawled under Billy's blow, Claggart's inert body resembles a "dead snake." But the Satanic snake is never really dead: Claggart's "soul" has no doubt taken flight to Hell, there to join the devil's eternal rebellion.

3 *Starry Vere*

If Billy is the subtly masked man of innocence, appearing
in the cloak of Christ's purity to the world and to himself
while in reality harboring the savage impulse of the barbarian, the child, the animal; and if Claggart is the deceitfully
masked man, deliberately and craftily misleading the world
as to his true evil nature; then Captain Vere is Melville's
maskless man, his man of forthrightness and frankness, who
by his balance of reason and emotion, mind and heart, recognizes evil and its inevitability on earth, comes to honorable
terms with it, and endures, albeit with a heightened tragic
vision.

Captain Vere is a middle-aged Jack Chase or Rolfe, past
their physical prime but exhibiting most of their fine qualities. As Billy Budd is a man of all heart and no intellect, and
John Claggart a man of all intellect and no heart, Captain
Vere is the man of moderation with heart and intellect in
ideal balance. He is wise enough to refrain from "developing" his virtues to that extreme at which they become vices.
He is mindful of the welfare of his men, but never [toler-
ates] an infraction of discipline." He is "intrepid to the
verge of temerity, though never injudiciously so." Though
he displays usually an "unobtrusiveness of demeanour" and
an "unaffected modesty," when the times call for action he
demonstrates that he possesses a "resolute nature." Though
he is "practical enough upon occasion," he betrays sometimes a "certain dreaminess of mood." In all things, that is,
Captain Vere avoids exaggerations, extremes. His nickname
—Starry Vere—might at first appear ironic to one who,
"whatever his sturdy qualities," is "without any brilliant
ones." But the stars themselves, unlike the sun, are not flash-

ily brilliant: they are held sturdily fixed in heavenly balance.

Like Melville's admirable maskless men such as Rolfe and
Chase, Captain Vere adds to an instinctive wisdom the wisdom of books: he likes "unconventional writers, who, free
from cant and convention, like Montaigne, honestly, and in
the spirit of common sense philosophize upon realities." This
love of books, though it deprives him of a certain boisterous
"companionable quality" common to his profession, and
though it gains him the reputation of possessing a "queer
streak of the pedantic," nevertheless underlines the dominant trait of his personality—his utter openness. He is interested in confronting the "realities," which he is so avid to
read about, without flinching and without a trace of deception. It is precisely this bluntness (characteristic also of
Rolfe and Jack Chase) which, though never cruel, frequently
puzzles or startles his colleagues and sets Starry Vere apart.
Melville carefully points out that in natures like Captain
Vere's, "honesty prescribes to them directness, sometimes
far-reaching like that of a migratory fowl that in its flight
never heeds when it crosses a frontier."

Captain Vere's crucial action in handling Billy Budd's
trial demonstrates that he is the only individual on board
the *Indomitable* who understands what White Jacket instinctively learned on his voyage and what Plinlimmon formulated as a philosophy in his pamphlet—the wide and necessary separation of heavenly and earthly wisdom, and the
"impossibility" of the application of the one in the province
of the other. Captain Vere understands further—and it is
this understanding that divides his sympathies and almost
unbalances this balanced man—that both kinds of wisdom
are right in their place, that the "failure" of one out of its
place by no means signifies its insufficiency. It is this insight
that enables Captain Vere to sympathize so profoundly with
Billy Budd while at the same time arguing so persuasively

the necessity of his conviction. At Billy's execution, Captain Vere's emotions, as compelling as the crew's, are simply more intellectually disciplined. As Billy's "God bless Captain Vere" echoes about him, Vere, "either through stoic self-control or a sort of momentary paralysis induced by emotional shock, [stands] erectly rigid as a musket in the ship-armour's rack." When, some time after the Billy Budd incident, Captain Vere lies dying on his ship in the midst of battle, he is heard to murmur "Billy Budd, Billy Budd." A member of Billy's drumhead court is present to testify that the refrain is not whispered with "accents of remorse." On the verge of death, Captain Vere still clearly understands the necessity of his action even as he cries out his affection for his departed sailor.

When Billy Budd climbs to the scaffold for his punishment, his execution appears to be more an ascension than a death. As the hangman's signal is given, "the vapoury fleece hanging low in the east [is] shot through with a soft glory as of the fleece of the Lamb of God seen in mystical vision," and Billy ascends, "and ascending, [takes] the full rose of the dawn." Miraculously there is no involuntary movement or muscular spasm in Billy's body—nothing but the rhythmical motion created by the roll of the ship. This phenomenon, combined with the appearance of the large sea-fowls—who with their "outstretched wings and the cracked requiem of their cries" circle close and continuously the burial spot in the sea where Billy's body plunged—impresses upon the awed sailors a vaguely superstitious realization of the transcendent nature of the event they witness. Although Billy dies, his continued existence, like Claggart's, seems assured, for as surely as Claggart descended to Hell, there to enter the service of the devil, Billy ascends to Heaven, there to sit at the throne of God.

The portrait of Billy completes Melville's gallery of Titanic Innocents—Taji, Ahab, Pierre, Mortmain—all of

whom suffer from some intricate disorder that renders them
ultimately non-human. Melville created these "heroes" in a
"descending order" of self-awareness: Taji, as he commits
himself to an eternal search for Yillah, recognizes and confesses his own hardheartedness; Ahab, in gazing down into
the ocean and searching Fedallah's steady gaze, discovers
and reveals, but does not confront the consequences of his
awful commitment to evil; Pierre glimpses his "unconscious"
motives, but the horror is too great for his mind to hold;
Mortmain recognizes the universality of evil and his despair
grows from his instinctive awareness of his inability to dis-
sociate himself from it; but Billy Budd is lacking not only an
intellectual consciousness but even an instinctive awareness
of his potentiality for evil, in spite of his stutter and his
quick fist: he is the one completely unself-conscious
"masked Innocent." And unlike the others, he has in Captain Vere a hero of humanity who shields society from the
cataclysmic consequences of his nakedly spontaneous and
raw Innocence. Since Billy's disorder is that which springs
from the dominance of an out-sized heart over an almost
non-existent intellect, his fate, although catastrophic on
earth like that of the others, ultimately partakes of a spiritual transfiguration.

12

The figure retraced

The universe, as Taji, Ahab, and Pierre could not or would not understand, is an incomprehensible and inextricable tangle of good and evil. The world, as the confidence man so amply demonstrated, conceals an interior corruption with an exterior innocence. Man, as Redburn, White Jacket, Ishmael, and Clarel came to know, inevitably becomes involved with evil as a condition of life. In direct confrontation of these harsh facts, Melville worked out a bitter solution—bitter because it is the only alternative to death through defiance, withdrawal, suicide, or to hypocrisy that by a veneer of innocence compounds the evil beneath. The solution is a frank compromise of the ideal and the practical, of unattainable virtue and inevitable evil.

Melville's moral imagination sought a synthesis of qualities which, though in isolation they tended toward monstrosity, in union created the conditions for survival and endurance. A favorite image was the Apostolic serpent and dove. In Matthew 10:16, Christ says to the disciples: "Behold, I send you forth as sheep in the midst of wolves: be ye therefore wise as serpents, and harmless as doves." Ahab had the wisdom of the serpent; Billy Budd had the gentleness of the dove: each in different—yet similar—ways brought about his own death. Only rare characters, like Jack Chase, Israel Potter, and Captain Vere, possessed these qualities in a balance that granted an equilibrium to their souls. The serpent and the dove may be matched with many other dualities which run through Melville: mind and heart, wisdom and love, the civilized and the primitive, guilt and inno-

cence, black and white, hell and heaven, Satan and God.
These dualities may be traced in Melville's intellectual
background to the two dominant American philosophies,
Calvinism and transcendentalism, both of which figured
strongly in Melville's personal heritage.

From these same sources may be traced the origin of the
two Christs in Melville, the human Christ and the dying
Christ. Although Melville used the Christ metaphor frequently, he was always careful to distinguish between the
figure of Christ that he admired, and the figure he feared.
The first was the Christ who became human, who linked
himself inseparably with the human fate, who took as his
own burden man's guilt. The other Christ was the unyield-
ing, uncompromising idealist, the spotless innocent. The one
is the Christ who bore the cross, the other is the Christ who
died. Melville's distinction is perhaps best suggested in the
ambivalence of attitude in *White Jacket*. Melville says: "To
be efficacious, Virtue must come down from aloft, even as
our blessed Redeemer came down to redeem our whole
man-of-war world." But he also says: ". . . there seems almost some ground for the thought, that although our blessed
Saviour was full of the wisdom of heaven, yet His gospel
seems lacking in the practical wisdom of earth."

In metaphorically delineating two Christs, Melville en-
abled himself to use one or the other Christ figure for all his
important characters. White Jacket and Ishmael are Christs
because, as symbolized by their baptisms in the sea, they
renounce their innocence (as Christ gave up his divinity)
and accept their burden of human guilt. But at the same
time, Taji, Ahab, and Pierre are Christs because they refuse
to come to terms with evil, unyieldingly pursue uncontaminated virtue, and end in death. In his two last major works,
Melville portrayed the two Christs in the two leading roles
—Clarel and Billy Budd. The American student Clarel, in
his pilgrimage to the Holy Land, finds himself at the end of

his journey ritualistically reenacting the Christ-drama in Bethlehem and Jerusalem as he works out his grief over the death of his betrothed. But Clarel becomes the human Christ as he reconciles himself to the human fate and joins the crowds—"cross bearers all"—who throng the *Via Crucis* in Jerusalem. Billy Budd, on the other hand, becomes the dying Christ as he is hanged at the yardarm for his primitive and spontaneous murder of the ship's master-at-arms. Clarel gives up his innocence and lives. Billy Budd maintains his innocence and dies.

1   *Primitives, rebels, and hypocrites*

In order to comprehend the intricate design of Melville's themes it is useful to trace the origin, evolution, and ultimate fate of Melville's major types of recurring characters. It is perhaps best to begin where Melville began, with the primitive, instinctive individuals—the natives of *Typee*. For though Melville's later work ranged far from the Polynesian islands, the primitive continues to appear. Savages are, of course to be found in *Omoo* and *Mardi;* many of their qualities turn up among the seamen in *Redburn* and the "people" (or sailors) in *White Jacket;* and the primitive returns in vivid array in Queequeg, Tashtego, Dagoo, and Pip of *Moby Dick*. He disappears in *Pierre* but returns in the blacks of "Benito Cereno"; in John Paul Jones and Ethan Allen of *Israel Potter;* in Black Guinea, the Missouri bachelor and the Indian-hater of *The Confidence-Man;* and he has his final, full portrait drawn in the protagonist—the handsome sailor—of *Billy Budd*.

Some forty years separate the Typees from Billy Budd, but the traits of the elemental savage remain startlingly sim-

ilar. During this period Melville makes it perfectly clear
that the barbarian is not confined to primitive tribes in
limited geographical areas but might well step forth from
the most sophisticated of civilizations. In one instance—
John Paul Jones of *Israel Potter*—the savage only thinly
veneered with civilization is identified as symbolizing the
essential national spirit of America. Paradoxically the primitive type in Melville might range in meaning from the grossest of evils, as in *The Confidence Man*'s Black Guinea, to the
greatest of goods, as in *Moby Dick*'s Queequeg.

Indeed, though Black Guinea may be said to portray the
devil and Billy Budd to symbolize Christ, they still hold in
common a number of linking characteristics. Set apart by
their darkness or fairness, they are both barbarians who live
on the elemental level of emotion and instinct. Both are
grossly imbalanced, and radically deficient in the essentially
human. Such imbalance is the central quality of major significance in all of Melville's primitives. Ultimately Melville
rejects them—he abandons the Typees; he allows Pip and
Queequeg to perish. Sometimes Melville appears to imply
endurance in another, non-human world, as in the case of
Billy Budd. But invariably in Melville, in spite of good traits
or bad, the primitive's fate is to perish.

At the opposite pole from the primitive is the over-intel-
lectualized, obsessed rebel. As Melville's barbarian appears
devoid of mind, so his Titanic rebel seems—at least ultimately—devoid of heart. Some of Melville's most memorable and heroic figures must be placed in this category—Taji
in *Mardi*, Ahab in *Moby Dick*, the protagonist in *Pierre*,
Mortmain in *Clarel*. They all have in common their monomaniacal obsession with the world's evil and their dedication to its eradication and to attainment of an absolute, personal innocence. They all end in death, deeply entangled in
the evil with which they refuse to come to terms in life.

Taji's heart hardens as he sets forth from Serenia on his

endless, suicidal pursuit of the symbol of his lost innocence. In his final absolute allegiance to Fedallah, Ahab seems to will his soul to the devil as he sets forth in suicidal pursuit of his symbol of all the world's evil. Yillah and Moby Dick, white maiden and white whale, are two halves of the same mythic whole. Taji believes Yillah all good. Ahab sees Moby Dick all evil. But as Melville knows and his readers discover, and as Taji and Ahab refuse to recognize, the universe cannot be so tidily divided. There are no neat halves, but only exasperating entanglements. Pierre and Mortmain suffer from like illusions. In his ambiguous attempt to prevent scandal from touching his dead father and proud mother, Pierre achieves fulfillment of the dark desire of his unconscious, causes the deaths of all those near to him, and, finally, fatally poisons his own sickened self. As Pierre, like Taji, seems obsessed with the ideal, Mortmain, like Ahab, is obsessed with evil. Seated on a camel's skull sipping the bitter waters of the Dead Sea, Mortmain declaims to Clarel and his companions of the utter wickedness of man. As his bitterness and despair become an intolerable monomania, Mortmain seeks his own annihilation, not in a monumental struggle, but in quiet isolation.

Related to these rebels in their obsessive revulsion for this world are the title characters of "Benito Cereno," and "Bartleby the Scrivener," and Vine of *Clarel*. But Benito, Bartleby, and Vine do not rebel, nor do they even rail against the human situation. They merely withdraw. Don Benito is startled to discover the appalling reality of evil as the black slaves mutiny and take over his ship. During their reign of terror, Don Benito seems utterly helpless, incapable of coping with a force he cannot comprehend. When he is rescued by the naïve but forceful Captain Delano, Don Benito sinks into himself, refuses further traffic with this world, retires to a monastery, and there makes the ultimate withdrawal into death. Bartleby the Scrivener, although his precise motives are never made entirely clear, makes a similar withdrawal. His decision becomes plain after we hear several times his single answer to every request: "I would prefer not to." This refrain eventually makes clear Bartleby's preference not to live. Finally he prefers the serenity of death to the complicated and entangling demands of life. Vine in *Clarel* creates in fantasy his own monastery of the mind and withdraws into it from the human scene. Although he continues to live, his utter isolation results in a paleness of spirit that seems drained of the vital juices of life.

Many characters in Melville neither rebel nor withdraw, but compromise their integrity and make a hypocritical adjustment to life's realities. These are the masked men, the pretenders. Their deceitful souls are even more repugnant to Melville than the Titanic rebels, who at least exhibit a heroic if wrong-headed quality in their actions. Indeed, most of society in Melville exists on this contemptible, shallow, superficially pious level. The missionaries in *Typee* and *Omoo* establish the pattern of concealing their evil beneath a mask of virtue. The pattern recurs throughout *Mardi*, but especially in Maramma, where Alma (Christ) is professed but wickedness practiced. Redburn discovers in London the rich, plush exterior of evil, and White Jacket finds on the U.S.S. *Neversink* the inhumanity and brutality which bear the name of law and order. In *Moby Dick* Ishmael and Queequeg swap their disillusioning observations of the virtuous, white "civilization," while Mrs. Glendinning and Glen Stanly in *Pierre* symbolize polite, hypocritical society. Such a society makes its appalling reappearance in all the works—in *Israel Potter*, in the short stories, in *The Confidence-Man*—and comes to focus finally in the sharply drawn English clergyman, Derwent of *Clarel*, who is a direct descendant of both Pani of *Mardi*'s Maramma and the confidence man in all his guises. Derwent's geniality, optimism, and faith are such a thin veneer that they cannot ward off reality, in whose presence Derwent's stricken soul shudders.

Of course Melville disapproves suicidal rebellion or withdrawal into death or hypocritical compromise. And he portrays his heroic figures, such as Taji and Ahab, as ultimately becoming Satanic in their rebellion. Closely related to their fate is Satan himself, as he or his descendants appear to be embodied in a series of Melville's characters. Most important of these are Bland of *White Jacket* (interesting primarily as a prefiguration of the master-at-arms in *Billy Budd*), Fedallah of *Moby Dick,* the masquerading racketeer of *The Confidence-Man,* and Claggart of *Billy Budd.* The earliest of these, Master-at-Arms Bland in *White Jacket,* sets the pattern for Melville's most successful villains. In his role as police officer of the ship, Bland presents a front of superior respectability to the world. But when the truth is out, he is discovered violating the very laws he was entrusted to enforce. Fedallah in *Moby Dick* seems as thoroughly evil as Bland. But symbolizing as he does Ahab's own evil nature, developing from Ahab's shadow into Ahab's controlling demon, Fedallah never has as independent an existence as does Bland. The confidence man is Melville's finest, fullest creation of the human embodiment of evil. In all of his various guises, the confidence man's constant pretense is virtuous innocence, his constant intent to gull his victim—and, like Satan, he claims every man as his rightful prey. Master-at-Arms Claggart, descendant of Bland, hides his colossal evil under the cloak of his petty virtue. His depravity is natural in that it appears to have no human motivation. Like the confidence man, Claggart is repeatedly characterized by the metaphor of the serpent.

With all Melville's purely Satanic figures, evil becomes an end in itself. They share with his Titanic rebels the imbalance of mind and heart, but their imbalance is absolute—

all fiendish intellect, no human heart at all. They appear eternally busy on all levels, making mischief, precipitating disaster, and winning souls for their demanding master.

2   Seekers, mystics, and maskless men

Alongside those in Melville who rebel against life, withdraw from it, or make a hypocritical or fraudulent adjustment to it, are those who work out some kind of tolerable and frank reconciliation. These individuals are by no means innocent of the world's evil. On the contrary, acknowledgment of complicity is the badge of honor which admits them to this rare company.

The characters of this kind first introduced by Melville are the Young Seekers: Tommo in *Typee-Omoo;* Redburn; White Jacket; Ishmael in *Moby Dick;* and Clarel. Taji, although a Young Seeker at the beginning of *Mardi,* must be excluded from this company, as he ends up not in reconciliation but in rebellion. Tommo does not really belong in this company, either, for although his abandonment of his South Sea Island vagabond life suggests a rejection of immaturity and an acceptance of reality, he nevertheless remains uncommitted as he is last seen sailing on another whaler into the wide Pacific.

Redburn-White Jacket (conceived as one character), Ishmael, and Clarel are the three Young Seekers who go the whole journey of initiation which concludes with the ritualistic baptism into evil and which signifies acceptance of a share in the human guilt and fate. When White Jacket falls into the sea, rips off his hated garment as if he would slit open his very being, and rises to the surface, he has completed an initiation begun the moment young Redburn (in his borrowed hunting jacket) set forth from home on his way to sea. When Ishmael, sole survivor of the *Pequod,* slowly gravitates to the center of the circle in the vacant sea where his ship has sunk, he has achieved a reconciliation to the human scene that seemed remote if not impossible when he appeared at the beginning with a "damp, drizzly November" in his soul. When Clarel at the end of his prolonged and sometimes tedious journey through the Holy Land joins the vast array of humanity struggling up the *Via Crucis,* he finally finds in communion with his fellow "cross-bearers" an end to his spiritual agonizing and isolation and a beginning of acceptance and involvement. All of these characters struggle with themselves and the world for a time, but then make an honorable peace. They endure.

Serving thematic functions similar to those of the Young Seeker, but without major involvement in the process of initiation, Melville's practical mystics play vital roles in his work. They are the vessels of his insight into truth's paradox. As such, they are both comic figures and serious philosophers; for in their very characters they exemplify both the paucity of man's real wisdom and the irony implicit in such small insight as man can lay claim to. All of these individuals are a complex combination of the practical and the mystic, of the everyday and the transcendent. The first to appear is Babbalanja of *Mardi,* the philosopher who accompanies Taji in his search for Yillah. Babbalanja's two natures are symbolized by two authorities he consults—the ancient oracle Bardianna and his private devil Azzageddi. Together these authorities guide Babbalanja to Melville's deepest insights, including that ultimate acknowledgment that man cannot know God's final purpose in the creation of the world's good and evil. And they also lead him to acceptance of Alma's Serenia, a society which, although short of the ideal, makes frank provision for the inevitability of evil, and which substitutes liberal tolerance for rigid dogma.

Plinlimmon of *Pierre*, Benjamin Franklin of *Israel Potter*, and Mark Winsome of *The Confidence-Man* are Babbalanja's spiritual descendants, combining, as does he, the comic with the serious and the real with the ideal. Plinlimmon's pamphlet, with its doctrine of virtuous expediency, provides a system of ethics born of a union of the transcendent and the practical, a system which neither excuses nor ignores man's inevitable wickedness. When Plinlimmon gazes with serene "non-benevolence" into Pierre's soul, Pierre is forced to glimpse, if but for a moment, the interior sordidness of his outwardly pure motives in living with his half-sister Isabel. Benjamin Franklin in dealing with Israel Potter shows himself a "household Plato," with both the shrewdness of a merchant and the insight of a philosopher. Franklin's combination of Yankee practicality and transcendental philosophy is identified as the national genius. Mark Winsome the mystic philosopher, in his incoherent babbling to the confidence man, sounds much as does Babbalanja in *Mardi* when under the influence of his devil Azzageddi. But also like Babbalanja, Winsome proves that he can cope on a practical level with an evil whose cunning has outwitted all others. Indeed, Winsome and his disciple Egbert, quick to see through the guise of the confidence men, turn the tables and gull the devil himself.

Perhaps the reason Melville always portrayed his practical mystics in a context of humor and even irony was that, as men of the mind, they had to be given some appeal to the heart. To present these wise men as a little foolish, in their abandonment of reason and appeal to the transcendent, bestows upon them an appropriate, because human, humility. Melville's humor in his portrayals is not critical so much as gentle. All of these realistic philosophers have by their very nature that balance of intellect and emotion necessary to survival and endurance.

Similarly balanced, too, are Melville's admirable men of

action, those characters who know and accept the world for what it is and assert their rightful place in it. These maskless men are the Young Seekers after the initiation is over and the baptism complete. There is a striking continuity in their appearance, too: Jack Chase in *White Jacket* is the first embodiment, and it is to Jack Chase that Melville's novel of his old age, *Billy Budd,* is dedicated, suggesting his appearance in the drama, not as the title character as is commonly supposed, but as Captain Vere, a mature and weathered version of the young captain of White Jacket's maintop. In the forty years between these books, variations on the character appear in *Israel Potter* (the exiled wanderer himself), in "Benito Cereno" (Captain Delano), and in *Clarel* (Rolfe).

All of these characters are balanced men, combining the wisdom of the serpent with the gentleness of the dove. Not one is innocent nor pretends to be. Courageous in facing the world's evil on realistic terms that mean involvement, they are all frank in acknowledging their own complicity, their own full share in the human heritage of guilt. They neither rebel against the human condition, nor withdraw from it, nor do they come to ignoble terms with it. They confront their situation squarely, frankly, and with the supreme poise that only an internal balance can bestow. And most frequently they are not controlled by circumstance but are in control of it. Not without humor, they may still take the tragic view—but without becoming unhinged with despair. The composite portrait of Chase, Potter, Rolfe, and Captain Vere must finally be defined as Melville's full, affirmative, and realistic answer to the question of existence posed by life's apparent cunning and hostility.

3   America and her destiny

Melville did not, of course, write in a social vacuum. What he said had relevance for his own time and for ours. He wrote in a day when American writers could not help but be concerned with their own country, its origin, its direction, and its fate. The prevailing view, which touched strongly a work like Whitman's *Leaves of Grass,* was that Americans were in some sense the chosen people, that their democracy, though to be fully realized only in the vistas of the future, was the inevitable form of the modern, and that somehow, someway, the defects of the present would disappear in the perfection of a distant day.

This idealism has come to haunt the America of our own time. No Whitman could appear in this century, for the intellectual climate has reversed and the prevailing winds are not blustery optimism but reflective pessimism. Probably no nation has ever spun through its adolescence and exhausted its youth so quickly, nor faced its maturity and approaching old age so innocently bewildered.

It is with some surprise, then, that we look back to Melville and discover his somber warnings. His criticisms were not, of course, unique, but a part of that conservative tradition which runs through Cooper, De Tocqueville, Hawthorne, James and the later Twain. But Melville seemed to embrace his concern for his country in his own personal ordeal, and to make his reservations significantly felt in his total vision.

In all his books, Melville seemed at one time or another, directly or symbolically, to allude to America and her possible fate. In *Mardi, Moby Dick,* and *Pierre,* the protagonist might in each case be identified as in part America—in her pursuit of innocence, or in her obsession to annihilate evil, or in her refusal to recognize it, especially in herself. In *Israel Potter,* although America's genius is identified with Benjamin Franklin, America herself, Melville says, may in the future become the "Paul Jones of nations"—"unprincipled, reckless, predatory." Captain Delano in "Benito Cereno," in his identification with America, may be both a warning and a tribute: his naïveté and slowness in the recognition of evil could lead to disaster; his courage and energy in coping with evil, once detected, may prove a salvation. In *The Confidence-Man,* if we identify the con man, in the guise of the gaudily arrayed cosmopolitan, as Uncle Sam, we gain new insight into the potential danger of the national persistence in a masquerade of innocence. The disillusioned Ungar in *Clarel,* for the moment clearly referring to America, speaks bleakly of the approaching "Dark Ages of Democracy" in which shall reign the "dead level of rank commonplace." In *Billy Budd,* the Handsome Sailor's instinctive, fatal action and resulting death may well be a suggestion to America of the possible catastrophe of her innocence.

Melville was not, of course, totally despondent in his view of America. He saw his country as vital to man's hopes —as, in a way, man's last chance. But Melville could not tolerate the smug optimism which befogged the intellectual climate of his time. His was a lover's quarrel with America: he would not have bothered to scold had he not so intensely cared. If his Ahab and Billy Budd could in their disaster serve as a national warning, his Jack Chase and Captain Vere might in their endurance serve as the national prototype. Like White Jacket, Ishmael, and Clarel, America might well take the plunge and through her baptism exchange her naïve innocence for the more profound awareness of complicity.

13
The quest for form

Rarely in America have we had a creative writer attempt such a variety of forms as those explored by Melville. His entire literary career may be characterized, in a very real sense, as a vision in search of embodiment, a theme in quest of a form. To suggest that Melville's theme remained constant while his form changed is to ask for a reversal of the common view—that he was throughout his life trying, with more or less success, to write novels to illustrate a constantly shifting moral view.

Melville's first two books, *Typee* and *Omoo*, represent the search for the primitive society which might in its isolation have preserved the values long lost to "civilization." It is seriously relevant that Melville's first books made no claims whatsoever to being novels. Their full titles suggested their major intent: "*Typee*: A Peep at Polynesian Life. During a Four Months' Residence in A Valley of the Marquesas with notices of the French occupation of Tahiti and the provisional cession of the Sandwich Islands to Lord Paulet"; "*Omoo*: A Narrative of Adventures in the South Seas." The British edition properly added to the title of *Omoo*: "being a sequel to The 'Residence in the Marquesas Islands,' [British title of *Typee*]."

In creating the unique form of *Typee-Omoo*, Melville drew from a number of traditions, foremost of which was travel literature. *Typee* and *Omoo* are travel books, related to any number of specimens of a form highly popular during the eighteenth and nineteenth centuries. But plunging beneath the surface of the travel book's semi-serious sociological examination of the various facets of a strange society, we find in *Typee-Omoo* the folk material, the salty, earthy humor, which at times capriciously captures Melville's imagination and carries him beyond fact into fiction as he exaggerates character or heightens suspense. And as we go deeper into *Typee-Omoo*, we discover as the skeleton form holding all of the disparate episodes together the archetypal quest, which relates the books to a tradition reaching from Homer's *Odyssey*, through the Medieval Romance and the search for the Holy Grail, to Rousseau and the romantic search for the noble society of savages.

Though it apparently begins in the real world, *Mardi* soon depicts a world of fantasy compositely created by Melville out of Polynesian mythology. As we travel deeply into this strange geography which frequently bears many all too familiar features, we find ourselves immersed in an abundance of history, poetry, and philosophy, all introduced naturally by the historian Braid-Beard, the poet Yoomy, and the philosopher Babbalanja, as they accompany the central character Taji in his endless search through Mardi for the beautiful, mysterious Yillah. Accompanying this weird group on its peculiar itinerary, we gradually become aware that though the landscape and the names are new, the voyage and the journey are as old as Rabelais and *Gargantua,* Spenser and *The Faerie Queen,* Bunyan and *Pilgrim's Progress,* or Swift and *Gulliver's Travels.* And though Taji's search for Yillah is thorough, it, too, has been made before— Menelaus sought Helen, Dante sought Beatrice, the medieval knight sought his lady, and the heroes of German romances sought their otherworldly women. The solid elements of the foundation of Melville's structure in *Mardi* are allegory, satire, and romance. The quest for a symbolic, ideal woman replaces the earlier quest for the symbolic, uncontaminated island, but both quests fail, as they must in fulfillment of Melville's theme.

Melville's next two books belong together not only in time but also in theme and form. Although one is not the narrative sequel to the other, as *Omoo* is to *Typee*, *White Jacket* is quite certainly the thematic sequel to *Redburn*. The full titles suggest their substance: *Redburn: His First Voyage. Being the Sailor-boy Confessions and Reminiscences of the Son-of-a-Gentleman, in the Merchant Service; White-Jacket; or The World in a Man-of-War.* A word from each of these titles suggests the major ingredients of both—"confessions" and "the world." First on a merchant vessel, and then on a Navy ship, Melville examines life at sea with the same sociological interest that he examined life in the South Sea islands. But under Melville's gaze the ship frequently becomes a microcosm of the world, and the significance of the observation is doubled. As the readers of *Typee* and *Omoo* recognized the familiar travel book, so the readers of *Redburn* and *White Jacket* recognized the sea story, familiarized by such writers as Frederick Marryat and James Fenimore Cooper, and exemplified best perhaps in Richard Henry Dana's *Two Years Before the Mast*. In this tradition, presenting information and leveling criticism were as vital as a good yarn.

But if Melville wrote stories of the sea and criticisms of the world, he also dramatized the "confessions" of a sailor boy. When Redburn dons his hunting jacket to make his first voyage, he is caught up in an initiation into the world and its ways that is not completed until White Jacket, near the end of his voyage, plunges into the sea and loses his ungainly garment. This ritual of initiation ending in baptism (immersion and resurrection) and symbolizing acceptance —White Jacket's of the world and the world's of White Jacket—is as old as myth itself. The garment symbolism is reminiscent of Carlyle's *Sartor Resartus,* but the trial of a youth in the temptations of the world, his terrifying experiences with evil and his final rebirth, granting deepened sympathies and greater human understanding, are archetypal patterns spliced together by Melville to trace out his own vision.

It is, perhaps, the secret of the greatness of Melville's next book, *Moby Dick*, that it links the archetypal quest of the early works with the archetypal initiation of the later, through the counterpoised characters of Ahab and Ishmael. Ahab's pursuit of Moby Dick, ending in destruction and death, and Ishmael's initiation into the world, ending in baptism and rebirth, support *Moby Dick's* structure with bedrock foundations. The superstructure that rises on these foundations comes not from the novel but from tragedy and the epic. The Bible's Book of Job, Shakespeare's *Macbeth* and *King Lear*, and Milton's *Paradise Lost*—and other such classic edifices—have supplied materials for this wondrous structure. True, much of the decoration or embellishment comes from whaling, its legend and its history, its science and mythology. But all of this substance, which memorializes an exhilarating area of experience fast fading from man's memory, shows the book to be more of an epic than a novel, to be properly placed not with Fielding and Dickens but with Homer and Virgil.

The work closest in form to a conventional novel that Melville wrote was *Pierre*, but he immediately obscured the tradition within which he seemed to be writing by adding the subtitle—*or, The Ambiguities*. Although this subtitle no doubt applies to the profoundly complex nature of the human psyche whose labyrinths Melville somewhat daringly explores, it seems also to characterize Melville's attitude toward the novel form he has adopted—an attitude that ranges from high seriousness to mocking laughter. It is as though he is gleefully and naughtily mixing the ingredients of Shakespearian tragedy and domestic romance, and then standing aside to observe the combustion. Readers of *Pierre* who have sat to ponder and to read again have

caught glimpses of a submerged form lurking beneath the
superficial, melodramatic, sentimental domestic tragedy—a
form whose prototype finds expression in the story of Adam
and Eve and the myth of the fortunate fall or in Dante's
Divine Comedy and the myth of the journey through the
inferno and purgatory into paradise. And moreover, beneath
the somewhat trivial level of the domestic in *Pierre*, out of
which most of the action was created, yawns the abysm of
the unconscious, teeming with dark and sinister figures.
These dimly sexual figures were Melville's joke on those
readers who wanted their pathos and sentimentality well
mixed with righteousness and virtue—a private joke which
Freud in our own time has made public.

Even in his short pieces, written in the early 1850's, Melville does not seem to place himself, as we might expect, in
the development of the American short story alongside Ir-
ving and Hawthorne and Poe and Twain. Instead, Melville
forges his form to fit his material, and rarely does he seem to
repeat either substance or shape. Each short work appears
unique and many of them are brilliant. From the series of
sketches set on the barren islands called "The Encantadas"
to the symbolically paired and subtly horrible episodes of
"Paradise of Bachelors and the Tartarus of Maids," from the
suspenseful and terror-filled "Benito Cereno" to the humorous
yet deadly serious "Bartleby"—although all reflect a single,
informing vision, each is cut from an unusual, sometimes
exotic, nearly always individual pattern.

From the short tale Melville turned to history in his
search for form. He found *Israel Potter* at hand and, by
taking over the tale of historical adventure, was able to
free his imagination for metaphysical flight. But Melville's
form is far from mere historical narrative. In recreating
Benjamin Franklin, John Paul Jones, and Ethan Allen,
and the exciting days of the American Revolution, Melville
was not simply reviving the romance of the past. He was

probing the national character, and discovering the national genius, the national spirit—and the national weaknesses. Nor did Melville miss the opportunity presented by the protagonist's name to make his modern history suggest a time more distant. *Israel Potter: His Fifty Years of Exile* is filled with narrative and thematic parallels to the story of the Israelites, their wandering in the world and the wilderness, their trials, tribulations, and prolonged suffering. Melville's history turns out to be as ancient as it is modern.

In *The Confidence-Man,* his final prose work for some thirty years, Melville abandoned history and domestic romance, tragedy and epic, and turned to legend and folklore, allegory and comedy. Within the text, Melville speaks of moving from the "comedy of thought" to the "comedy of action." And the hero—the confidence man who assumes the various guises—is drawn to comic scale. Far below Taji, Ahab, and even Pierre in the scope of his character and actions, the confidence man is reduced to minor mischief and petty racketeering. The joke, of course, is that the confidence man is the devil, and that he deals in just such devious and deceptive ways. Satan can sail on a small steamboat called the *Fidèle* down the Mississippi as well as reign in a magnificent Miltonic hell. And as the cosmopolitan confidence man, he can even assume the outlandish garb of that American provincial, Uncle Sam. As he gulls victim after victim in a dream-like voyage down the great brown, continental river, we become aware that the drama we are witnessing is nearest kin not to the humorous novels of Sterne or Dickens but to the allegorical comedy of *The Ship of Fools* or *The Canterbury Tales.*

It is perhaps not sheer speculation to say that the "long twilight of silence" that followed *The Confidence-Man* in Melville's career was in large measure caused by his exhaustion of the possible forms available to his imagination. He clearly never looked upon himself as a novelist repeatedly turning out "novels." It is more likely that he thought of himself simply as a writer ranging widely over the literary tradition, and trying his hand at a variety of literary forms.

Even during this thirty-year "twilight" period, the silence was repeatedly broken, although the sound reached fewer and fewer ears. Melville turned to lyric poetry, at first topical in content (particularly during the Civil War) and later nostalgic and reminiscent in quality. Three volumes of poetry were published during his lifetime (*Battle-Pieces and Aspects of the War, John Marr and Other Sailors,* and *Timoleon*), and a number of manuscript poems have been published since his death. Melville's most ambitious poetic venture, however, was his long narrative-philosophical poem in rhymed tetrameter—*Clarel: A Poem and Pilgrimage in the Holy Land.* Melville's pilgrims journey from Jerusalem across deserts and mountains, to Bethlehem; but, as Melville points out, his pilgrims bear certain similarities in motive, character, and aspiration, to those earlier pilgrims headed toward Canterbury. *Clarel,* filled with Old and New Testament materials, is, indeed, a far remove from the realistic novel, the dominant form of Melville's day.

And so, too, is Melville's final work in prose, *Billy Budd, Foretopman,* finished by Melville in 1891, but not published until many years after his death. Superficially *Billy Budd* is a sea story based on historical materials. But the sub-title—*An Inside Narrative*—suggests a form beneath or beyond the surface. Like *Clarel, Billy Budd's* real form is ancient and archetypal—the Christian myth. To discuss *Billy Budd* and its shape, we turn for examples not to Twain or Howells or Hardy, but to the story of Christ's Crucifixion. But *Billy Budd* is no mere retelling of the tale in modern dress. Here, as in all of his previous work, Melville is reiterating his basic theme of the tragic and compelling human necessity to abide by earthly rather than heavenly laws. It is Melville's intellectual daring that draws him to the Christ story itself to explore and question the Christian ethic.

In discussing the form of James Joyce's *Ulysses*, T. S. Eliot defined the "mythical method" as consisting of "manipulating a continuous parallel between contemporaneity and antiquity" in order to give significance to "the immense panorama of futility and anarchy which is contemporary history." In thus rationalizing the use of the traditional or inherited mythology, Eliot was touching on a problem which every modern author has confronted. Eliot himself followed the Joyce of *Ulysses*, but turned more and more to the Christian rather than to the pagan past. Joyce, in *Finnegans Wake*, finally found a modern myth in the Jungian collective unconscious that provided him a rationale for the synthesis of all myth of all time and place. W. B. Yeats departed the crumbling edifices of belief to enter mythic towers created out of only poetically-believed mystic philosophies.

Melville anticipated all of these writers in their sense of abandonment in an age of spiritual disintegration. Melville knew the agony of the loss of faith. He, too, sought earnestly for a cultural frame within which he could set his dramas and define his themes. As a writer, he felt acutely the need to find or create an ordered system with which to examine and evaluate the plight of man. Indeed, Melville's quest for form was in reality a search for order. In the long span of his career, Melville made four massive attempts to create a personal or a modern myth out of neglected or virgin materials.

The first of these attempts is the magnificent failure, *Mardi*. Melville's youthful experiences in the South Sea islands presented him with a vast, unexplored body of myth unavailable to most Western writers. After dealing with his experiences on the ostensible travel-book level, Melville marshaled his resources and energies for the imaginative exploitation of those experiences on the highest level of art. If he did not achieve the level for which he reached, we cannot help but admire the fullness of his grasp. The attempt becomes all the more impressive when we realize that the Polynesian mythology itself was a kind of chaos which Melville had to order by synthesis and invention. And this creation was to serve not as an end in itself—a merely romantic romance—but be a means by which something significant might be said about the world and the state of man.

In *Moby Dick* Melville had the impertinence to attempt the creation of a modern mythology out of the facts and legends of whales and whaling. And he had the brazen effrontery to succeed. Readers have long wondered about the relevance of those "Extracts" from the world's literature which stand at the front of *Moby Dick*. Whatever their intrinsic value, they serve in their position to remind the reader that whales, like gods, have an ancient lineage. At the beginning stands Genesis: "And God created great whales." The epic of *Moby Dick* may be without gods, but it has its whales—which serve the old function of the gods. Once we understand Melville's intention of evoking whales and their lore on an epic scale, we may more readily comprehend those recurrent "digressions" on the history, the anatomy, the sex and sociology of whales. If the characters and events of *Moby Dick* seem larger than life, if we feel that somehow the action—this old man chasing a whale—affects the fundamental structure of the universe, we must credit not whaling as in reality it was but whaling as transfigured by the mythmaking power of Melville.

In creating his whale, Melville spent his energies and exhausted his imagination. It was not until some six years later that he was willing again to delve deeply into new and native materials. Although *The Confidence-Man* is by no means of the same order of magnitude as *Moby Dick*, it nevertheless is a product of Melville's magical power of transmuting common clay into the fine china of art. If in *Moby Dick* Melville changed the materials of whaling into the materials of an epic, in *The Confidence-Man* he transformed the materials of folklore into the materials of an allegory. And his ingenuity is manifest in his preserving the native humor of the original frontier materials in the process of transmutation. As we observe the folk on the *Fidèle* gliding down the treacherous, muddy Mississippi, and as we listen to their lore, gradually we become aware that we are witnessing not just a frontier story, or, indeed, a drama of merely human conflict, but a cosmic drama, however diminutive, involving gods and devils, however outlandishly disguised.

Melville's supreme efforts were always followed by embarrassing silences. *Mardi, Moby Dick,* and then *The Confidence-Man,* each in its solid way, dropped quietly into oblivion. And Melville, when he was mentioned at all, was still referred to as the author of *Typee*—the man who had lived among the cannibals. It is no mystery, then, that in his last great effort at myth-making, Melville did not even bother to publish. There is a vital difference, too, between *Billy Budd* and its three mythic predecessors. Melville did not attempt in his last novel, this Benjamin of his old age, to create myth out of the raw materials of his experience. Instead, he gave to fragments of remembered experience an historical setting, and he gave the historical setting a mythic frame. There is perhaps some irony in this "return" by Melville to the very Christian materials whose unavailability in an age of religious disillusion had sent him forth on his search for form at the very beginning of his writing career some forty years before.

The final irony is not, however, in Melville's act but in the reader's hasty assumption. Because the mythic frame of the Crucifixion and the Ascension are so clearly imposed on the

story of the betrayal and hanging of the innocent Billy
Budd, readers have too quickly asserted that this final work
is Melville's return to conventional Christian faith. They
have missed the complex qualifications and subtle dissents
operative throughout the story. Indeed, Melville turns to the
Christian myth in *Billy Budd* not to revitalize and reaffirm
it, but, with some poignant sorrow, to demonstrate its final
inefficacy. Although Melville did not in this story, as he did
in the others, actually create myth out of the materials of his
experience, his achievement was no less impressive. In
Billy Budd Melville made the old myth serve as the basic
materials for its very denial and rejection.

If in his search Melville did not invent a form which he
could pass on to posterity inviolate, he still must be given
credit for the very highest powers of inventive genius. He
was not content to accept without question the dominant
form of his day—the novel. Instead, he adopted the outward shape but constantly pushed beyond the apparent
limits. There is hardly a kind of literature that he did not
sample or assimilate: travel book, sea yarn, sociological
study, philosophical tract, allegory, epic, domestic or historical romance, tragedy or comedy. Moreover, he expanded
the horizons of art when he explored new worlds in search of
usable myth—the world of the South Sea Islands, the world
of whaling, the world of frontier folklore and humor. Both as
heir and master of the old, and as explorer and discoverer of
the new, Melville must be granted a shaping imagination of
the very first rank. If our definitions do not allow him this
rank, we must rewrite our definitions. It will not be the first
time that genius has compelled criticism to look to its
terms.

Selected bibliography

The standard edition of Melville is *The Works of Her-man Melville* (London: Constable and Company Ltd., 1922-24). It is gradually being replaced, however, by the annotated volumes currently being published in the scholarly Hendricks House edition (see bibliographies for individual Melville works below).

Aside from the usual valuable bibliographical sources—The *Literary History of the United States* (Vol. III, 1949) and *Eight American Authors* (1956)—probably the fullest bibliography of works on Melville appears in Milton R. Stern, *The Fine Hammered Steel of Herman Melville* (Urbana, Ill., 1957); and the most serviceable, listing works on individual novels separately, appears in Donna Gerstenberger and George Hendrick, *The American Novel, 1789-1959: A Checklist of Twentieth Century Criticism* (Denver, 1961).

BOOKS MAINLY BIOGRAPHICAL

Raymond M. Weaver, *Herman Melville: Mariner and Mystic* (New York, 1921). A pioneer study which initiated the revival of modern interest in Melville and which is still valuable if corrected by more recent scholarship.

John Freeman, *Herman Melville* (New York, 1926). A brief account in the English Men of Letters series.

Lewis Mumford, *Herman Melville* (New York, 1929). An imaginative biography which exploits, perhaps too heavily, the fiction as source.

Newton Arvin, *Herman Melville* (New York, 1950). An admirably integrated biographical-critical study for the general reader, imaginative and perceptive.

Leon Howard, *Herman Melville* (Berkeley, 1951). Based on the Jay Leyda *Log*, this is the fullest, most detailed biography yet written. Also contains critical commentary on the works.

BOOKS MAINLY INTERPRETIVE

William Ellery Sedgwick, *Herman Melville: The Tragedy of Mind* (Cambridge, 1944). An imaginative, lyrical interpretation of the successive works as a dramatization of Melville's vision and mind.

Richard Chase, *Herman Melville: A Critical Study* (New York, 1949). A venturesome interpretation that imaginatively exploits Freudian psychology, myth, American folklore and humor, and which offers many startling readings which are always provocative if not always convincing.

Ronald Mason, *The Spirit Above the Dust* (London, 1951). A cogently argued English view of Melville which, though fresh in its approach, is somewhat conventional in interpretation.

Lawrance Thompson, *Melville's Quarrel with God* (Princeton, 1952). An unusual interpretation which identifies Melville with Ahab as a Calvinistic heretic in rebellion against God.

Milton R. Stern, *The Fine Hammered Steel of Herman Melville* (Urbana, Ill., 1957). An intensive interpretation of four works (*Typee, Mardi, Pierre,* and *Billy Budd*) in a demonstration of Melville's fundamental naturalism.

Merlin Bowen, *The Long Encounter* (Chicago, 1960). A sensitively written examination of Melville's novels as dramatizations of single individuals pitted against the universe and the strategies they adopt —defiance, submission, or an armed neutrality.

BOOKS: SPECIAL STUDIES

William Braswell, *Melville's Religious Thought* (Durham, N. C., 1943). An early investigation of an important but elusive subject.

Charles Olson, *Call Me Ishmael: A Study of Melville* (New York, 1947). A strange, dramatically written book which focuses on space as central to Melville's work.

Nathalia Wright, *Melville's Use of the Bible* (Durham, N. C., 1949). Full and useful treatment of a vital element in Melville's work.

Henry Francis Pommer, *Milton and Melville* (Pittsburgh, 1950). Exploration of an important literary relationship.

Edward H. Rosenberry, *Melville and the Comic Spirit* (Cambridge, Mass., 1955). A thoroughgoing analysis of Melville's humor as it affects his themes.

James Baird, *Ishmael* (Baltimore, 1956). An imaginative, wide-ranging examination of a central Melvillean theme.

Merton M. Sealts, Jr., *Melville as Lecturer* (Cambridge, Mass., 1957).

A detailed compilation of all the material relating to Melville's un-
successful lecture tours.

Hugh W. Hetherington, *Melville's Reviewers: British and American,
1846-1891* (Chapel Hill, N. C., 1961). A valuable analysis of all
the reviews of Melville's books.

BOOKS: MELVILLE MATERIALS

Willard Thorp, ed., *Herman Melville: Representative Selections* (New
York, 1938). An early collection of selected readings with a useful
bibliography and an important introduction.

Howard Vincent, ed., *Collected Poems of Herman Melville* (Chicago,
1947). Contains many previously unpublished poems plus all published poetry except *Clarel*.

Eleanor L. Metcalf, ed., *Journal of a Visit to London and the Continent
by Herman Melville* (Cambridge, Mass., 1948). Notations Melville
made on his trip abroad in 1849-50.

Jay Leyda, ed., *The Melville Log* (New York, 1951). An assembly in
chronological order of pertinent historical, biographical, and literary
materials in two large volumes to make *A Documentary Life*. An in-
valuable source and reference work.

Eleanor Melville Metcalf, *Herman Melville: Cycle and Epicycle* (Cambridge, Mass., 1953). A valuable collection of source materials with
a connecting commentary by the editor, Melville's granddaughter.

Howard C. Horsford, ed., *Journal of a Visit to Europe and the Levant*
(Princeton, 1955). The account of Melville's trip, dated October
11, 1856-May 6, 1857; which later served as material for Melville's
long narrative poem, *Clarel*.

Merrell R. Davis and William H. Gilman, eds., *The Letters of Herman
Melville* (New Haven, 1960). The most complete collection of letters available—a total of 271.

SELECTED CRITICISM OF INDIVIDUAL NOVELS

Typee and *Omoo*. Charles Roberts Anderson, *Melville in the South
Seas* (New York, 1939). A biographical-interpretative study useful
for all Melville's fiction set in the South Seas.

Mardi. Merrell R. Davis, "The Flower Symbolism in *Mardi*," *Modern
Language Quarterly* (1941) II; Tyrus Hillway, "Taji's Abdication in
Herman Melville's *Mardi*," *American Literature* (1944), XVI; Tyrus
Hillway, "Taji's Quest for Certainty," *American Literature* (1946),
XVIII; Merrell R. Davis, *Melville's Mardi: A Chartless Voyage* (New
Haven, 1942): a full-length study especially enlightening on the
composition of *Mardi*.

Redburn and *White Jacket.* Willard Thorp, "Redburn's Prosy Old
    Guide-Book," *PMLA* (1938), LIII; Howard P. Vincent, " 'White
    Jacket': An Essay in Interpretation," *New England Quarterly* (1949),
    XXII; William H. Gilman, *Melville's Early Life and Redburn* (New
    York: New York University Press, 1951): an interpretive study
    blending biography and fiction; John W. Nichol, "Melville's 'Soiled
    Fish of the Sea,' " *American Literature* (1949) XXI: points out
    probable textual error of "soiled" for "coiled."
Moby Dick. The bibliography on *Moby Dick* accumulates as rapidly
    as that on *Hamlet.* There are a few unusual and outstanding com-
    mentaries that must be mentioned. D. H. Lawrence, *Studies in Clas-
    sic American Literature* (1923): a psychological interpretation that
    identifies Ahab's vengeance against Moby Dick as the white man's
    destruction of his phallic consciousness; E. M. Forster, *Aspects of
    the Novel* (1927): a poetic interpretation that labels the essential
    in *Moby Dick* its "prophetic song"; F. O. Matthiessen, *American
    Renaissance* (New York, 1941): a sensitive, deep reading that shows
    Ahab's resemblance to the heroes of Elizabethan revenge tragedies;
    Howard P. Vincent, *The Trying-out of Moby Dick* (Boston, 1949):
    an exhaustive study that throws special light on the actual composi-
    tion of the novel; M. O. Percival, *A Reading of Moby Dick* (Chi-
    cago, 1950): a slender volume that provides a full and consistent
    interpretation, particularly useful on the smaller questions; Howard
    P. Vincent, ed., *Moby Dick* (Chicago: Packard and Co., Hendricks
    House, 1952): a book almost as big as the whale, crammed full not
    only of the text but of valuable commentary and notes; Leslie Fied-
    ler, *Love and Death in the American Novel* (New York, 1960): a
    Freudian reading of the sexuality and homosexuality in the novel
    that is always interesting though frequently wild and often annoy-
    ing.
Pierre. Henry A. Murray, "Introduction," *Pierre* (New York, Hendricks
    House—Farrar, Straus, 1949): a penetrating introduction by a "pro-
    fessing psychologist"; Charles Moorman, "Melville's *Pierre* and the
    Fortunate Fall," *American Literature* (1953), XXV; Nathalia
    Wright, "Pierre: Herman Melville's Inferno," *American Literature*
    (1960), XXXII.
Israel Potter. Life and Adventures of Israel Ralph Potter (1744-1826),
    The Magazine of History with Notes and Queries, 1911: Extra Num-
    ber 16, IV: the original story on which Melville based his tale.
Tales and Sketches. Egbert S. Oliver, ed., *The Piazza Tales* (New
    York: Hendricks House—Farrar, Straus, 1948); Henry Chapin, ed.,
    The Apple-Tree Table and Other Sketches (Princeton, 1922); Jay

Leyda, ed., *Complete Stories of Herman Melville* (New York, 1949);
Charles G. Hoffmann, "The Shorter Fiction of Herman Melville,"
South Atlantic Quarterly (1953), LII; Richard P. Fogle, *Melville's
Shorter Tales* (Norman: University of Oklahoma Press, 1960): a
sensitive reading attentive to the many ambiguities.

The Confidence-Man. John W. Shroeder, "Sources and Symbols for
Melville's *Confidence-Man,*" *PMLA* (1951), LXVI; Roy Harvey
Pearce, "Melville's Indian Hater: A Note on the Meaning of *The
Confidence-Man, PMLA* (1952), LXVII; H. C. Horsford, "Evidence
of Melville's Plans for a Sequel to *The Confidence-Man,*" *American
Literature* (1952), XXIV; Elizabeth S. Foster, "Introduction," *The
Confidence-Man* (New York: Hendricks House, 1954): an inter-
pretive Introduction with a valuable survey of previous commentary.

Clarel. Henry W. Wells, "Herman Melville's *Clarel,*" *College English*
(1943), IV; Walter E. Bezanson, "Melville's *Clarel:* The Complex
Passion," *English Literary History* (1954), XXI; Walter E. Bezanson, "Introduction," *Clarel: A Poem and a Pilgrimage in the Holy
Land* (New York: Hendricks House, 1961): a penetrating and
valuable critical analysis.

Billy Budd. E. L. Grant Watson, "Melville's Testament of Acceptance,"
New England Quarterly (1933), VI; F. Barron Freeman, ed., *Melville's Billy Budd* (Cambridge, Mass., 1948): an interpretive and
textual study of major importance which reprints text of novel together with text of a related, previously unpublished story, "Baby
Budd, Sailor"; Joseph Schiffman, "Melville's Final Stage, Irony: a
Re-examination of *Billy Budd* Criticism," *American Literature*
(1950), XXII; Wendell Glick, "Expediency and Absolute Morality
in 'Billy Budd,' " *PMLA* (1953), LXVIII; Harrison Hayford, ed.,
The Somers Mutiny Affair (New Jersey, 1959): an assembly of all
the documents surrounding the incident, involving Melville's cousin,
upon which Melville partially based *Billy Budd;* William T. Stafford,
Melville's Billy Budd and the Critics (San Francisco, 1961): a convenient combination of text and commentary in one volume.

Miscellaneous. R. P. Blackmur, "The Craft of Herman Melville," *Vir-
ginia Quarterly Review* (1938), XIV; Perry Miller, "Melville and
Transcendentalism," *Virginia Quarterly Review* (1953), XXIX;
James E. Miller, Jr., "Hawthorne and Melville: the Unpardonable
Sin," *PMLA* (1955) LXX; Milton R. Stern, "Some Techniques of
Melville's Perception," *PMLA* (1958), LXXIII.

Index